CAKES I'VE EATEN IN BED

OR CRUMBS I'VE SLEPT WITH.

SAM IVY

LifeRich Publishing is a registered trademark of
The Reader's Digest Association, Inc.

LifeRich Publishing books may be ordered through booksellers or by contacting:

LifeRich Publishing
1663 Liberty Drive
Bloomington, IN 47403
www.liferichpublishing.com
1 (888) 238-8637

ISBN: 978-1-4897-2021-4 (sc)
ISBN: 978-1-4897-2020-7 (hc)
ISBN: 978-1-4897-2022-1 (e)

Library of Congress Control Number: 2018962955

Print information available on the last page.

LifeRich Publishing rev. date: 11/05/2018

FOREWORD

I had thought about writing a book for a long time, and the older I got and before the Alzheimers sets in, the more I thought that I should do it. I have had an interesting journey and it would be nice to share it with friends. I hope it will be enjoyed.

Much of the spelling and phrases herein are British, and the characters names have been changed to protect my victims.

ACKNOWLEDGEMENT

I would like to dedicate this book to a few family members and friends. To my son, who had to spend his childhood years without me, and finally taught me how to use my p.c. to the full extent of a 79 year old brain. To my sister who has helped me more than I can say. To all the friends, (you know who you are) never be able to thank you enough, could not have done it without you.

CONTENTS

1 Growing Up In England

I was a tomboy like no tomboy ever. I climbed trees with the boys on my way to school, stealing apples, crawling on all fours under the window of the landowner to steal peaches from the vines on the wall and in the winter, jumping on frozen horse troughs, only I seemed to be the one that fell through, and had to take my socks off and try to dry them before I got home. Never did, always had a smack for being late, and green socks that were white when they started in the morning, HELLO!! My mother was strict (I am glad). I was an only child until I was 9 years old; not too spoiled but I guess growing up during WWII I was really taken care of.

My mother worked in a factory on the night shift, building airplanes, and Dad was on a battleship in the Royal Navy and so I lived with my Nan and Grandad. My aunt and uncle (Dad's sister and brother) also lived with us. I remember gas lamps in the street, and also in the house, like little egg shaped things that burnt oil and had to be replaced like a light bulb, and an outside toilet where my legs would dangle from the big wooden seat, as my feet did not reach the floor and squares of newspaper hung from the wall on a piece of string. Running down the garden holding my Nan's hand during an air raid to get to the underground shelter, was something I will never forget. The shelter was about fifty feet from the back door of the house. It was also called an 'Anderson Shelter' or 'dugout', a hole maybe twelve feet underground, which I'm guessing was about 10' by 20' with a wooden bench down each side, enough to seat 20, maybe 30 by squeezing in. It was solid packed dirt and smelled very musty, like a very old church. There were four or five wooden steps to get down into it. The roof was curved and made of corrugated metal and covered in grass and soil. It was very well camouflaged and could not be seen from the air.

One thing I remember vividly was slipping on the way down the steps one night during an air raid, and my Nan having to find a doctor to stitch up my eyebrow. I have no idea where she found him. Maybe it was a neighbour, who knows.

Another very scary thing for me was seeing a 'Doodlebug' (V2 rocket) fly by the bedroom window. One could hear them before they got even close. They made a very loud droning noise before they went silent and exploded. One night I heard one which had to be very close to the house because, as Nan ran up the stairs to get me, the sirens blaring, suddenly the bedroom windows blew in. We had to run down the stairs and through the house in the dark because no lights were allowed. I am trying to remember what we had for lighting in the shelter, maybe it was candles. We often ran through the brilliance of the flak from our guns that lit up the sky like fireworks. Once in the shelter it felt very safe even at times when the dirt would fall from the roof inside during a bombing.

Most of the women in the shelter used to knit, and I remember a lot of singing of old pub songs. I still know the words to this day of most of them. People were so close then. A neighbour would do anything for another, not like it anymore. Never will be I'm afraid.

One night when I was with my mother for the weekend when the German planes bombed an arms factory across from where Nan and Granddad lived. They were two of a handful of people that survived. The whole street, about ten houses, was demolished and I guess maybe being with Mum could have saved my life. Nan and Granddad were given a house (or helped) by the council in the district where they lived. That was a good thing about England. It seemed that people were always taken care of one way or another during the war years.

Me and Mum

Now we are jumping a couple of years. Dad is out of the Navy, I guess about 1947-1948. Mum is having a baby and I have the best friend across the street. I am now living in a flat with Mum and Dad, 2 rooms, a kitchen and a bathroom. My friend Joann and I play all the time. We were very close, but she had very bad Asthma attacks that used to really scare me. Her mother would let me in when she was sick and I really did not want to see her like that, but I guess one does things when young, that we just don't think about

Suddenly, it seemed that I was getting sick! I had a bad case of impetigo (skin infection). Then peritonitis nearly killed me, from what I was told, so the doctor decided to send me to a convalescent home in Hayling, which if I remember was about four hours travelling by train from Middlesex where we lived. This recuperation resort for kids was actually the start of my tomboy gone and young woman coming out. It took a week or two to get acting wild out of my system. In fact, the first week, one day before my 11th birthday, I was running and chasing a friend I had made, when a French door I was going to run through got stuck half open after a bolt on the bottom fell and jammed on a step, so instead of opening the door, I kicked it and missed the frame hitting the glass panels and putting my leg through one.

At 11 years old I guess one does not have the brain to break the glass around the leg, so after pulling my leg back through the jagged edges, it ripped the muscle in my leg, from the lower leg to the thigh. As I hopped down the corridor with a huge mass of flesh flapping in the breeze, I remember two girls fainting in the hallway.

Then off to a hospital on the mainland, about an hour away.

Poor Mum, and her first visit. I am on crutches and my long blonde ringlets have been cut off (part of the health rules, in case of lice). I'm sure she is wondering when am I going to NOT be a worry? Not yet Mum!

The next few weeks were more excitement for me, (not for Mum and Dad). My leg healed and I decided one night to celebrate by jumping up and down on my bed like a trampoline. Needless to say, I went through the springs and everything. Poor Mum and Dad had to pay for the bed.

Then I met a boy!. The home was co-ed. My girlfriend (Audrey), that I was close to, also met a boy . . We were not really allowed to hang out with the boys but Audrey and I used to find ourselves in closets and storage cupboards just kissing, which I guess was really exciting at that age. Now when I think back, I cannot believe it! 2011 is a different story, not like 1949! Next thing, I was released from the health retreat after three months, YEAH! No more greens at lunch which sometimes had little flies in it. Pills, pills, and more pills, but finally I am out of here.

The trip home was another one of my "accidents looking for a place to happen" incidents. After the train journey, then bus journey, and walking in-between, not paying attention to where I was walking, I remember turning around to talk to my Dad and walked into a very large telephone pole. Needless to say, I did not make it home in perfect shape. Very large black eye!

Well my spa vacation over, it was time to take my exams to see if I could get into Grammar School. I could not take the exam when all the other kids did, as I was confined to the Island! So I was allowed to take it on my own in the headmasters office. Very frightening when one is a kid. I Passed! Off to Grammar School. Mum and dad, very proud. Mum, maybe not as much as when I got an honours certificate in January 1949, from a London college for playing Beethoven's "Fur Elise" on piano.

I enjoyed Grammar School and I was into athletics big time. Even at the age of 12 and 13, I was swimming, running, and captain of the netball team, (like basketball in America). That honour I kept for the next three years. The first year I entered the swimming gala as a junior. I believe I was about 12. I had to swim in a variety of events, diving, breaststroke, backstroke, and freestyle.

At the end of the day, when everything was finished, the whole school congregated at the end of the pool to hear the results of each event. I heard my name and, junior champion, with whatever points it took, and saw Mum and Dad jump up and down applauding. What a day!! I received a little silver medal and a bronze shield.

2　The Boy Next Door, And More

I forgot to mention, which is pretty obvious, but I had lots of boyfriends before meeting Phil, the boy next door. Most of them, like me, were very young! Part of the growing up included silly stuff like kissing (little pecks), holding hands, and an arm around your neck at the movies. Mum allowed me to go to the pictures now and again, as long as it was early and I was brought home at the time she said.

I had the worst crush on this boy at grammar school. He had beautiful blonde hair and long eyelashes. His name was Brian. He rode his bicycle, as I did, to school every morning. I think we were 14 years old. Every chance I got, I would try to get his attention. He finally took me to the movie, and he explained that he could not put his arm around me, as that was the one he played badminton with!!! Anyway our dating never went any further. Think I know why! No Way!

My music career lasted until about 1950, as we moved into a 3 bedroom council house, much further for me to go to my lessons once a week, and now, I have two sisters, Ellen nearly 3 years old, and Sue a year and a half younger than her. I remember my mother being very embarrassed that she had two children so close together. She used to try and avoid our neighbours, but it was when dad came home from the Navy, which makes sense to me now! The new house was great! We had neighbours on one side with two sons, Wow! I took a liking to the younger of the two and we started riding our bikes together but we had to leave separately because Phil's mum always had her eye on everything he did. Our bedroom windows were right next to each other and we used to hang out and talk a lot. When mum cooked roast beef we would always have meat drippings which were great on bread or toast with salt and pepper and I would share with Phil as our windows were so close together I could pass the bread to him, until his mother would open the back door and yell "PHILLIP, ARE YOU HANGING OUT OF THAT WINDOW? GET TO BED!"

Our bike riding and laying in fields of bluebells lasted until I was about 15, then sadly the family moved again. Phil and I still stayed great friends, but no more bike trips!

My father played soccer and we would travel to little villages in England. It took a couple of hours, by coach, from where we lived, to watch him play. This led to me meeting my future husband, Jimmy who played for the team. I had met him at school earlier, then he went into the Royal Air Force (RAF), in the meantime Phil went into the Army.

I am now 16 and having fun, except Mum is strict. I think I mentioned that previously, and my time to be home at night was usually about 9 pm. I am really, really, glad it was like that, especially when I see how young people are now-a-days in lots of places around the world, wild and loose, no self-respect!!

Phil and I communicated, but it seemed that it never got serious. Jimmy finally came out of the RAF and we started dating about 1956. Now, if we went to the movies etc., I was allowed to say goodnight in the alley in-between our house and the next door, but Mum would still come out and yell if she thought we had been there long enough.

3 Marriage and Motherhood

Suddenly, or so it seemed, I am 19. Jim and I discussed getting married. Not a good idea according to Mum and Dad. To get married before 21 years of age in England needs written permission from the parents. Well we had to keep asking and asking until Mum and Dad gave in.

. Anyway, the plans went forward. Our first thing we had to do was go to the Vicarage, which is a house close to the church where the Vicar lives that is going to marry you. We were counselled on subjects to do with married life, and our options. Next thing was to deal with the actual wedding plans, church, reception, bridesmaids, etc., etc. Mum and Dad, bless them, paid for just about everything. What was sick, was the fact that Jimmy's father had a very good profession and could have helped, but he never helped with anything. My two best friends, Joann and Rita, were my two adult bridesmaids. Rita and I went with the same boy when we were 15 years old, and I thank the Lord we both dumped him and are still friends after 57 years. My two young sisters were my lovely little bridesmaids. After a few months of dressmakers, caterers, and a vicar that I heard drank a lot (don't blame him), we were ready to do the deed. What do we know at 19 years of age? We think we know it all. WE KNOW NOTHING!!!!

Finally with mum and dad's help, the big day arrived, March 29th, 1958. Amazing, the weather was great in England. Can you believe it? The whole wedding was very nice, except Jimmy's father treated my Dad like a bar tender when he went to get somebody a drink at one end of the bar. Guess Dad was on the wrong side, but I know he got a little pee'd off.

Jim and I stayed at my aunt and uncle's house for the night after the wedding. The next day we went on a train to the seaside for a few days. While we were on our honeymoon Jimmy showed me a letter that my dearest Mother wrote to him, asking him to take care of me, etc. etc. It was a beautiful letter! Thanks Mum! Miss you very much.

We spent a really nice few days walking on the beach and going out to eat, the only thing that was very embarrassing to me was that the bed creaked in the Bed and Breakfast we were staying in. I am twenty years old, and have never been in bed with a man before. I certainly did not need a creaky bed. Maybe the proprietors of the place knew about this and it was the subject of conversation for them after those particular guests checked out. Not that funny to me!

We are now back at home, living with Jimmy's mum, in a 2 bedroom flat. Jim works for a telephone company, and I travel to London and work for a company that prints plates and cards for insurance companies. We both have pretty good jobs, and we are very close with my friend Rita and Pete, who Rita is now married to. The boys both play soccer and cricket And Rita and I are busy most weekends at the cricket club making tea and sandwiches with the other wives, sometimes it's like a bloody soap opera, listening to all the gossip from the old dears!

It is now May '58. I have only been married for a couple of months or so, and I have a bad feeling that something is wrong, so I visit my doctor, who gives me a few tests. I am pregnant! I was actually upset. How am I going to tell Mum and Dad? I remember waiting one or two weeks, and then catching a bus to get to their house. I wore a trench coat tied around the middle because I thought my belly may show on the bus. What do I know? I thought everybody would notice. I was only three months, silly girl!!!!

I got to Mum's house and we went into the living room. I blurted it out. "Mum, I'm having a baby"! She shouted up the stairs to Dad, who was in the bath. He shouted back down, after realising he heard he was going to be a grandfather, "No, not already"! I started crying my eyes out until Mum reassured me that it was Wonderful!

Now the wonderful beginnings and the nightmare follows. During the next few months I got bigger and bigger. I was a very slim athletic person, and suddenly I felt like a Xmas pudding. The Doc told me to cut down on sugar in my tea, so I stopped altogether. To this day I still do not use it.

Well the day is approaching fast. It was supposed to be Valentine's Day, February 14. We are now 3 days past. Then about 2 pm on the 17th, I am sitting with Mum, in her house, in Portsmouth, where we have moved to. Jimmy and I have a flat on the top floor of a 3 story house that Mum and Dad, and my Granddad (Mum's Father) have purchased in Hampshire. Big House! I worked until I was 8 months, in London, running for the train, after a 15 minute bus ride, then an hour and 20 minutes. So when Jimmy and I had the chance to move to the south coast, we took it.

Back to the 17th, at 2:00 pm, I suddenly found myself covered in warm liquid and found out my water had broken. Twenty and a half years old is not old enough to accept this phenomenon, but cannot cancel it! Mum called the midwife and got me to bed in her room upstairs.

The young midwife showed up about 3 hours later and tells me "not yet"! So keep gritting teeth and moaning, and in between pains, have a cup of tea, and a piece of toast and marmalade. Don't forget, this is 1959. A little gas and air, that's all you get! No shots in the back to numb you, so that the pain is insignificant and not a big deal. The midwife came back I think round-about 10:30 - 11:00 pm and now the real work starts! Finally about 12:30 am, here comes the most beautiful baby one has ever seen. He was 8 lbs. 12 oz. Big little bugger. Then the doctor showed up to stitch me up. No freezing, no anaesthetic, and tells me "hold still" after I came off of the bed about two feet. My mother went berserk! "Hold still" she screamed, and it did not make any difference, he still stitched me up. Well he will be one we have to deal with again in 1961, two and a half years down the road.

So now my Father has a boy in the family, he is over-the-moon. He had 3 daughters and always wanted a boy. Guess a grandson is as good as having a son, when one has a very close loving family as we had. Now we have gorgeous Leslie, little chubby pink cheeks, and a very pretty baby for a newborn (still very handsome at 53). Time flies! I remember the midwife held him up in a net with a weight attached. That's how it was done in those days if one had a baby at home. Wow! Fabulous!

It doesn't take long for the physical and mental stuff to start. Milk coming into breasts, belly hurting, and now find out after a week that my milk, gallons of it, was not any good. So we start on Plan B, bottles! Easy to warm up a bottle from the fridge at 2 am in a dark, cold kitchen, right? Yeah Right! Put the bottle in a saucepan of hot water and bring to a gentle boil. (No microwaves then girls)! Then cool the bottle down, until one can drip it on the back of ones' hand and it has not scalded you. Feed baby for an hour, burp for another 30 minutes, and maybe, just maybe you will be able to go back to bed and sleep. OK! Sounds like hell, but would not have changed any of it for the world.

Leslie is now growing like a weed. Had a lot of help from Mum (bless her) and my two beautiful younger sisters, now 10 and 11 and a half, who helped when really needed.

March 1961, found out I am pregnant again, due date September 11th or there-about. This time not quite so big, but sick, sick, sick, and more sick. Maybe seven months, Purgatory! Mum and Dad are still in the house and Jimmy and I moved out, and went back to London for a while, staying with his Mum.

We finally decided the coast was it, came back and found a

flat, 2 doors from the house Mum and Dad had. It was a house converted into two flats. We rented the 2nd floor with a living room, a bedroom, and a kitchen with a toilet in the corner. Glad there was a door on it! There was no fridge, big old ceramic sink that I washed everything in, including sheets. Then I hung them in the garden to dry, except when the weather was too cold, or the sheets would freeze, so after I got them in from the garden I hung them on a wooden clothes horse in the living room in front of the fire. If they were left too long outside, when they were brought in they would defrost on the carpet. It's a wonderful life (a great name for a movie, think I will ask James Stewart to play the leading role).

Moving on, it is a couple of days from September 11th 1961, no baby. It is now a week later and I tell the midwife that I am very sure that I should be having this baby. I absolutely know when I got pregnant it was the previous New Years' Eve, had a little too much celebrating with Susie and Pete. The midwife tells me that it is not ready yet, as much as I try to tell her and the doctor, that I am sure of when I became pregnant and that I should be ready. This was one time that I really was sure about. Now it is nearly the end of September, no baby!

Mum and Dad have sold their house and bought another one 3 or 4 miles away, I will be having my baby in the new house. I am now calculating that I am nearly 3 weeks overdue. Sitting in Mum's living room and close to the beginning of October, I had the most excruciating pain in my belly, and the baby did a 90 degree turnover that moved my whole stomach. My mother called the midwife immediately and she came and finally started to induce labour.

A few hours later, maybe six or seven, (who was counting?), two midwives showed up. Then the doctor (Frankenstein himself) came in and the last words I heard for maybe a day or more, were from the doctor (the man of a thousand bedside manners), who said, "you won't do anything with that", the "that" he was referring to was my baby daughter, she was DEAD! Face to pubis and breach. Evidently she fought very hard and died about four hours before birth. She strangled to death, trying to be born, my Mother who had watched the whole horrible scene, told me some time later, that the poor little girl was tied up in the cord like a parcel, it was not easy giving birth to a 7 lb. baby that was dead, I still blame him (doctor monster) 51 years later, but life goes on.

My mother was the best in the whole world. My baby was in a very fancy cradle next to my bed for two days without me knowing, as I was given pills and knocked out after she was born. Mum had to put that dead little girl in a box and take her to the funeral home on foot, at least a mile and a half away may I add. We did not own a car, ever! Mum's hair turned white within a month, guess after being a witness to that ordeal, not surprising. I think I may have cried for months, it just would not go away.

I moved back to the flat. I found out that Jimmy had started gambling on horses, dogs, and whatever., it got to a very serious stage when my wallet would be empty after he had given me money for groceries etc. I would go across the street to the little grocery store, and when I got to the till (register), no money. I was very embarrassed. Our rent that I would leave on the bottom stair of the flat, as the lady in the bottom flat would pay it along with hers, came up missing, and the life insurance money that I would save in a clock provided by the insurance company, would not be there when they came to collect every month. Finally, after what I had been through and having to deal with this problem, I became very stressed and disillusioned about a person I had known since I was 13 years old. What is love? It is respect, trust, and caring. That is my definition! I was not getting any of this. All he wanted was sex, and when I refused I was called a whore. We were too young for this sort of life, we never went out very often and social life was nonexistent. He was the only person that I had sex with in my life, that did not help the situation one bit, scary eh?

It finally came to an end. I had had enough of lying to the bill collectors, my little grocery store manager, and my Mum who had lent him money after he told her I had asked for it. Never did! I managed to sell furniture, which was not much, and moved into Mum and Dad's house with my son. The final straw was when I found a part time job in a cinema and had to go on my bicycle and find Jimmy in a betting shop after I had left my son asleep in the flat, and a fire in the fireplace. I know I must have embarrassed that man as I stormed into that betting place and screamed at him, "if your son dies in a fire while I am at work, it will be your fault".

It was three weeks later that Jimmy moved into Mum and Dad's house with me, but it did not last long. I could not deal with him in any way, shape, or form. I did try, but when someone treats you really badly, you can go off on them pretty fast. HE LEFT!

Not so fast Sam It's nearly Xmas and Jimmy called and asked if Leslie could spend it with him. I talked it over with Mum and she said "It is his son as well as yours, so maybe you should agree to that". Worst decision I ever made, and have made to this day. If only I would have said no, you come here and visit.

Jimmy had Les for one month, and when I called to see when he was going to bring him back, he told me he was not at the moment, as there was a rail stoppage due to snow. This was a start of a long fight to get my son back. He never intended to bring him back, and suddenly I was so traumatised, it is something one cannot put into words. I immediately hired a solicitor (lawyer) Suddenly it is June and Jimmy has had our son for 6 months. Seems like six years. We finally get to court, surrounded by these professional experts, in their wigs and gowns. At last, after Jimmy's mother not giving me one word of praise, the decision! Custody to my husband. the end of my world!

Two weeks or so later, one of the judges from the custody trial came to my mother's house to talk to me. He did not agree with the verdict and wanted me to try again, for a second trial. NO, NO, NO, I could not take it. The answer came out the same. My little beautiful faced 4 year-old angel was gone as far as I was concerned. I had reasonable visitation, not reasonable to my mind, after a 3 hour journey to have my son for eight hours, it was not acceptable, too painful! The last time I visited him, I took my two younger sisters with me and we spent a wonderful day in London. I bought Leslie lots of new clothes and we went to a lovely restaurant for lunch. What lovely manners my son had. Hope Jimmy keeps this up, teaching him the right way, as the future is telling me I will be out of this country within the next couple of years, over 5000 miles away. Something I will have to do.

On returning him to my Mother-in-Law's flat on this last day, he would not take his little arms from around my neck, his fingers dug in and I had scratches. What a devastating finish to the day. I cannot say how long I sobbed.

Went back to Portsmouth and Southsea and my part time job in the cinema, which now has turned into full time. I was working as an usherette, showing people to their seat with a torch, (flashlight), then got upgraded, I guess is the word, to selling ice cream during the intermission. Then again I was suddenly in charge of the ice cream room and kiosk, candy and cigarette concession. I guess it doesn't sound like a big deal, but I was responsible for all the takings in both places. I finished up going in to work on my day off to make sure everything balanced, amazing what one will do for 5 pounds a week. In 1963 that was about $15.00. Crazy, eh?

4   And Then Along Came Dave

My next experience was dealing with the assistant manager, Mr. David Robbins. The manager arranged a little get together in the lobby at the theatre one evening, before the place opened, to wish his assistant a Happy 21st Birthday. I thought that's funny, my birthday is four days away. Maybe we have something in common, anyway never thought any more about it. He turned 21, I turned 24, and I felt much older.

Guess he had his eyes on me. Yeah! Did not know at the time that I would love this man 50 years later! His pick-up line, as we lived in a naval town, was "Is your husband at sea?" I remember answering "No, I wish he was". Well suddenly it's "Would you like to meet me for a drink?" "Yes I would". "O.K, meet me in the off licence in the pub across the street". An off licence is a small little room where pubs sell off sale beer and liquor from, and most of them have somewhere one can sit and have a drink. I went across after the cinema closed, and sat in the off licence for about 15 to 20 minutes wondering if he would show up. He finally arrived about 30 minutes later. We sat and talked, just small talk, and then I told him I had to go home, it was late and my Mum had been watching Les for me while I was at work. We shook hands, strange but nice. I knew that he would ask me out again, woman's intuition, or maybe vanity?

Guess I must have tickled his fancy. He came after me again (very soon!). Well, I think I fell in love with him from the start. Had not even had a date, but there was something about him that just grabbed my heart, still does to this day, and we are now in our seventies (long story).

Our first date was a surprise to me. I did not know what to expect, as his family was a little upper class (England does have this class thing, it is not money, it is breeding). Our family was working class, his was ex-military. His father with an O.B.E., brother, teaching at a very exclusive school etc. etc. Anyway, I did not really let that interfere with my decision to go. It was my day off and I had gone across to the cinema, which was very close to Mum and Dad's house, to watch the present movie playing, Sodom and Gomorra. I was about half way through the movie, and enjoying it, when the manager came to relay a message from my Mother who had walked across the street to let me know that my husband was there and wanted to talk to me. Funny really, I did not think it strange that he would be here from London at this time of night, so I left the movie and went to the house. I will never forget what I found when I walked in. Dave was sitting there and Mum was ironing, and evidently they were saying my husband at the house was the excuse they concocted between them to bring me back home, I had introduced him to my parents a couple of weeks earlier as far as I can remember, and they loved him straight away.

OK now the date. We went to a really neat little bar in Old Portsmouth, where one could see ships going in and out of the docks or harbour, the bar was upstairs with big windows and very cozy atmosphere. Had a great evening and after finding that Dave had a sense of humour like mine, felt suddenly lifted out of the doldrums.

It is now well into 1963 nearly the end of summer, and our dating has continued (secretly), as working in the same place we were not supposed to date, management were not allowed to fraternise with staff. We were never found out and even after revisiting the place on a holiday from the Bahamas, no one had ever known or suspected. How Dave's little Mini car was not spotted outside the house I don't know. (Dave has told me since, that the cinema has been demolished about 2010 and manager gone, he would now be 104). Dave now lives about a three hour car ride from there in England and has visited the town on many occasions. Sunday mornings were really special. Dave and I would get to have 2 or 3 hours on a little beach across from Hayling Island where the ferry started from, (that is the island I was prisoner on when I was eleven, health retreat gone now.) and we would have a drink in a local pub on the way home to Mum and Dad's. Sometimes he would stay for Sunday dinner, (lunch) extra treat for me. Then we had to go to work at 4pm.

My father worked in a small nightclub which one had to take the ferry on across from Portsmouth, or drive the long way around, which is what Dave and I would do occasionally after finishing work in the evening. What a fun place it was! Dad worked behind a small bar, and there was a band, and the 'piece de resistance' was "Chicken in a Basket with Chips" (fries). Superb!!! We danced, we ate, and we had a drink or two. Sometimes we would take Mum with us, and then Dave would drive us all home and he would spend the night on the pull out couch in the living room. I spent a few nights creeping in there from my room, which was down the hall. Naughty girl! It was quite a long time before I had sex with Dave, I think he was about to give up on me and I knew I couldn't lose him, so I finally gave in. It turned out to be very different to what I had been used to and I think it was good for both of us,. to be hugged all night is still one of the best things in the world!

September, and it was Dave's birthday. I had saved up and bought him a portable radio. Now our beach trips were even better.

One time, I guess we were both off, we went across on the ferry to Hayling. Beautiful sandy beaches, and when the weather is warm it was idyllic. I remember meeting Bob, David's brother. Nothing like him, but really nice guy!. Amazing how different two brothers can be. I like my one the best!! Summer hurrying by. Dave having fun with Mum on a Sunday morning, shutting her in the pantry and then picking her up when he let her out. Good fun times!

Something now comes to mind that was really sad, and upsetting. It is November '63 and Dave has been sent on a course by the company. I am at work one Friday, and Dave is on his way home by train. Cannot remember where from. Anyway, halfway through the main picture, an announcement was made that President John F. Kennedy had been assassinated and the theatre would be closing. I seem to remember a lot of people in tears. How awful! I went home and still did not believe it!

Dave arrived home the next day. I guess he heard from someone on the train about the tragedy that was an event that affected the whole world.

Nearly Xmas. I told Mum I had seen this beautiful nightdress in 'M and S', one of our stores in England. I wore night clothes in those days. It was pale blue with dainty white spots on, full length, and made from material that looked like organza, very feminine, never thought anymore of it. Now December 24th. We have family at the house, my Dad's brother has come from London, so we have seven for Xmas. Dave has popped in before work to give me a gift! Guess What? The gorgeous blue nightdress. I think Mum must have told him. What a lovely surprise!

New Year's was not quite so nice as Xmas. The cinema held a party for staff and guests Dave brought an ex -girlfriend, he obviously could not bring me, and the manager had met her before so I guess it looked good for Dave to bring a date.

1964. Still trying to see my son who is five now, for more than one day at a time. This is where money would speak loudly, don't have any!

This year, not knowing that it would change my life forever, was actually very exciting. David was transferred to another cinema, about five or six miles away, so I would visit him on a Saturday after

I finished work, and after he finished we would go to the club in Gosport where Dad worked.

I am not sure what convinced me to change jobs, but I did. Decided to work in a local hospital, that's if I got hired. I did, and started. I was put on a geriatric ward on the male side, about 30 beds in one large ward and mostly older men with very bad health problems. The uniform was like a nurse's, even though I was not trained, I could have been mistaken for an R.N. or equivalent. The dark blue pinafore, the white starched apron, and the white cap, black stockings and black shoes to finish it off. I think this outfit turned Dave on I'm sure, as every chance he got, he would pick me up from the hospital after my shift, just to see me walk across to the nurses' locker room where we put our uniform in the laundry. Had to wear a clean one every day. One was never allowed to leave the hospital grounds with a uniform on. Good rule!

My mother told me "you won't be able to do that job", taking care of sick people with cancer, gangrene, and many more bodily malfunctions, would be very hard to deal with. Well I did it! She was right, not easy, in fact the first man that died on my shift I had to help lay him out. He was about 75 years old and the sweetest man, how sad! I had never seen a dead body before, and when they told me that I had to stuff all his orifices with cotton wool, and tie a tight bandage around his penis, that was the night I did not eat dinner. I guess it was like any other job, when one does it every day, it becomes routine and seems normal. The thing was, there was nothing normal about this man who died. His name was Mr. Long (true story) and when the male nurse pulled the sheets down for me to get started on this nasty job, I nearly had a nervous breakdown. His penis was laying across his thigh, I had not seen more than a couple of penis's in my life, but I knew this was something unusual. It was enormous! How did he ever make love to a woman? Glad it wasn't me. Finally, the male nurses standing in the doorway laughing at my predicament, all went about their work, can anyone blame me for not wanting my dinner?

Going along for a few months and everything is OK. Suddenly, Dave tells me he is moving to London to go to Croupier School, and hopefully get a job as a crap dealer in the Bahamas. I was very upset at the thought of him going to London, which was out of my reach at the moment, but I would be working on that. It seemed like an eternity, before I would see him again.

We spoke on the phone a few times, and then I made a decision! I was going to quit my job and go to London, which is what I did. I am sure Mum was worried about me making this move, but I was adventurous and in love, and Dave agreed to it.

Off I went on a train, 2 hours the first leg of the journey, then on to the underground, not really sure of where I was going, anyway after a few hours of trains and tubes I made it. I was over the moon to see this man who had stolen my heart, big time! Not sure how he felt, he was not the type to really express his feelings, only physically I guess!

He was staying in a 3rd floor flat that I believed was owned by a friend of a friend. It had one bedroom, living room, bathroom and a small kitchen. Very small, but all one needed to live quite comfortably. Roger, who owned the flat, lived elsewhere. I supposed that was why Dave had rented it from him.

I suddenly found that I was going to the local butcher shop and buying meat to cook for our meal at night. I did not have a job yet, so I had all day to do stuff. I loved it, felt really needed!

I had not had much experience at cooking for other people, just Jimmy and Leslie. I think it came to me very easily because I loved to do it, and I think I was going to turn into a pretty good cook somewhere down the road.

My mother cooked basic English fare and whatever she cooked always came out well, her Victoria sponge cakes were really delicious, and our Sunday roast, whatever meat it was that she roasted even cooked well done, was very tasty. I know I am missing that already.

I am looking through the paper every day for a job, not sure what I want to do yet. I suppose it would be great if I could find something similar to what I have done already, don't think I will try hospital again, even though I was told by a Sister, (that is a high up R.N. in England) who was in charge of the ward I worked on, that I should pursue nursing as a career because I had a lot of compassion for people, nice compliment, but I don't think I want four or five years of training, and how would I afford to keep myself? So I just keep looking.

Roger (the guy who owned the flat), sometimes joined us for dinner, he was very nice and easy to get along with. I remember him mentioning that at some time he was going to paper the bedroom that Dave and I were in. One morning, being on my own and having time to spare, I found rolls of wallpaper in the spare cupboard in the bedroom, and some pots of paste to put it on the wall with, also a trestle table for laying the paper on. So, what did I do? I papered the bedroom, of course! Had it done before Dave and Roger arrived home for lamb chops, and roasted spuds and peas that I had cooked that afternoon, which like the bedroom wallpaper job, came out superb! David was tired most nights, as he was working in a large store (famous one in London) during the day in the Xmas department, and going to school in the evening. Roger and I sometimes picked him up from the dealers' school, and we would go to a local pub for a drink.

December is approaching and I know what is coming. Dave has passed his training to become a croupier, and will be leaving before Xmas to work in the Bahamas. .

We drove to Portsmouth two weeks before he was due to leave, so that he could say goodbye to my Mum and Dad. Is it really going to happen?

He bought Mum a box of Xmas crackers, (a cardboard novelty that is tube shaped and covered in pretty paper, then pulled apart by two people holding one end each, then it makes a small pop like a Chinese firecracker). This is an English tradition that has been going on since 1850. Invented by a sweet and candy maker named Tom Smith. His sons took over, when he died, and the cracker business grew. Small paper hats shaped like crowns were inserted into the middle of the cracker when they were made, and after it was pulled apart the hat fell out and it would be worn. Then they started having really nice novelty's in them, which would make some of the boxes one bought very expensive. Every dinner plate at the Xmas table would have a cracker on it. They normally sold in boxes of twelve, so if one had more than a dozen people for dinner, two boxes were needed. A lovely tradition that is still going!

We left my parent's house and drove back to London, having a very close call on the drive back. It was raining very hard and dark and dreary, a typical English winter night in December. A woman in a car in front of us, suddenly slammed on her brakes and we swerved and spun around a couple of times before finishing up maybe 12 inches from a large tree. I remember we went up the curb sideways and luckily came to a stop before we hit the tree. Silly Cow! What was she doing? I think if I remember correctly, after sitting for ten minutes looking at each other and sighing big breaths of relief, we went for a stiff brandy! We were very lucky, a mini is a small car, and I was really thankful that Dave was a very good driver. I think God had plans for us.

It is the night before David is due to leave. I cannot sleep, and the bus garage across the street has a red neon sign in the front of the building that flashes all night and shows through our bedroom window. PLEASE, please don't let it be morning! Well morning came, and Dave did not want me to go to the airport with him, so we are saying our goodbyes at the top of the stairs on the 3rd floor landing. I am not saying goodbye, I am not saying anything, I am crying too hard. He is Gone!

5 Fate Opens a Door, Bahama Bound

The next chapter of my life takes a wonderful, unbelievable turn, I really believed in fate from then on!

I had found a wonderful job before Dave left, in London, very close to the BBC. My first job in London at 15, working with printing and multi-graph machines helped me procure this job I believe. Now, with Dave gone, I have to find a second job so that I can save up to go to the Bahamas and see him, even for a week's holiday. I searched and found another job, which I had also had experience at, and that was working in the cinema near the coast. I now got hired in London in a very prestigious theatre. After I left my daytime job, I could jump on the tube and get to the theatre in time for the evening show where I served ice creams and juice drinks. In those days we had a tray, basically a small box with a light attached, that would have a strap which went over the head and around the shoulder so the box sat at the waist, not too heavy to carry. During the intermission, the girls selling the ice creams and drinks would stand in the middle aisle in front of the stage, and the patrons would go and buy their choice, and then two or three times during the movie we would walk up and down the aisles backwards so that people could see the small light if they wanted to buy something. The light on the tray helped to see the money and give change, and obviously let people know we were there! Working upstairs in the circle was a bit more scary in the dark, if one lost ones footing," lights out" to coin a phrase, but a fun job really! The first movie playing in the London theatre when I started, was Mary Poppins with Julie Andrews, great entertainment!

I finished in the cinema about 11 pm every night and would get back to the flat around 11:45, depending on the underground trains. One night while I was taking a break in the girls lounge, one of the people I worked with came to tell me that there was a young man asking for me. I went out to the lobby and this lovely looking chap said he had a message from Dave. What! How great was this. I remember I had written to him a couple of weeks previously, and told him I would do anything to get over to see him. Well actually no surprise to me, the message was on the back of a pack of matches, THAT'S DAVID!, and it said, 'I hope you don't mean you would do anything xx (kisses)', and that is all it said! I was happy with it though, it meant something to me guess he does care! A very sad thing happened to the nice young man with the matches from Dave. From what I found out he was on holiday with his girlfriend in England, taking a break from the island. Evidently one night they sat in his car with the heater on and the windows closed (January can be bitter cold in London) and were overcome by carbon monoxide fumes, they both died, and I may have been one of the last few to see this nice person alive. God works in mysterious ways, and we never find out why!

I am now leaving the flat in the morning about 7 am, going to the office, and leaving there about 5 pm and rushing to the cinema. Heck of a long day! One morning I woke up and felt very ill, think a touch of the flu. I called in sick, and sat in front of a small electric fire in the living room until about 10 am, turned the thing on and off as I am paying the electric bill, then I went three floors down to the front of the building to buy a newspaper from a stand. Went back upstairs and made a cuppa, and wrapped in a blanket sat and started to read the paper. Suddenly, half way through, I turned a page and there in big bold black letters it read, 'Bahama Island, New Hotel Opening needs staff in every department, call this number for an appointment for an interview'. I cannot believe it! My flu suddenly just feels like a runny nose at this moment. The phone was in my hand and I was dialing. Could this be the fate I have wondered about?

The phone rang half a dozen times, and I was ready to put the receiver down, when a voice said "Hello! This is Major Blah, Blah" (cannot remember his name, one would think I would never forget it, told you-I was a good candidate for Alzheimer's). He then said "may I help you"? I told him I was calling in reference to the ad about the Bahama position and I would like to get an interview set up. The interviews were held in a Hotel in London. I managed to get one a few days later during my lunch hour. Very nervous, I showed up to a suite in the hotel for my interview. Major Blah-Blah was sitting behind a beautiful desk and stood up to shake my hand. How wonderful! Manners oozing! He looked like a Major should look. Very smart suit, shirt and tie, tanned face with a rather large moustache, and tall and slim. We chatted for a few minutes and then I had paperwork to complete. When I finished, the Major looked it over and then said "This looks fine Samantha, but I have to tell you we have all the staff we need right now". "Your name will go on the extra list, so-to-speak". The air went out of my balloon, and my heart sank to my thighs. I was too late! We said "goodbye" and I went back to work feeling very down, I think at the theatre that night I ate three chocolate ice cream sandwiches, two would have done the trick, but they tasted so good I had to have another one. I did not need to worry about my shape in those days. That night I dragged my ass to the underground, got home, fell into bed really depressed, and a miracle, I fell asleep even with the neon sign flashing. Why wouldn't I?. long, hard sad day!

Three weeks later, I am at my desk in the office, and the girl who worked next to me passes the phone saying "Sam, it's for you". It was Major Blah-Blah. What!! "Hello Samantha, are you still interested in going to the Bahamas"? Is the guy crazy? I think I said yes at least five times. He tells me a person that they hired became very ill and is in the hospital, so I could take her place working in the housekeeping department if I was interested. I did not care which place or what department I would be working, I accepted the job. The hotel would pay my fare from England to the Bahamas, and I would pay it back from my pay cheque every week. Fine with me, I am going to see the man I am in love with. Do I care about the job I will be doing?

After that phone call, I went to the post office in my lunch hour (seems I have not eaten lunch during my lunch hour in a long time). I found a telegram form on one of the counters, and started to write a couple of lines to Dave. In 1965 the post office had little ink pots filled with liquid ink, and pens with pointed sharp nibs on, consequently one had to dip the pen in and out of the ink pot to write on any postal paperwork. I got halfway through my message when the pen nib caught on the edge of the pot and pulled it out of the hole it was sitting in, enough to spill ink all over my telegram. Do you think this deterred me? No! I blotted the paperwork and took it to the clerk at the counter to send it off. The man who took it looked at me a little strange and told me that it was very difficult to read, and was I sure I wanted to send this? I was not to be put off. I sent it!

At 2 am in the morning or about that time, I had a phone call from Dave to say he had received my telegram, but he could not read it. Why? I blotted it didn't I? I then told him I had got a job and I would be arriving in about 3 days, hard to believe eh? He never really had much of a reaction, but that was David, He will never change!

Now I have to get to Portsmouth and say goodbye to the best Mum and Dad, and sisters that anyone could ever have. Fabulous family and I'm not sure when I would see them again. I found myself in the mail car on a train from London to the coast about 2 days after I talked to Dave. The train was so packed, when I ran onto the platform about 5:30 pm, the mail bag car was the only option, and I was very lucky that the guard let me on there. Mum (I loved you Mum) was so worried about me going 5000 miles with about £5.

That was roughly $14 dollars in my pocket. I convinced her I would be fine, and Dave would meet me when I got to the Bahamas, which seemed to settle her down. OK, goodbyes over with, over two hours back to the flat, and next morning packing bags and so excited I can hardly breathe. Roger has offered to take me to Heathrow airport. We became pretty good friends after Dave left. Shame we never kept in touch.

The day has arrived. How do I try to explain what I feel? I can't! Arrived at the airport and Roger has helped me through the checking-in process. Time to get the shuttle out to the plane. In those days the planes never pulled up to the gates, one had to take a small courtesy bus out to the runway and board from there. A huge 707 Scary! How does this thing get off the ground? I am very cool, pretending as I board that I am a routine traveler. Book in hand, I take my seat next to a rather middle aged, well-bred lady, who knew I was a novice by the way my knuckles turned white as I gripped the arm rests during takeoff. I watched out of the window as this ginormous machine picked up speed and gradually lifted very smoothly off of the ground into the air. Unbelievable feeling! (Now days, I do not watch take off, I close my eyes until I hear the cocktail trolley coming round, that's about an hour in the air). Got a little cowardly in my old age.

What an experience on a 707 with about 300 other people, eating, drinking, and watching movies. The turbulence got to me a few times. Instantly thought we were going to crash, but the guy next to me on the other side assured me that this was all part of flying in a big bird. OK, guess I feel better.

I think if a person does not believe in fate, a good part of my story may make a lot of people change their minds. The first part of this fate was having the flu and taking off work to sit and read a newspaper. That was something I never did, now I am on my way to the Bahamas. "Yippee"!

The first part of the journey will take me to New York (I think I've heard of it!). After that to Nassau, capital of the Bahamas, also called New Providence. One night stay there, and then on to Freeport, small out island. All very exciting and also a bit scary on my own. I have never been out of England. David on the other hand, was on big liners (ships) going to South Africa and other port-of-calls when he was very young. For his 23 years he was well travelled.

It is now about 2 hours into the first leg of my adventure and a really strange thing, small world! Still is. One of the stewardesses (they were called that then), came to me and said "Excuse me, are you the lady that is going to the Bahamas?" I said "yes", wondering what was going on. Then she said "I have another lady on board who is also going there would you like to meet her?" "Of course, yes I would", I said. This could be the start of a friendship. Her name was Sarah, and as I mentioned earlier "small world". She would turn out to be my roommate, working for the same hotel, and she was British, which made it easier in many ways as we understood each other's humour, etc… The Bahamas were British Islands until they claimed independence in 1972.

We are now landing in New York's Kennedy Airport, how ironic! J.F.K. I don't think most of the world, especially America, have come to terms with the assassination of the president John F. Kennedy, and when I think about the night I was working and they closed the theatre, this sure does not feel real that I have just landed here. Did I mention fate?

6 New Friends, New Food

I have hooked up with Sarah, she seems a pretty nice person, and we are getting along fine. We sit and discuss the job we have both taken, and so much we are not sure about, and we are both a little apprehensive of what is to come, I am very lucky, I have Dave living there and watching out for me, she has nobody. At this time we have no idea that we will be roommates along with two Canadian girls. I am finding out that I am very adventurous, didn't know I had it in me! It seems the only thing I am nervous about is seeing Dave when he picks me up at the airport.

Sarah and I have a couple of hours to kill before the next flight to Nassau. "Sam, (seems everybody calls me that now), what about a coffee", Sarah says. I have to be very careful with my money, and make sure it lasts until I arrive on the island. Anyway, found out the coffee was not too expensive so we had one. Finally our flight was called, and we were boarding.

Another few hours in the air, but getting closer. I think we landed in Nassau Bahamas early evening. We found the hotel we were booked in, nothing special, but we were not paying so who cares? Suddenly we had a bit of an issue at the front desk. It was cleared up after an hour or so, when the hotel that hired us called and clarified our booking, "Thank God". Did not want my first night in the Capital of the Bahamas to be on the street.

We had an enormous ceiling fan in the middle of our room, and Sarah and I found it a real novelty. Neither one of us had felt 80% humidity or seen ceiling fans before. Sweating wasn't the word, are we going to be living with this every day (Afraid so)!

Never thought I would love cold water! Think I had at least 3 cold showers in the next 8 hours, never seen a shower before either. Cannot remember what time we left the hotel, but I know it was before noon. We get to the airport and finally are about to board our last plane. This long haul was nearly at an end. Did I tell you that I had a tweed coat and gloves that I put on to save carrying them, I cannot say how uncomfortable I was, this is not how I wanted Dave to see me when I arrived, (I am blond), I left it on!

"Excuse me! Is this the plane? Propellers?" Have to walk uphill to our seat? Oh Lord! Am I going to meet my maker? Woe is me! In a tweed coat and suede gloves. Well, I didn't know, did I? And nobody mentioned the humidity!!!!!

We are approaching the island, looking down at the ocean, it was unbelievable! Green, blue, and turquoise even better than postcards I'd seen. Nearly there, nearly there! My heart is pounding and I feel very light headed (could have been the extra clothing I have on), even though I am sweating, glowing for ladies, please! Sorry, sweating is definitely it. This machine is landing, bumping, and jumping along the runway, but on the ground. Hallelujah!

In later years I learned the plane was a DC 3. Very safe, from all accounts, got me there! As the plane door opened the heat came in like opening an oven door. Here I am in my winter attire (well it is January in England and I am blond, I did tell you). Off came the coat and the gloves and it really didn't feel much different. The air is sticky and heavy, and very hot compared to where I came from.

Cannot see Dave as I approach the very small terminal building. Have customs and immigration to go through, no problem there. Then I see him. Coffee in hand, which nearly went as I rushed him.

It's only been a couple of months or so since I last saw him, but felt much longer.

We say our Hi's and he walks me to his car. Wow! It's one of those American jobs with the big wings front and back, and how strange to hear American voices on the radio. I felt a bit like a celebrity in this huge car, and on this little desert island.

The hotel where I had acquired the job had sent a representative to meet us. A young good looking guy with a (I learned this), crew cut, typical American boy next door look. He took Sarah in his car, and Dave followed behind, to the hotel. This was not what one would call a pretty island, only the beaches were beautiful. The landscape was rather barren, but the palm trees made it look tropical. I heard a rumour that a lot of the palm trees were imported, and that most of the island was made up of pine trees. It turned out to be true.

The man who supposedly bought up hundreds of acres of this island years earlier, frequented the only casino on the island at the moment, very exclusive place. This is where Dave worked.

We now arrive at the hotel that I am going to work in, and the boy next door (Buzz), shows us to the room where we will all gather for orientation and all the other stuff we need to know, like where our apartments are, and hours we will work, and when. Dave leaves, and informs me he will pick me up later, evidently, knowing where I am going to be.

Cannot remember exactly how many of us were there for this pre-work meeting, but I think at least 25 to 30. Very mixed bunch of people. A lot of Europeans, French, Italian, Spanish, and Brits. Actually it was a very interesting couple of hours. We were all told of our busy schedules (early morning!) and then issued with nylon overalls to those of us in housekeeping. Picture this! Ninety percent humidity, and clean 15 rooms while wearing a nylon overall. This is where the expression "glowing" completely left me. Sweating does not even cover it either, but here I am in paradise, so work hard, get a tan, and enjoy every minute. This was a dream come true, "Yeah" but in the next few months it would turn into a nightmare.

After the two hour meeting at the hotel, we were taken to our living quarters, apartments about 2 miles away. Sarah and I were delegated a 2 bedroom apartment to share with two Canadian girls. We all got along pretty good.

That evening Dave picked me up and I believe our first stop was the apartment he shared with Barry, a friend of ours from England, who by the way, lived in the same home town as we did. He happened to be at work when we arrived. (Barry passed away a few years ago from cancer, another good friend lost).

No! This was not planned was it? After about an hour in bed, Barry came home. Glad he did not walk in on us. I had not seen the man in months. We said hello and had a conversation for a while, then Dave and I left and went for a drink. Then Dave took me back to the apartment and I had to prepare myself for the bus that would pick me up at 6:30 am, that came around very fast!

My first day was very hard, cleaning and changing sheets in 15 rooms in a nylon overall with that humidity would definitely help to keep one slim, and now I am 75 I have great respect and admiration for hotel maids! Some hotel guests can be very ugly, dirty and demanding, also forget to leave a gratuity!

My first day off, I went to the beach with a girl I befriended in Housekeeping. We had to walk maybe three miles or more. No transportation at this stage of the game. When we reached the beach, next to the hotel where Dave worked (he was on the day shift at the moment), we met some croupiers and spent a fun couple of hours. We then went to the dealers' cafeteria in the hotel where I met Dave for lunch.

The guys from the beach showed up and found out I was Dave's girlfriend. Guess they were a little dashed, all the work they put in trying to make good impressions. The ratio of men to women on this island was about 20 guys to one girl. Pam, my girlfriend, on the other hand was having a ball! Pretty soon I remember Dave working a swing shift now and again, and that meant that I did not get to bed early, but I was very young and "I could handle anything baby!"

One night Dave took me to this little steak house where some of the dealers hung out. This would be one of my first American meals that to this day I love. Hard to believe one can enjoy a meal at 11:30 pm, but everyone did it then. Steak and Caesar salad to die for! Next thing I would love would be escargots, "Excuse Me!" Who in this world would eat snails? I would! After two friends took us to dinner one night and convinced me to try one that was it! Same for David. To this day one of my all-time favourites. If you have never tried it, don't knock it! I think this was probably the start of my education to food, and how to act properly in a gourmet restaurant. I had never been to one before. Learning which fork to go for first! I now consider that I can mix with the high and the low and I am very happy with that. I tasted food that I had never heard of in England, so glad I tried it, made life much more interesting.

It is about six months since I made it to the island and the hotel. I have just been promoted. I am now in charge of the housekeeping department, working the late shift behind glass windows and a locked door. There were a few shady characters that would hang around the back door of the hotel where the staff came out from, I don't think I have to explain anything further than that. Dave would pick me up at the end of my shift. Oh relief! To the pub, or the steak house. What a life eh? Then the "Caca" hit the fan.

There had been quite a few people complaining about the staff food, rice four or five days a week, and also from the girls who cleaned 16 rooms a day, not allowed to take their nylon overalls off during their lunch break (30 minutes). This whole scenario started to really look a lot like slave labour! Lots of the workers wanted someone to write a letter to one of our politicians in England about the conditions, and suddenly I was the chosen one, oh please why me? well I wrote a letter to the best of my ability explaining our working conditions and our food and everybody involved read it and agreed we should send it.

About one month later, believe it or not, a very British man, bowler hat, umbrella the whole deal, showed up and arranged a meeting with the workers. Everybody had a say, and it boiled down to our very British government man, telling us even though we were living on a British island the government could not intervene with problems of any kind unless there was a war!

I think this could have started one! Well, the very proper "Limey" government man left, and we had to carry on and deal with it whatever it was.

7 Facing Deportation

One morning, Pam and I went to the beach relaxing on our day off. About an hour after getting there, a van from the hotel showed up, and two guys jumped out and told us we were going to be deported that afternoon, about 4 pm. What? It was like a movie scene. This was very scary and very real. These men were not very pleasant and had no compassion for us at all. We were told to get into the van and we would be taken to our apartments to pack our stuff. What? Why? How? We got to our apartments, I called Dave at work, this was not a habit of mine, but I considered this a time to do it, and in a hurry! I think writing to the proper Limey man was a mistake!

I had about four or five hours left before I would be shipped off. Was it something I said? Why did I get picked? Why did I speak out loud? I really was speaking for all of us! Guess it got me into Big Trouble. It seemed like an eternity before Dave called me back and said "sit tight, everything will be OK". Another hour goes by and, finally I get another call from him telling me that I have been given a Culinary card, (I have no idea what that is, or from where or who) but paid for. I cannot be shipped off without a union hearing which could take weeks!

Guess the word got through to management and security, as soon as I heard, they heard and left our apartment. Dave had made friends with a bouncer, come security guard, who worked in the casino, he once was a famous heavyweight champion in the boxing world Joe was his name, (died in Vegas years later), lovely man. Well he knew a man that was up high in the union, and I guess he put a word in for Dave and certainly me. Never knew how to thank him, and that deed was not all he did. Next thing we heard was the union guy went to the main island for some sort of meeting, and was killed. Is this a script for a movie or what? Am I coming or going? Literally!

There was this strange law on the island, one could not leave one's job and work somewhere else, unless a release was issued from management. Well our friend the boxer, unbeknown to us, was also close with the owner (or one of them) of the hotel I was working at. He got in touch with one of the main men who lived somewhere in the U.S, I believe. The man came to the island and called a meeting at the hotel for us poor souls who were very confused. He was the nicest person and apologised for all the problems and stress we were experiencing and issued releases for all who wanted to leave and work somewhere else. Needless to say, I was one of them.

8 A Wench Saga, Big Skirt, Little Money

I did not have to wait long before finding another job. I managed to find a food waitress position in our local pub, this time the manager was from Switzerland I believe. The hotel manager was German, only difference was that this one could occasionally be pleasant! I started work on the lunchtime shift, and being as the pub was British themed, the waitresses had to wear an outfit like an old English wench. Long skirt, off the shoulder white blouse, and a white cap, that seemed to come off All-The-Time! What a SHAME!

The Navy would come to the island about every couple of months and then I had to work evening hours. They used to drink upstairs and that meant carrying about 10 pints on a tray with one hand, and picking up the skirt with the other, or "you're a gonna down the stairs"! The manager sometimes showed you up for no reason, so one was careful to do things right.

This next episode will probably be one of the most embarrassing moments I can remember.

Dave and I made friends with a couple who lived above us on the second floor. Sid and Abby, she worked in the casino where Dave worked, and he would take over the job of manager in the pub after the "Swiss Miss" was deported for reasons unknown. Before this happened, I was working the lunch time shift, and Sid and Abby came in on my shift one weekend to eat pork chops, which was a favourite on the menu. The chops were served with mashed potatoes or chips, (fries) applesauce, peas and two little red crab apples for decoration purposes. Very attractive tasty meal (NOT BY THE TIME I WAS FINISHED WITH IT), I went to their table, served them with a cocktail and a beer, and we had a conversation for a minute or two before I went to the next customer. Lunchtimes were very busy in this establishment and waiting time for a meal was at least 25 to 30 minutes.

The cooking area was in view of customers as it was an open pit with a grill and ovens etc. and there was waist high red brick wall that separated the chef from the servers. Condiments and sauces were also in an area at the end of the wall for us to take to the tables for people who requested them.

It is now about 30 minutes since I took the order for my neighbours and the chef has beckoned to me that I need to pick up. The tray most of us carried did not hold two dinner plates side by side. It was not quite big enough. Anyway I went to the wall and the chef put the dinners on my tray, balancing one plate slightly on the edge of the other and a little over the side of the tray. I got to the booth with my precious cargo, and suddenly the plate that was slightly over the edge of the tray tipped a little and touched my arm. It was red hot! So up in the air the whole thing went, splattered everywhere in front of me. I think I wore a lot of it. This was one of the worst hours I could remember, especially as I was hoping Abby would get me an interview at the hotel for a job in the casino.

These two people had to be one of the nicest couples I had met on the island. Not only did they not make a fuss, but they helped me clean it up and ordered another pork chop lunch. They must have been VERY hungry. Blew my mind! This time everything went perfect, I made sure of that.

9 Casino Story, No Skirt, Big Money

Abby got me an interview and I was hired as a cocktail waitress in the casino. I was so excited, but I really did not know the difference between a Screwdriver and a Rusty Nail (Do we have a carpenters' convention in?). One had to learn in a hurry or it was "go to the end of the line" from the service bartender, with the line being nine girls in front of you in the service bar getting their drinks before you. Now your customers are waiting. I think I went to the end of the line for three weeks, nearly every night I worked. Amazing how fast one learns when ones tips are in jeopardy, and when someone thinks a cocktail waitress is dumb then I need to say that I think this is very unfounded, trust me! If you cannot remember what alcohol goes into what drink, and where you deliver the order, then you are dumb! Memory is really important when one is serving cocktails. The service bartender needs the drinks in a special ordering way too, starting with whisky, scotch, rye, etc…, then gin, vodka, and lastly, mixed drinks that need cream or are on a blender. The whole thing boils down to him not picking up the same liquor bottle more than maybe one time for each drink ordered, and 10 girls are waiting on him for their orders, so one dummy can really hold up the conveyor belt, if you know what I mean.

I guess this is the start of my serving drinks for a living (for the next 50 years and still going). Making money was suddenly very easy, and the outfit we had to wear was definitely a help towards the cause. Black stockings, Danskin elastic high cut elastic panties over the top, a black tuxedo type jacket, with short tails at the back. White blouse, black bow tie, and high heels finished it off. It was actually very classy, but also pretty sexy and expensive. We had to buy our own uniforms, which existed of two black jackets, 100 dollars apiece, made by a Chinese tailor who had a small shop downtown. The stockings and black panties we had to buy in Miami, and that meant we waited for someone to go there on a shopping spree on a weekend getaway. The stockings turned out to be the most precious thing to our outfit as they probably were the most abused. Gamblers flicking cigar ash on them, putting them on in a hurry, taking them off the same way (for some of the girls I'm sure) And at 5 dollars a pair, which was quite a bit in those days, it could get a little too much, but I guess we were all making enough money not to worry about stockings.

Not only is this job a money maker, it is also a red carpet of sorts. Movie stars and celebrities coming in all the time. Very exciting for a girl from England, waiting on a Hollywood star.

Most of them were very easy to wait on, but there were one or two who really let everybody know that they were famous, and they were the ones who would stiff you (stiff you means they did not tip). I learnt lots of phrases in the casino. One of the first being "86 him". I always went to one particular waitress to find out what these sayings meant. When a pit boss or someone in charge said "86 that person", that meant help him or her leave from the place now, plus with help from security. It was an American saying that I had never heard of.

I cannot divulge cocktail waitresses secrets, but my source for learning taught me lots of little tricks. She had been doing this job a long time and was full of tricks of her own. All the girls seem to look up to her.

There was a small lounge or show room adjacent to the casino, and all ten waitresses had to take turns working there a couple of nights a week, unless one worked the day shift in the casino.

The show room held roughly about 80 people or so and had good live entertainment. I remember some of the groups were great! This was also a place for big gamblers to leave their wives while they lost or won a fortune. Some of these wives were a pain in the butt! Because their husbands were big players we basically had to kiss many BUTTS.

10   Sun, Sand and Loving

Our days off were really great! Dave and I would go to the casino's gourmet room about once a month. Employees from the casino were given a good discount in the restaurant and the food was fabulous. We would dress up, and both of us with a good tan were a couple to be envied. I used to feel very attractive. Lovely feeling.

Weekends, specifically Saturdays, were great fun. About eight of us used to meet on one of our gorgeous beaches and play volleyball. The court itself we had all played a big part in putting together.

One morning, I'm guessing it had to be a Saturday, a few of us sat around and thought what if we had a net and a couple of poles to put in the sand, we could play volleyball. Well a few weeks of figuring this out and we came up with a plan.

There happened to be a construction site not too far from the beach where we hung out. So we picked the one in our crowd who we thought would make a good burglar and sent him to find two poles tall enough to bury in the sand and attach a net to, we would have paid for them, but we could never find anyone working there when we were on the beach. Some of the guys actually studied the height and width of the court, the rules and the whole thing. This was a serious project! Well our pretend burglar got the poles not long after.(another friend deceased) Then we found a cement truck driver that had a little extra cement on one of his loads that was going to be dumped anyway and gave him a nice tip to give us the spare he had. So we all worked hard and dug the holes (after reading up on the distance between, etc.). The truck showed up, poured the cement, and now we have to come up with a net and ball.

This was a small underdeveloped island. There is not a store to buy volleyballs and nets, so we have to wait until someone goes across to Florida to buy what we need. About two or three weeks later, we had our net and two balls. A couple of the guys, drilled holes in the top of the poles and put hooks in them to attach the net to, now we are ready to play. We did make our own fun on this island, that's for sure! but I think this is the first time any of us had played volleyball. We were all young and athletic, this will not be a problem.

I thought it would be a great idea to buy mugs for all of us to have a drink after the game. (not alcohol, we all worked on Saturday nights) and I painted everyone's name on each mug. We took it in turns taking them home and washing them. We also had one of us in charge of taking the net and ball home every week, keeping them safe just for us. Super times! Lots of fun and great exercise (with all the drinking after work and parties we had, we needed it).

All of a sudden we have a new place to drink. A new pub was opening, and very close to where we all worked. Very handy. Actually it was a really welcome change, and the place was always packed, even at 3 am. It was on the waterway and only about half a mile from the marina, where there was a fantastic little bar that served pizza, best I ever had. The cheese would literally hang off of a slice and the crust was thin and crispy. Good thing we had jobs that kept us moving, and parties that kept us hopping, plus the swimming and the volleyball, otherwise we would have been able to start an extra-large people club without hesitation!

11   R and R in America

It is now around 1967-68. Dave suggested we go across to Miami on the boat, about a four hour journey, then drive up the coast of the United States in our car for a vacation, at least three or four weeks if I remember correctly. Wow! Can't wait. We both managed to get the time off, and so we are set to go. I think it was early June when we sailed into Florida. Our Lincoln would be a very comfortable car to travel in, but neither one of us had ever driven in America. I am very glad Dave did all the driving.

We started our trip overnight in a hotel on Collins Avenue on the beach in Florida, already relaxed we went for a meal, I believe we had oysters, and then we went back to the hotel bar and spent a couple of hours chatting with the bartender and having a few cocktails. The next morning we went for breakfast and then started our adventure. This man of mine is very capable at driving on a freeway, and really being in charge. Amazing for a 26 year old, handsome, sexy, and with a brain. How lucky could I get?

I cannot remember our first overnight stop. I believe it was somewhere in Georgia. We drove through a lot of states, and the first "Dry State" came as a real eye opener. What is a Dry State? NO ALCOHOL? You have to be joking! After hours of driving and looking forward to a beer, we finished up with orange squash (crush?) in our room, and a vibrating bed that took two quarters for about 10 minutes of shaking. That was a novelty that made our night.

We are now heading towards Virginia and I have the map, (oops!), think I messed up. Suddenly we are in a fight. We did not do that very often, but this one was suddenly very ugly!

Guess I did not come up with the right exit or entry, think I had the map upside down. Either way, we were screaming at each other. I yelled "stop this blah-blah car and let me out". He did, on the freeway. I started walking on the side of the road and all of a sudden I see Dave backing up towards me, BACKING UP! That is not something drivers do on freeways in America, anyway he got level with me and said "Get your f^#!&* ass back in the car". I did, in a hurry. That was the last of it, peace for the next few weeks. The Southern states were very enjoyable, very different scenery and buildings.

We are now in Washington D.C., pouring with rain, pitch dark and Dave has turned onto a one-way street the wrong way. Turned out ok, no traffic coming towards us. We found our hotel, very nice, very old with a lot of atmosphere, and we are both ready to eat, drink and relax David must be tired, driving for hours at a time can really take its toll. Needless to say, our sex life for now has slowed down a little.

We really enjoyed Washington, great restaurants, and the Smithsonian, very interesting and educational. Next stop New York. THE BIG APPLE, YEAH!

Our first impression of Manhattan, Honking, Honking, and more Honking, from cabs. We live on a small British island in the Caribbean, two lanes and dirt roads, never heard anything like this before, a little unnerving when one is not accustomed to this much traffic, also on the wrong side of the road to what we are used to.

Dave and I had become friendly with a guy who came to the Bahamas quite a bit, and he lived in Queens, a suburb of New York. He invited us to stay with him anytime we were in his part of the world, so we took him up on his invitation. He had an older house, but comfortable. We would go on the subway when we went into the city, easier than driving and trying to find a place to park.

We did the usual tourist places, Empire State Building, Statue of Liberty, which I might add, we walked up all those tiny winding stairs, (Whew!), then the East side food markets. New York is an exciting city.

Next stop will be Connecticut, and we will be visiting Dave's brother, who took us on a tour of the school which was great, and as it was June the school was empty, so we got to see more than if the students were there.

The three of us had a nice meal that evening and then went to see the movie' Mash.' That show is still one of my favourites.

Next morning we said our goodbyes, and started the haul to Vermont. Dave has booked us a room in a hotel in a beautiful part of the state, already for when we arrive there. As we got closer to our destination, rolling hills, green landscape and as it was early morning with no traffic, fabulous surroundings.

We suddenly came upon a small chalet type restaurant that made their own maple syrup. Dave pulled in and we ordered, ham and eggs, pancakes with syrup. To this day I can still taste that. "To die for breakfast"!

A little tidbit of knowledge I learned about maple syrup. It takes about forty gallons of sap from the trees, boiled down, to make about one gallon of syrup. Worth every penny one has to pay for the real thing. Off we go again full of ham and eggs and maple syrup, feeling great!

Stowe is very close now, looks just like Switzerland without the snow. Plenty of chalet type buildings here, even a pub, which obviously we visited a few times. The local golf course beckoned us, maybe David more than me, but off we went carrying our clubs around eighteen holes. No cart here baby! Just one thru eighteen hills or so it seemed. I will never ever forget this golf course as I had one of the best holes I ever played, and really bad blisters hands and feet. I cannot remember which hole it was, but I teed off and had to make it across a long lake to the fairway, which I did, (miracle right there). Then after the fairway, maybe three or four strokes more to the green. Another miracle comes up. I hit a three wood to the edge of the green, chipped up and putted in. I parred a Par 5, Holy Cow! Never done it since, could have been all that maple syrup slowed me down to a very relaxed state!

What a beautiful place this is! Dave drove us up a very high hill, actually a small mountain I think about 2500 ft, until we found a couple of streams and places to sit and relax in this very clean air. I decided to take off shoes and pants and put legs into water. Am I crazy? Guess I was then. Absolutely freezing, but amazingly very exhilarating. To the pub for dinner, warm and cozy. What a super day. Thanks David, I love you!

Next leg of our journey will take us across the border into Canada, and the famous Niagara Falls. What a sight to behold. No picture can do this scene justice. The Canadian side of the falls is the most picturesque and the most visited and photographed.

Before we went to the hotel, Dave parked the car and we went as close as possible to the railing on the sidewalk to see this wonder without getting too wet. The spray from the falls can stretch a very long way and soak people lining the street maybe fifty yards away or more.

Our small little hotel/motel was only about a mile from the main attraction, so tomorrow we will explore and see wondrous things! I think we are staying here at least three maybe four days, not a lot of time to see and do everything, but how lucky am I to even be here?

Our first attraction was donning the yellow raincoats and boots, as in the movie "Niagara" (Marilynn Monroe), and going down to the overlook where the water hit's the bottom, and crazy tourists are on the "Maid of the Mist", a little boat that goes very close to the main water dropping down to the river level, are they Nuts? Being where we are was brave enough for me.

From there we went about a mile downstream to see relics that remain from people using them to go over the falls, or get across the river that is travelling, (I am guessing) about 150 feet a minute or 30 to 40 miles an hour. Many lives lost here.

Dave thinks it would be great to go across on the aero car, it's a contraption like a ski lift car only it goes across whirlpools, fast whirlpools! I am not too keen, but don't want to be a spoilsport, he wants to do it, I'll do it.

Very scary, looking down into the swirling black water. What if this thing fell off the lines it was attached to? Didn't happen, I'm still here obviously.

Next day I thought I would like to find a beauty shop and get a haircut etc., it's been a while since I looked a little prissy. Found one in the phone book close to where we were staying, and luckily they could fit me in, so Dave drove me there and would pick me up in an hour or so. Had a nice relaxing hair wash, cut, and blow dry and felt renewed. Paid and left the shop. Only had to wait a few minutes for Dave, then we drove back to the hotel. What I found next in our room was something I have treasured for 45 years. Evidently while I was having my hair done, Dave did a little souvenir buying. He bought me the most beautiful Eskimo Indian doll dressed in a suede leather outfit with fur trim, very real looking, about twelve inches tall with eyes that opened and closed, and he had sat it on the bed leaning on my pillow. One of the nicest gifts I ever had. It still sits on my piano and is really in good shape after all these years. It has been with me every single place I have lived.

Another wonderful day and it's not over yet. Dave is taking me to dinner at a restaurant in the sky so to speak. It is similar to the needle in Washington State, and it rotated very slowly while we're eating dinner so one can see the views of the falls lit up at night, which is breathtaking. After a couple of drinks and a great meal, we head back to our hotel. Tomorrow we are driving to Toronto a couple of hours away, how do wealthy people get bored? Give me a shot at it. So much to see and do in this world and Dave and I are only seeing a tiny little portion of it. David is driving liking a trooper everywhere we go!

I really don't remember too much about this leg of the trip, just remember arriving, and taking a small break after we checked into the hotel and then off to a restaurant. This restaurant was gourmet, very cozy, very nice. Dave ordered two whole Maine lobsters. Neither one of us had eaten a whole Maine lobster before. We were used to spiny tails from Freeport, which were out of this world because we ate them maybe a couple of hours after they were caught. Well the whole lobster was really an experience. First the large bibs, then the instrument to crack them with, and lastly the waiter showing us how it should be done (bet he thought, English dummies), and at that age we were drinking Neirsteiner and mainly sweet white wines and German hocks. We have both been educated since, and I know Dave is like me he likes a good dry Italian or French maybe (wine that is). Tasted great to me at the time though, and now I have really progressed I love a good martini or a glass of Pinot Noir occasionally (Am I educated or what? A REAL CONASSER of fine wine)

Next morning we are on the road again very early, and this time to Montreal which is about three hundred miles. The hotel there was great! Old and worldly, if that's the right word, it even smelled old, I loved it. There were even old people sitting in the lobby reading newspapers, and a sort of real homely smell, but lots of charm and character. I loved Montreal, would go back if ever I got the chance. I guess June was not a bad month to visit this city, and we decided to see the old exhibition "Man and His World". Well let me tell you it was bloody cold. I had a very thin silky dress on, mini of course! (What do you think? I'm young with beautiful legs, so there!) No sweater for me, froze my ass off.!

This worldly fiasco out of our hair, we go back to our comfy hotel. "Dave, I love this place"! Shower, shave, change clothes, and we go on a mission, restaurant hunting. We find an underground shopping centre called 'Place Ville Maria', and after walking around for five or ten minutes we came across a fabulous restuarant, Oh

Wow! Only thing on the menu was escargots. Guess what? Our little butts were on seats in there instantly, and maybe one hour later had eaten snails six different ways. Who invented this? Better than sex! Well, not all the time. Dave and I had a great sexual partnership, I'm sure he would agree with me, and now friendship and love until we die. (fifty years later). Goodbye snails! See you again one day, 20 different ways to cook these little suckers. PLEASE! Who'd a thunk it!!!!!

Now on our way back home, do not really remember any of it right now, did not want to. Arrived at the ship from Florida to the Bahamas, docked in Miami, the end of our fabulous holiday. Once again, thank you David Robbins I will never ever forget it, and I love you.

Back to reality after five or six hours across the gulf. No seasickness, thank the Lord. Couple of days after docking and driving home, we are both back to work. Did I just have a wonderful dream? Nope, back to waitressing, volleyball and pub every night. Not so bad, white beaches and turquoise water, who gets the chance to live this?

12 Halloween, A Nightmare Begins

Jumping ahead maybe two years. It is Halloween, and dealers and waitresses are invited to a party after work, in a house on the beach that a couple of dealers rented. Costume optional!

I found a very short silver dress and a pair of boots to match. No idea where I got them, then I painted my face green, and made a small antenna to put on my head out of aluminium foil. The outfit turned out pretty good, who really knows what a Martian looks like anyway.

My friend and work mate Jamie (also very sad to say died of cancer as well as Barry, we were great friends) had a cat outfit, whiskers and all, very cute. This house we were in was packed to the rafters, seemed like half the island was invited. Great music, and I mean MUSIC that had a tune to it and one could understand the words. Stones, Beatles, Bee Gees, Sergio Mendes, Beach Boys, and more. I could go on and on. I miss all that old stuff. The drinking, dancing and total partying was really in full swing at 3 am, pretty normal for most of us.

Someone tapped me on the shoulder. I turned around and looked into a really beautiful face. Black curly hair, brown eyes and pure white teeth, and this handsome young man was asking me to dance. I had never seen him before, and during our dance he told me he worked in the hotel across from where I worked. He was front desk and bookkeeping, he told me. Just before the song ended he made a comment. "You have beautiful legs." Dave happened to be standing within earshot and suddenly we were on our way to the car and home. A few minutes after driving, Dave says, "You have beautiful legs", very sarcastically. I replied, "I didn't ask him to say that". Never knew Dave had this jealous streak, kinda nice! We did not speak until the next morning. Funny when you are young, how the moods take on as a big deal.

About two weeks later I was working in the lounge, and serving drinks before the show started. Suddenly I see the young man I danced with on Halloween. His name he told me was Geoff. He was sitting with a friend of his, and on my station.

The next few weeks he seemed to be everywhere I went...the pub, the lounge, where I worked, and a small night club I used to go to with the girls from work. The group that was performing in our small showroom sang one or two Herb Alpert songs. One being, 'This Guys in Love With You'. Geoff must have seen this group more than I did, he was there every time I worked, and he always requested that song. In those days stalking was unheard of, but I guess that is what Geoff was doing to me. He was six years younger than me, I found that out when he brought his parents to see the show. I think his Mother told me during a conversation about her family. They lived on the other end of the island, lovely people. His mother worked in a perfume store there. Pretty soon I would be introduced to 'Lair du Temps', Geoff bought me a bottle for a gift, beautiful fragrance, still wear it to this day, along with Christian Dior 'miss Dior', my all-time favourite.

The inevitable was about to happen. Geoff has shown up at the pub one night, and sat next to Jamie and me. Dave is sitting in a booth behind us with a couple of the guys, we are sitting at the bar. I am getting a little tense here as Dave is watching Geoff sitting next to me. Wouldn't it have been wonderful if Dave would have said something to him, but I guess he was not that type, or what would he say? Then Geoff asks me out. I explained that I live with Dave, and we have been together for eight years, thought this would be the end of it. NO! NO! He is still appearing everywhere I go, even in the lounge when I work.

I called Dave from the nightclub on the beach one night when I went with the girls after work, to tell him that Geoff had shown up and would he come over from the pub and be with me. He told me that he was happy where he was, so guess I'm on my own. It does not end here. Another week later I am at home on my night off. Dave has been transferred to the other casino that has been built on the Island. He has been there for a while now on swing shift. I have one night off on my own. The phone rings, I pick it up. Unbelievable! It is Geoff. I'm very surprised. I know I never gave him my number, so where did he get it? He wants me to go for a drink with him, my first answer is no, so I hang up. He calls back and wants me to listen to a new song, sung by Perry Como called 'It's Impossible', which is playing right now on one of our radio stations. That did it! I decided to go for a drink. Do not know what came over me, I think I feel that Dave is maybe bored with me and treating me like a chair in the corner. He did tell me once that I was not a challenge, should have become one sooner! Drove to Geoff's apartment after he told me how to get there and off we went to a small bar on the beach between the town and the West End of the island, cute little place, only about six bar stools but a patio that hugs the ocean. We are the only two people there, very romantic. What am I doing? I think I must have arrived home about 3:30 am, and went in and sat on the couch.

David came out from the bedroom, he was never home at this time, usually in the pub or sometimes he would be invited to a dealer's apartment maybe for a card game or whatever, strange! He says "Where have you been"? I say "I have been out for a drink with Geoff". Then he says, "Well you can't go out for a drink with Geoff and live here can you"? They were the exact words Dave said, I will NEVER forget them. My world just crumbled! I believed in love and fairy tales which I thought I had. Did he really say that? He went back into the bedroom and I sat there in a daze, who knows how long? Maybe half an hour or more, guess I have to leave now.

I then picked up my keys and left the house and drove to Geoff's apartment, I had nowhere else to go. By this time I am bawling my eyes out. It is about 5 am in the morning, and lucky for me Geoff answers the door. Tomorrow will change my life, maybe forever!

I wake up in Geoff's apartment and hear him calling the hotel where he works. He is calling in sick to take care of me obviously, how nice! I am a total wreck, not sure what to do, where to go, how to deal with this situation. It actually hurts me to remember this and write about it.

Geoff was a very mature person for his age. He took over everything that he thought I should do. If only Dave would have said, "I love you", or "come home and we can sort this out" Guess his pride got in the way, and I know he was hurt. Seemed all he was concerned with at the time was had I been to bed with this guy? Which I found out later from friends of ours. I too have my pride!

I am now apartment hunting, one small mistake and telling the truth and this is where it got me. Guess the dealers can go to the beach and get BJ's from somebody I knew, including Dave, so I heard. I have only been out for a drink!!!!!

Geoff is really great, driving me around from place to place and then taking me to breakfast. It's hard to believe, going for a drink with a man that obviously Dave wasn't keen on, would put me in this new world, I may have lost my love! A two-room and kitchen would be my next home, from a lovely house with three bedrooms great garden, a lot more than this, but my own fault I guess.

I have to get to the house and get my belongings. I don't want to do it when Dave is there. Geoff gathers a few of his friends and suggests we go after Dave has left for work. So that is what we did. Within a couple of hours I had retrieved most of what I owned, amazing! Seemed I had a lot more than this. I also took one or two cooking utensils and a pillow and sheets. I never would think of taking anything that was not necessary for my use. Dave and I had a very comfortable place, and plenty of every home comforts, some which I had made myself, so what I took would not even make a dent!

Finally get all my stuff and my dog, excuse me our dog(Dave bought me this dog), into the apartment. Poor dog! It must have really stressed him. I know how he feels, I am so sorry Gus to involve you, but trust me I will take care of you whatever and however. I decided to see if I could work the day shift for a while, my manager helped me out and got me a day shift in the casino.

One evening before I started my other world, I was at Geoff's had been there for dinner and he was at work. I stayed for a while to clean up and wash the dishes.

Suddenly, I looked up and saw Dave through the kitchen window. He knocked on the door and I opened it. He stood there looking lost and forlorn. I invited him in even though it was not my apartment. I figured it would be the nice thing to do. We sat on the couch and started talking. Next thing I know, the front door opens and Geoff walks in. He said he had a feeling that something was going on and he needed to come home. It was a very tense and awkward moment for all three of us.

These two men were not the really aggressive type, so getting ugly was out of the question. I cannot remember any of the next ten minute conversation between Dave and Geoff, but all of a sudden it was very quiet.

David was gone and Geoff decided to go back to work, and I am going to my apartment and my dog. Oh my Lord, save me!

My day shift started and was a little boring until Dave showed up in the back service bar one lunchtime, which was empty during the day. We had to pick up the drinks in a bar near the hotel lobby, real pain. Five minute walk to get drinks. Anyway, it seemed as though he was really miserable, even though he would never admit it. I am thinking, why don't you ask me to come home? No? Ok, I stay where I am. I find it hard to believe that he is unhappy but he will not ask me back. It has been about a month or so since I moved out, and Geoff and I go to the pub and play darts and have a beer etc. It seems that Dave always comes in when we are there, very hard to deal with and for the next couple of months it does not get easier. I actually lost quite a bit of weight, could not eat and finished up weighing around 100 pounds.

R.I.P. Ellie

I then get a phone call in early March from a girlfriend that I work with. Evidently my mother had called me at Dave's not knowing that I had moved out, couldn't tell her at the moment. Anyway, she called to tell me that my sister Ellen had a 'Ewings Sarcoma', a rare bone cancer, and that she was given three months at the most.

I rushed to the house and Dave was waiting for me as Mum was going to call back. No one told her about our problem, which was good. I sat on the sofa waiting for the phone to ring. Finally, about thirty minutes later it rang. Devastating, how does one deal with this? How are Mum and Dad going to handle this? I need to go home to England right now. I leave the house, Dave and I not saying much but feeling very, very, low, with our crap still with us and now this!

I drive to Geoff's and tell him the news. He is very sad for me, but he is going to take charge again and help me to book a flight home. I will never, ever, forget March 4, 1971! Geoff takes me to the airport, and tells me as we sit waiting for my flight that I have to be strong, my Mother needs me. He then asks me if I could renew his passport for him while I am in London, which I agree to, he has all the paperwork and pictures taken care of.

The flight to Nassau is called, first leg over with and I will have a three hour wait there until my flight to Heathrow. Geoff walks me to the gate and tells me he cannot wait for me to come back, he is a very romantic guy. He kisses me goodbye and I am on the worst journey of my life.

After I get to Nassau I decided to call Geoff, but no reply. So I settle down with a book and a coffee for the next two and a half hours. Finally I am on the plane to London.

The journey is about 8 hours as far as I remember, as most of it was a daze. Cold air is the first thing I really remember after landing. I get a cab to the British Embassy to renew Geoff's passport, that job done. I now have to get a train to the South coast of England, about two hours away. I find the train to Portsmouth and Southsea and am now travelling another sad journey. Getting close now, don't want to get there but I know I have to. Finally pull into my station and get a taxi to Ellen's little house. Mum and Dad had sold their house near the seafront and moved into a flat close to this house to take care of her. Mum came to answer the door, Ellie was laying on the couch. She did not know I was coming home so I made up an excuse about taking a short holiday. She was not told that she was dying. It was very hard to deal with this and act normally. Another hard thing to deal with was knowing that Patrick, her two year old, would lose his Mummy.

The second morning after I arrived Mum and I took Patrick to a daycare so that we could give Ellen a few hours of relaxing. While we were at the daycare dropping him off, Jan, the owner, told me that there was a phone call from the Bahamas. It was Dave, guess he called Ellens neighbour and she gave him Jan's number. I took the phone from her hand and said "hello", he answered, "I want to speak to your Mother", I couldn't believe he did not want to speak to me, anyway Mum spoke to him for a minute or two and we headed back to the house. She never said anything about the conversation with Dave until about three or four hours later. I sat with Ellie and made her some lunch and a cuppa (which is a cure-all). Then joined Mum in the kitchen to help her get dinner ready for Dad. He was at work still, even with Emphysema riding a bike in all weathers, what a man he was!

Now Mum blurts out something about 'killed in a car crash'. I did not really grasp what she said. I thought it was something to do with my dog. Geoff was going to look after him for me, but then, MY GOD!! Geoff has been killed in a friend's car whilst going to visit his Mother and Father at the West end of the island. This happened three hours after I left. That is why I could not get an answer when I called him from Nassau. I screamed and screamed, and Ellen got off of the couch and came to the kitchen to see what was going on. It cannot be true! Please, please, no. I cannot be consoled. The rest of the day was a total blur. I do remember the next day. I spent hours on a pay phone to the Bahamas, never did reach David. I spoke to Geoff's roommate and he assured me that Dave had picked up the dog, he then told me that Geoff's Mum and Dad were shipping his body back to the North of England where they came from. His best friend was with him, they were both killed after being thrown out onto coral rock, going too fast round a bend in a small convertible sports car. I remember it well, it was red, a two seater. I had been in it once or twice and had been very nervous about the speed Geoff was driving. Ray, his friend, loved speed too. It was his car, I guess he was driving. What a waste of life, two lovely young men.

I knew roughly the district where Geoff came from a small town up North somewhere, so I spent half a day calling funeral homes until I found out where he would be taken, and i also managed to get his sisters address, not sure how and I then decided to get a train and go there. It was a three hour train ride that seemed like ten. I arrived about noon and got a taxi to the funeral parlour. Geoff's body had arrived the day before. I asked the man in charge if I could see him before I went back to the Bahamas. He informed me that it would be a closed coffin, the injuries were too severe. He and his friend were thrown out of the convertible sports car onto the coral rock along the roadside on their heads, from what I learned.

I made my way from the funeral place to his Sister's house. I stopped in a really nice store on the way there and bought her a gift.

I remember it was a very fancy teapot. 'So what do you buy someone you have never met?'

As soon as Pattie (Geoff's sister) opened the door, I knew this was going to be much easier than I ever imagined. We hugged, we cried, and then we talked for a very long time. She told me that Geoff had mentioned me - little did we know that we would meet under these circumstances. Then a big surprise! Her Mother and Father were due to arrive later in the day and they had no idea that I was there. I was dreading their arrival, I knew seeing Geoff's Mum would be very hard for the both of us.

The last time I saw her was in her apartment in the Bahamas. Geoff had taken me to meet his folks, which was really nice, we had a very relaxing evening, and he had also brought them to the lounge where I worked on a couple of occasions. They were all very close. The worst thing of all about this tragedy was not only was Geoff's death, but five years earlier his brother was killed in an accident at work when a large piece of machinery fell on him. I never knew the whole story. It was something that Geoff never discussed for too long.

Now these two wonderful people have lost both of their sons. Where was God? Geoff was 25, and his brother 30, died five years apart. Mum and Dad finally arrived about three hours after me. I knew I would get hysterical, but I was not alone. Hysterical arrived for all of us, I don't remember so much sobbing.

We are now calm, and Patti made tea in her new fancy teapot. That teapot was the greatest gift, it seemed to help diminish the sadness, and us Brits are known for a good cuppa. Tea fixes everything! I spent the night on a spare couch and left early next morning.

Another long journey to a sad house. Three days left and I go back to the island, cannot imagine how I will deal with that. It's amazing! Three days go so fast when you don't want them to. I am off, telling Mum "I will be back soon". I kiss Ellie and tell her

"Get better, I love you", had a job getting those words out without breaking down.

Dave was at the airport to meet me, I cannot explain the feeling of joy that came over me, I've needed him more than I ever knew, this man is the love of my life. Where have I been? What world did I go to? He takes me back to my apartment and spends the night. He wanted to make love to me but I was just not ready yet to act as though everything was back to where it was.

The next day Dave and I sit and discuss a lot of things, he wants me to move back into the house. I have to think about it, but it doesn't take too long, 20 minutes or so. I'm back, the dog goes berserk! How wonderful, I am home!

13 Sweet Dreams Again, Maybe

Pretty soon it's April and things are feeling a lot better. It's going to take me a while to heal I know that, but being back with Dave is really helping and I am back on my regular shifts in the casino. Life goes on!

June is here, time is flying by. Suddenly something came over me, creepy feelings that seemed physic. I have to go back to England. So I booked a ticket and left the second week in June, I have taken a leave of absence. Ellie is now confined to the couch in the living room. Paralysed from the waist down and unable to walk. When I see how much weight she has lost and survey the whole situation I know it won't be long. I take over for Mum, dealing with nurses coming every other day, and doctor as needed. I will always defend our National Health system. It did right by our family. We had to use the neighbour's phone as Ellen did not have one, but I did manage to get one for Mum and Dad before I left, and that was also through our national health system for terminal cases.

June 19, 1971. Called the doctor in the morning, Ellie had pain in her arms. My girlfriend Rita picked up Leslie in London so that I could see him while I was there, bless her. They arrived before noon, and Dad took Rita and Les to the seafront for a couple of hours.

Maybe it was meant to be that they went when they did. I had to go next door again and borrow the neighbour's phone to call the doctor.

Our doctor was one in a million. He was at the house within an hour. I let him in and went to the kitchen with him. Mum is not dealing with any of this. He said "Sam, I will not let her suffer" and he filled a syringe with morphine. She had been on this for a quite while, but I guess there comes a time when the body needs more and more. The bone cancer she had was a rare and painful one. The doc went into the living room and injected Ellie and told her this would help. He then left. About an hour later, she started gagging and trying to speak. I grabbed the oxygen mask and covered her face and it was just a few minutes before she was gone. I guess I knew but I would not take the oxygen mask from her face. Mum finally convinced me to stop. It had made a mark on her cheeks where I kept pressing it on her mouth.

I have not mentioned this before, not sure why, but she was living with a boyfriend she met in her early teen years, her marriage like mine, did not work out. She was really in love with this guy, who was there when she died. I took his tie and wrapped it around her chin to the top of her head to keep her mouth closed. Mum has disappeared. Guess I am alone with my sister. Funny, I did not cry, not then anyway.

Dad came back from the beach with Les and Rita, so glad they were not here at the final moment. Is my life ever going to be really happy again?

My Mother insisted that Ellie would be brought back to the house after the Funeral Home had taken care of her. She was in an open coffin in the living room so that all friends and relatives who wanted to say goodbye would see her one last time. I still have not cried, even though I am the one dealing with the coffin, the people, the funeral etc… Mum and Dad could not deal with any of this. Mum has fainted twice and the funeral is coming up. My sister is going to be cremated and her ashes put in a beautiful crematory garden about an hour out of town. My other Sister Sue has flown in from the Channel Islands, unfortunately she is not so tough either. Finally it's over!

14 Sweet Dreams, Ellie my Love!

Rita took Les back to London before the funeral so he never had to see anything. He was only eleven years old he, did not need that picture in his mind forever. Sue also left a day or so later after the funeral and went back to the Jersey.

Before I left to go home, I called Leslies father to ask him if he would let him come for a holiday, even though I wanted to pay for the ticket he would not agree to it. Guess he thought I would keep him there. I think he might have been right! What a shame to deny him a month in the Bahamas. Nothing I can do about it. I don't have custody.

Another long journey ahead of me. I leave England again. Dave picks me up and is very sad about Ellen. He has known my family for over nine years. I try to relax for a couple of days and then back to work.

The summer months are going by very fast and life is about back to where it was six months ago. At the end of September I have a big surprise! I had no idea that Dave was planning a wonderful surprise for me. He was in touch with Mum and Dad and he was arranging for them to bring Patrick and come for a holiday. He wrote a wonderful letter to my Mother which I still have to this day, never have told him that. One day before I die, I may give it to him. I have treasured it since Mum gave it to me years ago. He was suggesting that they come in October, and not to worry about the tickets, he would take care of them. Also they would not have any expense once they got here. He wanted them to come without telling me as he thought it would really cheer me up. How wonderful, they really needed a break! The Bahamas would be a dream for them. Dave did not tell me until the last minute that they were coming. Now I am getting excited.

It is early October, I have to get the house clean and tidy and arrange bedrooms, who is sleeping where, etc. Pretty easy, really. We have three nice size bedrooms, and the two in the back of the house are connected with a bathroom in between. Patrick can have a room on his own, and Mum and Dad can have the bigger of the two. There is a sliding door in the room I am putting them in, and outside the door is a huge gardenia bush that smells like heaven. The smell of that drifts into the room and it's fabulous, especially first thing in the morning.

15 Family Vacation

They arrive on an evening flight, Dave and I are at the gate to pick them up. Dad had a wheelchair supplied as his breathing was not too good due to his Emphysema. We pick up their bags and take them back to the house. Three weeks of fun and entertaining starting right now.

Mum is very impressed with the house and having a washing machine, and a dryer was the icing on the cake. In England, she had to walk and catch a bus, with the washing, to the laundromat (big loads). Not an easy life walking and riding buses to get groceries and do washing. The small stuff could be hung outside on a clothes line but that was depending on the weather. Anyway, Mum and Dad are already in heaven seeing this place, and it's only been a couple of days since they got here.

The next plan for me is to take Mum to the salon, where I get my hair cut and get pedicures. I feel she is going to love being pampered. I am not even sure if she ever had a pedicure and her toenails painted. I booked an appointment for both of us for the next day. She had no idea what she was in for, total pampering!

Dave has the night planned at the gourmet room where we go, he has asked a friend of ours if she will come and babysit for us, she will. Great!

Mum and I are off to beautify ourselves. Even walking into this salon gives one a feeling of being wealthy (I wish). I introduce her to Kurt, the guy who cuts my hair, best hairdresser I ever had, and then the girls that do the nails. Mum is having feet done while I get my hair cut. One of the girls sits her in the pedicure chair and puts her feet in the warm pulsing water, she is already very relaxed, then they ask what sort of beverage she would like. A few choices in this place, tea, coffee a few different ways, juice, or sodas. Fancy coffee, as she calls it, was her choice. The phone was placed next to her chair in case she would like to call Dad at the house and tell him that she was really enjoying this morning, she did. Next, her hair, my feet. I think it was about four hours later when we were both released, feeling like a million dollars, amazing what a little pampering can do for the Bod!

I decided a little lunch is in order, and we go to an 'International Bazaar', where there are a couple of places for a coffee and sandwich, cannot have too much lunch as we are going gourmet tonight.

We arrive home later than the men expected, but boy do we feel good. While we were gone, Dave took Patrick and Dad for a ride around the area, and showed them what the place looked like, nothing spectacular to us, but to people that have never had a holiday on a tropical island, I guess palm trees and beaches were very exciting, like they were for me when first arriving here. We spent a lazy relaxing afternoon talking and walking around our garden. We had avocados, limes, lemons, tangerines and small bananas (plantains). Dad worked in a nursery and greenhouses for years, so he was amazed that all this fruit, etc. just grew without a problem. With 85 percent humidity anything grows, mostly mold (in our closets, that's for sure). We had to buy these smelly bags to hang in the closets that made our eyes water, or leave a light on 24/7, this did help a little.

The beaches and the ocean in the Bahamas are to die for, but (a big but) one has to be tough to deal with moths as big as swallows, flying bugs, cockroaches that could carry a baby off, and scorpions which I used to find in the house. I was more scared of the moths than the scorpions, which I would smash with a broom. If a moth got into the house, I mean one of the big ones, I would run out into the garden and pray Dave would come home and deal with it. Funny thing, never saw moths or bugs or anything the whole three weeks Mum and Dad and Pat were there. We did get the house sprayed about a month before, so guess that did the trick.

It's now about 6 pm on the day of pampering, and I tell Mum I have something for her. I bring her a long dress from my closet, perfect for her. Gold coloured dress, with long sleeves, and lapels and buttons to the waist. I had it made, and guessed her size, fits her perfectly. She is ecstatic, I added a pair of gold sandals, and a small black clutch purse, she looks wonderful. Men are easy to outfit, jacket, tie and a nice pair of pants. About 7 pm we all get into the car and off we go.

We get to the hotel and Dave valet parks the car, something else Mum and Dad have not heard of. This is not only a holiday for them, but an adventure for Mum. She is sixty years old and never been out of England, this is so wonderful for her, actually both of them, thanks again Dave.

We have to walk through the casino to get to the little gourmet room. We all look so nice, and lots of hellos to Mum and Dad from our friends and workmates. The Maitre d' shows us to a booth and for the next two hours we introduced them to escargot (that was fun, glad they were both adventurous), Caesar salad, and Steak Diane cooked at the table in a flaming pan, think it made them both a little awestruck. Coffee and liqueurs finalised the event. It was a memory I have to this day. Our local pub also had the pleasure of their company before we headed home.

The next two weeks flew by. Dave and I were pretty good vacation planners. We arranged a trip across to Miami, Sea World, and shopping, and a nice hotel to use as a base.

We took Mum, Patrick and Dad to the West end of the island for a day trip, beautiful beaches there, older part of the island, had a lot more mangroves and original greenery, also hundreds of piles of conch shells lining the road on the drive there and back. The Bahamians used to sell them, I preferred to swim down and get my own.

The conch that comes out of these shells is made into fritters and salads that most restaurants especially the pubs, serve. The fritters were great with English draft beer that we could get in the pubs. Last few days we spent on the beach, and drinking and eating. Saying goodbye was not easy, but this is a holiday Mum and Dad will not forget. It had to be a once in a lifetime for them.

16   The Split, Back To Blighty

October has gone and we are half way through November, I am very restless and Dave and I are getting into a stagnant stage. It has been a hard sad year for both of us. At the beginning of December I decided I had to leave and go back to England. Regretted that decision to this day.

Three of my girlfriends came round to take me to dinner about a week before I was due to leave. They are taking me to a new restaurant that had just opened. We arrived at the place on the third floor. We get out of the lift and it looks as though it may not be open yet. We walk out into a very quiet hallway, and get to the door supposedly into the restaurant, it was very dark as we went in, obviously not open. Suddenly all the lights came on and about fifty or more people were waving and cheering. What on earth is going on? I was really awestruck!

This was a real surprise! Friends and workmates had arranged a going away party for me. I know I don't want to leave, but Dave will not commit, even now. After nine years I thought he may have at least said "I love you". I guess I knew he did in his own way, but a woman wants to hear it now and then. This party was a great night. Friends making speeches and toasts, a couple of them calling Dave a fool for letting me leave. Guess we were both too young at this time.

I was given a one dollar casino chip that had been gold plated and put on chain as a going away gift. I gave it to my son when he was 21.

D-Day is here. Dave says to me as I get ready for the airport, "I am not going to say anything", and he didn't. If only he would say don't leave, don't go, guess we were too young, or he felt that way, and I guess he did not want to be tied. Seems as though everyone around me is crying, including me, not David. As I go through the door to board the plane it seems suddenly I am alone in my seat and in the air, the most horrible feeling. Not sure why I did it, guess I wanted to be really needed and loved, and I was not really feeling as though I were getting it or going to. Only had one relationship, and that was a marriage that did not work.

Miserable journey! Seems I have had a few of these in the last year. Landed in London, after changing planes and sitting around in an airport for two or three hours, at least in those days one could smoke a cigarette. (I have since quit, I'm glad to say). Anyway, back to London, weather freezing. It is about two weeks before Xmas, won't be a happy one here, or on the other side of the ocean I'm sure. I must not think about it, depressing!

My sister Sue is coming home to Ellies little house (where Mum and Dad are still living) for Xmas. That will really cheer me up. My mother was a great cook, only English food, but it was always delicious, and so for Xmas it was turkey, sage and onion stuffing, lots of veggies, mince pies and Xmas pudding with custard or brandy butter, best dinner ever. I did not check to see where Dave was spending Xmas, it was too upsetting for me. For the past maybe six years I used to cook for a bunch of friends, usually about a dozen of us including single guys that did not have girlfriends, then we would clean everything away, relax with a brandy or a drink for a couple of hours and then all go to work. Not too many of us ever got to have Xmas or New Year's Eve off, so Christmas day dinner at our house was special.

I did get New Year's Eve off once, but nobody else did, so I spent most of the night on my own until about 3 am when I met Dave and friends in the pub. We were all used to very late nights in the pub as the casino did not close until early am, great life, drinking, partying and beach nearly every day. The liquor, cigarettes and beer were very cheap to buy on the island, so parties were very inexpensive to hold in one's house or apartment. There were some wild ones! I remember a party that really stands out in my mind. The usual crazy guys were there, some of them used to really entertain us. Dressing up as women with wigs and the whole female gear and acting the fool, they were great fun.

Anyway back to this party. It was held in a house on the beach again, (but not the same one as the Halloween party). I will never forget the outfit I wore, it really was very sexy. A bright yellow dress, thin straps over the shoulders, mini length, and from under the arm to the bottom hem each side were strips of the dress with about a two inch space all the way up and down. The bikini panties to match the dress came level with one of the strips so it looked as though I had no underwear on (so, I am young) I finished it off with a pair of yellow boots just below my knees, and having a wonderful tan I know I was a sight for sore eyes (so I was vain as well). I think a woman knows when she has GOT IT, and this was one of those times. It started off with Dave and I having a good time, super music, snacks, booze and fun company. Suddenly I realised a couple of the dealers were trying to put the make on me getting a bit bold, and so did David, suddenly I was walked hurriedly out of the house. I thought, oh no we are leaving, now what have I done? Next thing I know was Dave walking me down to the beach, very dark but very warm and very sandy, if you get my meaning!! Suddenly in between a couple of dunes, Dave was making love to me, or maybe a quickie I think was the right scenario. Guess with the dress and the attention I was getting it made his testosterone really jump high. In the words of Johnny Ray, "Oh what a night it was, it really was such a night". One party I will never forget. Those were wonderful years in my life. Still reminiscing I'm afraid. Now back to where I was, my mind keeps wandering and it makes me very happy thinking of all these memories.

After Xmas is over in England, my sister Sue suggests I move over to where she lives. A small island in between England and France, part of the Channel Islands. There are about eight islands off of the coast of Normandy in the English Channel, a British Crown dependency not ruled by England though.

Late January, I decided to go, not a good time to move to a small island in the middle of a cold ocean, it was freezing, especially in the bathroom. I have just left the Bahamas, what am I doing here? Am I in a movie that I don't remember signing up for? What! No shower? Actually glad, taking ones clothes off in the morning in a cold bathroom was enough of a shock to the system.

One of my first purchases has to be a heater of some kind. I finished up buying an oil heater, easy to use and inexpensive. Better than running up an electric bill. I had a mattress on the floor in a room which Sue's roommate gave up for me and then she shared the other room with Sue. There were only two bed rooms and there were three of us. I was pretty comfy and how nice of her to do that. Next thing I want to do is buy a car. I have come home to England with enough savings to keep me going for a while so I don't have to worry about finding a job right away. I found a car a mini stick shift, this is going to be a new experience my car in the Bahamas was an automatic. Dave bought it for me one year as a birthday gift.

I started taking Sue to work and picking her up when she finished. Luckily I did not have to take a driving test as I had an international licence that I got in the Bahamas.

The first few weeks of my driving this car were hilarious. It seemed every time I got in, I somehow always hit the horn, have no idea how but it would start honking. Sue and I would start laughing, and there were times when I had to pull over and park because we were in hysterics. There was one time I parked on a hill, luckily out in the countryside, because after we stopped laughing and I tried to get going I kept rolling back trying to put it in first gear, well that started us off again. Sometimes when we were out together we got really stupid. What fun we had.

My sis was 21 and I was 31. That did not stop us going everywhere together. We enjoyed clubs and pubs, and in the summer (coming soon), beaches. Before I get to that a lot more to talk about. One night we went to a place that Sue knew that had dancing and a bar, not too big. This is where I met the best sex in a long time. His name was Danny.

I was sitting on one of the many couches in the place, about to light a cigarette (they were the days of smoking), when a voice said "Would you like to dance?" I was about to say no thanks I am going to have a cigarette, when something made me really look up. I changed my mind about the cigarette and got up to dance. It was instant chemistry. We danced a few dances and Danny said "Shall we go?" I replied "Where?" He tells me that he walked to the club, so did I have a car as he left his at his flat. He said, "What about a drive to the beach?" "Fine with me", I said, being very brave. Then I made sure Sue had a ride home, and off we went.

We drove a few miles and had great conversation along the way. Finally stopped at a little parking space near a beautiful beach, one of the nicest on the island. A cigarette was in order and after a smoke the groping and kissing followed. I still find it hard to believe how compatible we seemed to be; I guess I was very lucky with one or two relationships in my life, most of them were happy get along ones.

On the way back Danny wants to see me again, so we arranged a date in a local pub near where I live. He then tells me he has a girlfriend but it's not working out, they have been together for some time and he thinks she is going to end it soon. In the meantime I have found a job in a local cinema, who would have guessed? The date I was looking forward to was cancelled, evidently Danny remembered where my sister worked and went into the shop and told her to tell me he wouldn't be able to make it. I had told him about myself on our drive to the beach, and that my sis worked in town.

A few days later I was at work sitting in the employee's lounge, when one of the girls I worked with came in and said there was someone to see me in the main lobby. I went down to the entrance and Danny was there. He said he was sorry about cancelling on me but could we make another date. Of course I agreed, and had a feeling this would work. We had a quite a few dates, then the obvious happened, I went to bed with him. It was the most fantastic hour I had spent in a long time. Nice to hear a man compliment you on your body and other things.

From then on we saw a great deal of each other. We had lots of friends, most of them Danny's. He was a telephone engineer, strange, the second one I had. He suggested that I should apply to become a telephone operator, which I did. The classes lasted about eight weeks and there was a ton of homework. I had to take books home every night and learn all about an exchange on an island.

Sue and I have a new flat which is great, but at the top of a hill and I don't have a car right now until I replace the mini. So it was walking uphill with books, groceries, and anything else. Kept us fit I guess.

I passed my exams and was hired as a telephone operator. The switchboard was one of the plug-in type so when a light came on I had to plug in and say "trunks number please", then I had to transfer the call to the mainland from the island. My first day was very funny. There were about 10 operators in a row as far as I can remember, the girl next to me was very helpful and like me a sense of humour.

I had a supervisor watching me for the first couple of hours on my first day, then I was on my own. I watched the girl next to me for a while and at one point I thought I heard something weird. I asked her if I was correct in hearing what she said when she plugged in, and I was. Instead of saying trunks number please, she said "trunks rubber knees "very fast, that appealed to my sense of humour so we hit it off big time.

There were some very funny moments. I had an old lady on the line one morning, or she sounded old, calling from a phone box.

I had already said trunks number please, and I tried dialling the number she gave me, it was supposedly her sister in England. I went back on the line and told her, I was very sorry there was no reply, would she like to try again later. Her next statement was one that got me laughing. She said "well excuse me dearie, but did you 'ear the dog barkin"? Another day with lots of laughs.

I finally got another car, big old tank with the gear shift on the steering wheel and a great radio, much bigger car than the mini, but who cares? Gas was cheap then. I had lots of great times with the mini, but it started to need repairs so I thought it was better to trade it in. Danny and I took it across to England before I got rid of it, and we went to Brighton for a five day holiday. Had a really good time and he decided he wanted to marry me. A few months later I found out when he took me to dinner for my birthday, that he was still living with his girlfriend, the one who was supposedly leaving soon, so our relationship ended after a year. What a shame! It was great. Heard he married a girl much younger than himself, he was about 36. Hope it worked out for him. Suddenly I became very, very depressed, lost Dave, Geoff and my sister both died, lost custody of my son, and now Danny. Why do men have to do this? Don't ask me to marry you if you are living with someone! What the hell is your problem? I am now reaching 34, suddenly I felt old.

17 Forgive Me, Please

One night I was alone in the flat. Susie had gone to a party. I sat in front of the fire and began to drink straight scotch, I hated scotch, not sure how we got it in the place, anyway needless to say I got drunk, really drunk. It is true booze is a depressant and in the frame of mind I was in I decided to take a handful of migraine pills thinking my sister, bless her, would not be home until late. Wrong! The party she went to was not that good so it was a lot earlier than I had anticipated. I remember leaving her a note, and the next thing I remember was waking up in the hospital. This episode in my life is not something I am proud of, and I'm glad my parents and son never knew about it thanks to Sue, guess Leslie does now, forgive me Les! Nothing bad that happens in one's life is worth doing what I did, and I am very thankful that Sue came home early. I guess I owe her my life.

I had a couple of weeks in the hospital and was treated for extreme depression. Had the whole ugly treatment, shock machine twice a week and all. After a couple of months of pills and doctors, I decided to go back to England. I asked Mum and Dad if I could stay with them, they said of course, so I quit my job and left the islands. I hated to leave Sue in a bind, but it was the only solution to healing myself.

I moved in with my parents and straightened my life out. I went for an interview with the telephone exchange in a district outside of Portsmouth. I secured myself a job as an operator, only difference between this exchange and the one in the channel islands was the size, this one is much larger and I did not have to say 'trunks number please' as it was on the mainland. I think the excellent reference I was given from the last exchange got me this job. I still have the reference somewhere in my junk and paper case, cannot believe it has been nearly 47 years.

Xmas is coming and I found out that I have to work the day shift on Xmas day but I will get off about 4 pm, so Mum is getting the dinner later for me. Xmas day is here and I am sitting at the board along with a huge line of girls working. I have never seen so many flashing lights. Obviously people call all over the world at holiday time, especially Christmas day, it was really hard to keep up with all the plugging in and out.

I get home and as usual have a wonderful meal, me, Dad, Mum and Patrick. What wonderful parents I had. If I had to pick them from a line without even being told how they were, I would have chosen them immediately. The job is good, but I miss the Bahamas and Dave.

18 A Prayer Answered

A girlfriend calls me at the house one afternoon and says she may have a job for me. She is still living on the island. Is this what I have been waiting, hoping and praying for? I have to borrow my fare from Mum and Dad, about four hundred pounds, plus a little to keep me going when I get back there. I booked a ticket and have high hopes. I think I have a job and maybe I can see Dave and we could get back together, well neither one worked out.

I arrived sometime in April or May, cannot quite remember, but it's a year since Dave sent me a telegram telling me we were getting married, not will you marry me? That might have helped. Why did he wait so long after I left? Suppose he had to have a fling. I don't know why I turned him down, because I will always love this man. I think deep down I had a feeling that maybe he felt lonely, or he was influenced by my friends to ask me, but I felt he really did not want to get married, guess I was right he never did marry anybody. I know the man loves me to this day but not enough to ask me back when I returned. That would have been a little difficult for him anyway as he had found himself a new live-in girlfriend. Crushing blow for me. Amazing how fast it took for someone to move in with him, not really. She was attractive and I heard her family had money. Hope that did not influence him, don't think so.

Now I have to find a job. What, Where, and How? If I do not find one, I am out of here. The job Michelle found for me did not work out, so I am getting a little concerned.

I see Dave in the pub with his new girlfriend. It's a nightmare for me. Seems the tables have turned, I have to watch him with her when I'm drinking with friends. Guess payback is a bitch!

A friend who introduced Dave to his new score, has told me she thinks she can find me a job looking after a couple's daughter and doing housework for them, etc. This is what I needed, but not what I need! This child is thoroughly spoiled, just about a brat and not young. I don't think they realise that an outsider wants to give her a good smack. I found myself as a chief cook and bottle washer, although these people were nice to me I did not know how long I could put up with this.

They allowed me to bring in a date one night and cook a nice meal for him while they took the daughter out for a few hours. My date was a very nice handsome guy who was an engineer for a very large company hired to do some sort of power project on the island, which meant that he would not be around too long. Who really cared, he and I had fun together.

My girlfriend Michelle (the one who helped me get back to the Bahamas) and I made up a foursome one night with the engineer that I cooked a meal for and a friend of his. We went to the little bar that Geoff had taken me to, a couple of years earlier. The owner had hooked up speakers from the juke box to the patio outside, so we could sit there and listen to music or dance. It was a very small place, but unique in the fact that the ocean lapped up to the edge of the patio, very rocky, no beach, but that was the novelty, smashing little place. We danced to 'Me and Mrs. Jones'... love that song.

During the next few weeks I had a couple more dates with Mr. Engineer. His name is not important. Then he left and went back to the states I believe. I never went to bed with him, just had lots of nice dates, parties, dancing, etc. Shame, I think he was spoken for. I really enjoyed his company without strings.

Our trips to the little bar on the ocean did bring back a few memories and one or two of them were not good. I could never get a statement out of my mind that Dave made when Geoff was killed. I know he felt very rejected and maybe deceived, but that part was not true, I did tell him the truth, he can never deny that, sad that he had all that pride, it does get in the way and true saying, 'goeth before a fall'. After I moved back into the house it took a while for both of us to enjoy each other again. One morning about a month after I moved back in, after the whole horrible episode, I remember him saying he wished he would have found Geoff's (Geoffrey's) broken body on the road, he would have kicked it. He was the one who took me away, that is why God took him. This was not David speaking, he felt very hurt and bitter. I remember I shut myself in the bathroom in the back of the house and broke down. Dave banged on the door for a long time, trying to get me to come out. I must have been in there crying for an hour, until finally Dave says "Sam, come out please, I will make you a cup of tea". Told you all, tea is the cure-all if one is a real Brit! No more about Geoff was ever mentioned again, and as I have said before, I will love Dave until I die!

Moving back to my return to the island. This babysitting job I have has to go. One morning I am walking along the road near where I am living, and a car pulls up and stops. It is one of the guys I worked with in the casino He asks me if I need a ride. "Yep, sure do" I said. So I hopped into this old Jaguar convertible that he is refurbishing and he drives me to the apartment where I live. On the way there, we chat, just small talk, then he asks me how the job is going. I tell him that I am not too happy with it. He then asked me if I would like to come and work for him.

Evidently him and his wife are separated, and he needs a live in person to look after his three daughters and four dogs. Wow! I am not a Mary Poppins but I think I can do this. The girls are 7, 9, and 11 years of age. . I am going to find out soon how capable I am, didn't know I had it in me. The dogs, Great Danes and Yorkshire terriers, are about the most obedient and well behaved dogs I have ever seen. John is responsible for this, the man I am going to work for.

19 Me And The Dane

My first night in his house was long and strenuous. My first task after I looked at the kitchen was to clean it, that's after I unpacked my stuff in the bedroom where there was a small four poster bed with pink chiffon over the top. Hope I have not taken the room from one of the girls! Looks like it. As I start to put some of my undies in the drawers, I noticed the black Great Dane has come into the room and is watching every move I make. She starts showing her teeth when I walk from the bed to the dresser, so I start to move very, very slow. I get my unpacking over with and go to tackle the kitchen. The huge dog is still following me, a little unnerving as this animal must weigh about 150lbs. I remember her name meant Greek goddess I believe, yeah! Only when I stand still for a few minutes she starts to look a little calmed down. After I spend about four hours cleaning grease from the stove and eggs that exploded from the microwave (found out later), and when I started to clean egg shells from the ceiling did I start to see the end of this first project.

Something amazing happened next. I mopped the floor and stood back and admired my work, looks wonderful, now made my way to my room, black Dane following. I got myself undressed and very slowly got into bed. I was so tired it could not have been any faster. I laid down with one eye on her, (you know who I mean), and suddenly she jumped onto the end of the bed, am I going to be ripped to shreds? Held my breath, no? Hallelujah! This was a one person bed, trust me, but she got herself comfortable and settled down at the foot end, unbelievable! I think I finally dropped off, body screwed up into a ball and scared to move, and woke up in the morning realising I have a new big beautiful black dog friend, and what a friend she turned out to be. John said when he came home he thought he was in the wrong house after going in the kitchen, it was a great job! The dogs accepted me very quickly, the girls, not so fast, to be expected, I am not stupid and will be as patient as possible.

The first dinner I cooked, I believe a roast, which I know was good. I know I am a pretty good cook. The nine year old decided she did not like it and she was not going to eat it. Well, dad is pretty strict and he told her, you will sit there until you do eat it. She looked at me and said "you are not my Mother, and you can't tell me what to do". I did not say a word. I think I knew how she felt.

I had lots of duties involving the kids, drama classes, swimming lessons at the YMCA, and driving them to and from school, besides washing, ironing, cleaning, cooking and feeding and walking dogs. Kept me in good shape. It did not take too long for the girls to come over to my side. Then we all got along great. We spent a lot of time together and they knew who to come to when they were being scolded for room not clean or some other chore not done.

We had little secrets from Dad and I guess this brought them closer to me. John did a lot of scuba diving and all the girls were very good swimmers. We all spent lots of time on the beach or in the ocean, and John was great at spear fishing. We ate fresh fish a couple of times a week. Red snapper, yellowtail and the occasional spiny lobster, it really can spoil a person. I managed to get the girls to like roast lamb, took me a while, most people in the states are not keen on lamb from what I hear, but if it is seasoned with garlic and rosemary and cooked properly it is delicious.

20 The Ugly Yacht

About a year after I first moved into the house, John told us all that he had bought a boat, not just any boat, a galleon looking thing that was used to take tourists who wanted to buy land, on tours through the waterways. It was docked in a small marina close to the hotel I used to work in.

It was not a pretty sight! Not sure why he wanted to live on this ugly monstrosity, but I had no say, nor did the girls. We moved out of the house that was 50 yards from the beach, onto the YACHT on the water. There was a large room on the lower level, one small room upstairs, and two rooms at the back. A small toilet and basin near the main entrance. Windows extinct, bathroom extinct, kitchen also extinct, a small hotplate and a toaster oven was the extent of my gourmet appliances. I am not sure how I cooked meals, but I do remember cooking a roast lamb in the toaster oven once, not an easy task, but guess what? It came out great and tasted really good. Not having a bathroom meant that we all had to wash in the room where the basin was, heating up a pot of water first, or wash down on the dock with a hose, wearing a swimsuit. One or the other, we were always clean.

This floating palace did not seem to upset the dogs too much. There was a small fenced area off the front of the boat where they could run, and as long as they were fed on time, no problem. They also had a pretty large deck in the centre of the boat where they loved to lay.

Life is wonderful!! Robinson Crusoe and family had nothing on this!! John starts work on fixing up the 'ugly lady'. I must say he was a very handy do-it-yourself man, and he could fix most things that broke. He was also good fun and very thoughtful, taking me to dinner and buying me little gifts occasionally. The first thing he is working on is the windows. This is a tropical island. We have storms that can blow up in an instant, and chances of hurricanes living on this structure without windows or reinforced rigging that is holding us to the dock could be very scary if the weather did turn nasty.

John is doing a great job, and suddenly it feels much more homely. Very strong glass of some kind made up the windows. Are we going to sail the Caribbean? God, I hope not!

I have tried to make this place as comfortable as is possible with what I have to work with, but when we are all happy, tanned, and well fed luxury living is the last thing I think anyone cares about. I think John is very happy he bumped into me that day on the road, and the man loves me, not in love with me, same from my side, that's two different things. We shared a few very intimate moments which were good for both of us. Me seeing Dave with his new girlfriend, and him thinking of his ex who he is not over, guess it took away a little of the pain.

Our yacht never leaves the dock, heaven forbid! We have a dinghy that we take out into the ocean when John goes spear fishing, and we all have a spear. I did learn to do a little scuba, never pursued it though. I think I was a bit nervous about bumping into sharks, and the barracudas were prolific. Didn't seem to bother him, he really loved scuba diving. This was the time of tans, bikinis, smoking a little pot and eating fresh fish. This style of living lasted about a year, then after John had fixed up the boat he decided we were all going to move back on to dry land. I must admit I had got used to this. Made one feel very beatnik and free.

He found a nice four bedroom house, two bathrooms and a big kitchen, luxury for me. I have an oven, Yippee!!

Now the girls have to worry about making sure their rooms are clean, trust me, Dad inspected them when he came home from work, and if not to his liking they had to do it until it was, but this man was a really wonderful father. He made sure his girls were well mannered and respectful. I loved them, still do! And still in touch over forty years later.

One day (I knew it was coming), John wants to take me to the pub, we did not do that too often, he didn't drink like most of us, the occasional half pint now and again was his limit. Anyway, I had a feeling that something was about to happen, I was right. We got to the pub and sat in a booth. After he ordered us a drink he informed me that he was going to try and get back with his wife. It did not take long before I started to cry, another crash in my life! I pulled myself together and we went home to tell the girls. It was like a bomb had dropped. They all broke down. They want to be with mum, but they did not want me to go. The middle one now really loves me, sat on my lap and cried hysterically. In the meantime John had called his wife in the U.S. and wanted the girls to talk to her. This was one of the saddest evenings one could imagine. They talked to their Mother, but it seemed not much help at the moment even though I knew they wanted to be with her, and so they should, nothing I could say or do, not my business. I am now wondering where do I go? What am I going to do? I should have known, this man I am working for is one of a kind, I do not have to worry about anything, he is going to make sure I am taken care of and safe. He suggests that I go to Las Vegas, he will get me a car and then I can drive there from Florida, how terrifying will that be?

21 Call Me Gulliver, Driving On The Wrong Side

I have never driven on the right hand side of the road or been on a freeway in my life, do I have the guts to do that? The girls are getting ready to leave, this is a very solemn house right now. I am helping them pack and trying to cheer them up, I think they know, we may never see each other again, tears are inevitable. John tells me he is going to put them on a plane and their mother will pick them up in the U.S. He will then take me to some friends in Florida for a weekend and I can leave from there to drive to Vegas. He buys a Pinto station wagon, stick shift no less, making my trip even more scary. He then tells me that he wants me to take Circe the Dane with me for protection. Good idea methinks!

This journey I am about to embark on will influence the next 38 years of my life. John leaves to go back to Grand Bahama the day before I am supposed to drive off into the sunset. Very sad saying goodbye, hope it works out for him he is a really good guy, deserves the best.

My last night in Daytona Beach with friends was very relaxing, bloody good job the way I'm feeling! Peggy, my girlfriend from the island and her husband Jack cooked a great dinner for us, pasta with garlic and olive oil, and the greatest garlic bread. I am going to be driving over two thousand miles with a dog. Do I have to worry about my breath? Only the dog will know.!

The three of us had a few goodbye cocktails, helped put me to sleep and then the next morning arrived, I am off. I really must say that I have never been so nervous about anything in my whole life. Jack bought me a compass to put on the dashboard, not sure if that will help, but it's the thought that counts. Peggy helped me pack my boxes in the back of the car, guess a wagon did help as far as packing belongings in a car goes. It took me a while to get used to the stick shift, amazing I did it at all. Now I have to find out how to drive on the wrong side of the road, and how to get on a freeway or toll road, also have to have the right change! I wish I could have had a few lessons on this stuff, guess everybody had confidence in me and did not think I needed it.

Wow! Again, to this day do not know how I did that, but wait, it is going to be three times total I do this. My first stop after about eight hours of driving but letting Circe out in between, was obviously somewhere in one of the Southern states, and the Holiday Inn Hotel, will always love them, allowed dogs. I had enough cash on me to order room service, nothing fancy, a burger and fries and coffee, and I had brought along dog food and her dish so she was happy.

For the next couple of days I learned how to overtake big trucks, that the traffic lights were up in the air, and to make sure I had plenty of small change in front of me. I also found that my driving a gear shift was getting better and better. I am driving about ten to twelve hours a day, but not as fast as most of the traffic around me. I would rather take it a little easy. A trip tic book from AAA is on the seat next to me, letting me know what exit numbers I have to watch out for.

My next worst nightmare was in Dallas, Texas. There were four lanes of traffic doing about seventy miles an hour. I was in the outside lane. I glanced at my exit number and suddenly noticed it was only a little way off. How do I get across three lanes? I don't. It was at least twenty more minutes before I could manoeuvre across to manage to get off on an exit. Now I have to find my way back, what a pain!

I think that ordeal could have killed me. Did I mention that I finished up on a median between eight lanes at one point? Most drivers probably did not think that there could be a Brit driving amongst them that is a real novice on freeways. I could use a large brandy after that performance, had not started drinking vodka and tonic in those days, in fact hardly drank at all. Cannot wait to get this day over and check into a motel.

The next morning I started out very early, I wanted to get out of Texas, miles of nothing. All of a sudden I see a sign post saying El Paso, but I then see a big sign that reads Mexico. I think I will take a detour and visit another country. What do I know? I am now going across the border into Juarez. I was already nervous before I got out of the car that I had parked about one hundred feet from Immigration on the Mexican side. There was a man standing next to the door before I had it fully opened. The dog was going berserk, and I tried to tell him "no thanks" whatever he wanted. Obviously he did not speak English and when I started to point at the immigration officers he took off. Nothing deters me mate! I am in Mexico and I am going to take a stroll down the main street, not a good decision. At least four men tried to get my attention, and it did not really feel like a place I wanted to be, so I made my way back to the car. The dog was happy, so was I. When I tried to drive back through the border crossing, I was pulled over to one side and my car was thoroughly examined. Border Patrol emptied boxes, looked under seats, checked my passport and left my wagon in a mess. Maybe they thought I went into Juarez to get dope or something illegal. I was so happy to get out of there. Today I hear that place can be pretty scary for tourists, but I did it didn't I?

I am now in New Mexico, what a beautiful state. It's about nine hours of driving and I am out in the countryside in a small little town and looking for a motel. The first one I checked out was full, are you kidding? Some sort of festival going on. Well after not finding one I decided to drive to the next town, about two hours more, don't have a choice really just do it.

22   Could This Be The Bates Motel

About another hour of driving, Cerce wants to do her thing, so I pull over onto a grassy patch just off of the road and I let her wander around for a while to stretch her legs, etc. I am out in the middle of nowhere and it is very dark. Then I get her back into the car and I get in and turn the key, nothing, dead. Oh my God! What do I do now? I lift up the hood of the wagon, get out my flashlight and look around. About fifty yards away across a field I see a light coming from what looks like a small shack. I decide to check it out, so I lock the car and start to make my way there. When I finally get there it is a small little shack type house. I knock on the door and an old man opens it. "Do you have a phone I could use please"? I ask him, "I need to call the highway patrol as I have broken down". He tells me he has a phone and to come in. I go in and the surroundings look like a movie set from 'Psycho'. There is an old lady sitting in a rocking chair with a shawl around her shoulders, and the whole place is pretty dark and old looking. I was thinking that they are both up in age and nice of them to let me in. The old man shows me where the phone is, and I have to find out the number for the highway patrol which I do. I call and tell someone that I need help, and thank the old man and leave. I make my way back across the field to the car, get in, and wait. It is very dark and creepy, nothing around just very quiet. I must have sat nearly an hour, no highway patrol yet, great help they turned out to be, so I guess I sit a bit longer. Suddenly I see the old man from the shack coming across the field with a huge friggin' knife in one hand and a flashlight in the other. Is this really going to be a true horror movie scene? Terrifying! I quickly made sure all the doors were locked and the windows were up. The hair all over my body was standing on end. When he finally got close to the car he knocked on the window on my driver's side. I rolled it down about two inches so that I could hear what he was saying. He pointed to the hood and walked around to the front of the car and proceeded to mess with something underneath with the knife. He then came around to the window and told me to try and start the car, which I did. It started. Am I happy or what? This old man told me it was the battery cables corroded, nice of him to come out and help me. I thanked him and off he went, and off I went about fifty miles an hour. Why did my imagination run wild thinking I was going to be chopped up and scattered in New Mexico, how stupid! But who knows? Shit happens!

I drove another hour and finally found a motel. I am so worn out room service is in order. Tonight I celebrate my being alive, it's going to be a steak which I share with Circe. She will not get any of my baked potato though, too yummy for dogs and too much butter. If one of us is going to put on weight, it is going to be me. Who'd a thunk it?

She and I are now laying down and relaxing, heaven! Sam don't feel too good. Famous line from a poem, 'and miles to go before I sleep'.

Get an operator call about 6 am. Here we go again. You were right Robert Frost, a lot of miles to go. What wonderful company this dog is John was right, protection more than once, and love and companionship, and on our first encounter I thought this dog didn't like me. DUH! She loves me and I love her. Shame humans cannot feel love like dogs do.

Ok enough sloppy stuff, we have to drive through New Mexico

into Arizona. I made one big slip,(no! no! not another one). I spotted a sign that said Las Vegas, so I started towards it without looking at my AAA book. Travelled a few miles before realising that there is a Las Vegas in New Mexico (very strange thing, my future husband that I have not met yet went to school in New Mexico, fate is unexplainable!). Luckily found out I was wrong before I went all the way, more miles and gas wasted. Back on track going towards Kingman Arizona, way, way off in the distance, but I am making it. What are the odds on this? I am obviously a lot more capable than I gave myself credit for. So far this has been one incredible adventure. Glad I did it! Seems as though me and my pal Circe are driving into oblivion, it will come to an end, I know it.

I realise the desert can be beautiful, but I am an ocean person, and the Arizona desert is a little boring to me. (Virgos are earth, weird that I love water), it is not as bad as Texas though. Am I going to be able to settle in the desert? Not sure. Guess I have to give it a try first. According to my calculations I have about ten more hours of driving to reach Boulder City Nevada, so I am going for it in one stretch.

I reached Hoover Dam in the dark and it was pouring with rain, and there are big trucks overtaking me coming down doing more than the posted 25, could have been 15 I cannot remember, so I have decided to stop for the night in Boulder City instead of driving into Las Vegas. I found a little motel that would let me in with the dog, and after the hairy ride down from the dam, I was very appreciative.

Tomorrow is going to be very interesting, after five and a half days of driving over two thousand miles, and now I have nearly arrived!

Before going to sleep for the night I decide to find a motel for when I arrive in Vegas tomorrow. I found a reasonably priced one on the strip and made a reservation, now I can sleep. Thanks for yellow pages I think, not knowing I have a hard day coming.

23 Where Is The Vegas 'Strip' (Blonde at Work)

Up and at 'em early the next morning, last leg of my cross country journey coming to an end. I know Circe will be very happy not to be in this car for hours at a time, she has been a fantastic companion for all those miles.

I drive into Vegas and am now looking for 'The Strip'. I am on Las Vegas Boulevard at the moment and driving up and down looking for the strip, HELLO! Nobody has informed me that Las Vegas Boulevard is 'The Strip'! (it's a blond thing) I finally found out by pulling over and asking someone, feel really stupid, but now I can find my motel. I check in and start to take some of my stuff out of the car, unfortunately have to go to the second story on the outside stairs. Lastly I go down to bring Circe to the room and a voice shouts at me as I am getting her out of the car. "You can't have a dog in the room", the voice said. Oh no, what am I going to do now? The desk clerk had seen me get the dog out of the wagon and start for the stairs and he was the one yelling. I thought I had mentioned the dog when I booked the room the night before. Guess the night guy had neglected to tell me no dogs, or he just ignored it. Is this my first impression of the Entertainment Capital of the World, or so they say. Well I am not a happy camper right now, where do I go?

First thing I do before driving anywhere is to call John. He is very happy I made it. We have been in touch along the way, now I tell him what sort of predicament I am in and ask him to help me. He gives me a phone number for a friend of his who has a house on the other side of town west side of the strip, and tells me I should be able to stay with him for a while. Then he gives me another number to call, this one is a guy he worked with, who now lives in Vegas with his wife. We say goodbye for now and I take off for the address given to me after I made a phone call to his friend Mike.

I finally find the house and boy am I glad to be done with driving for a while. The freeway was easy compared to driving in Vegas, now I really have to pay attention to the right side of the road. I think turning left on a green arrow is the scariest. I keep wanting to go on the wrong side of the road. I find it hard to believe that I am still alive! Into each life a little rain must fall! Lately I have had a few downpours, but this is Las Vegas the sun will come out, and trust me one can get a bit fed up with constant sunshine.

I stayed at Mikes for about a week and then I moved in with some of John's other friends. I found a cleaning job, working for a big boss of one of the casinos. The job included cleaning a large house on the golf course, doing the laundry, changing the beds and then dealing with dog feedings and making sure the patio was washed down, along with the outside furniture. This man's wife was from Europe I think, maybe that was a help in securing this job, but WOW! She was a bit careful with the money she paid me, and I think they were loaded.

They each had their own bedroom and bathroom, plus a huge walk-in closet nearly as big as their bedrooms. He had a huge study next to his bedroom on the second floor, and downstairs there was a large dining room, living room, a huge kitchen, and a laundry room. Once a week I did this mansion cleaning for $35. Yep that's right, thirty five dollars. Two words for that, HARD WORK.

One week I remember this woman asking me if I knew how to cook a leg of lamb, of course I said yes, (dumb shit Sam). She was having a dinner party and wanted me to cook the lamb for her, so I said I would (dumber blonde!). The following week on my cleaning day I went in and I took care of her lamb, putting garlic cloves under the skin and rubbing fresh rosemary on it, then smearing a little olive oil all over and wrapping it in foil. I did all this a day ahead so that I could cook it the next day(my birthday), also I am doing her a favour.

Her company arrived and I had cooked her lamb and accompaniments and waited on these people about six total, also serving coffee. It was suddenly about 7:30 pm and my friends were taking me to a show on the strip for a birthday treat. The show was at 8 pm and I am not even there yet. I explained to this woman I worked for, that I have to leave now and she hands me a bonus and thanks me. Guess how much for all that work? Fifteen dollars, could not believe it, bit cheap eh? I need the job unfortunately. It's amazing in life sometimes one has to kiss ass!

Staying with John's other friends turned out badly too. One morning I overslept and left the condo without making the bed or tidying up and I was worried about the rich woman firing me for tardiness, so I thought I would take care of it when I got home. Unfortunately hubby's wife came home before me and had a fit. I was told that I was a dirty person and that I had to move out. Another storm has come my way, now what? A dirty person! That was a real insult, and the second time. Where do these people get this from?

I called John, I think he must be fed up with me by now, but he tells me to come back to Freeport, thank the Lord. Unfortunately I don't have the dog anymore, a family member of his has picked her up, miss her! Now I have to think about that five day drive back to Florida. John tells me he will arrange to have me flown back from Miami in a private plane, another friend of his has a son who is a pilot and he will fly me back as soon as I arrive.

I am to leave the car in a long term parking place and he will pick it up later. Guess he will leave it at our friends place up the coast. I visited AAA to get my route back planned, and pick up my little book with the freeways and exits I need to take.

A little change on the way back may be good for seeing other towns, and also break the boredom when there are miles of nothing and I don't have Circe to talk to. Guess I will have the radio on a lot more. One thing I am happy about is the fact that gas is cheap. I don't have too much money to spend on hotels and food, so I decide I will drive for as many hours at a time as I can handle. I am off!

I asked AAA not to put me through Dallas. It scared me on the way out here, so they routed me through Houston. Thank God! What! Are you kidding me? I went early in the morning, it was just as bad or worse for traffic. I think the journey back is going to be faster as I am driving longer hours and really concentrating on exits, etc. I love the Bahamas and cannot wait to see John and my friends.

The Florida panhandle is coming up and I think I am going to find a motel before going on to the last leg of my drive to Miami. I find a nice Holiday Inn (my favourite), get a burger brought to my room and sleep for the night. I am looking more like a burger every day. Six am is a good starting time. The weather was pretty cool and humidity lower.

I find the freeway that my little black book told me to find, and after about three or four hours of monotonous landscape I pulled over for a cigarette. It is now a different weather story, getting hot and very sticky. I get back into the car and happen to glance down at the seat on the passenger side. This is where my stuff is, cigarettes, AAA book and a few snacks and candy. Help! Help! My AAA book is not there. I turned everything over and inside out, still not there, so I assume I left it in the motel. Now I am really having to concentrate. Luckily my brain is still working pretty good and I remember the number of the freeway I have to get on. I also have the common sense to realise that I am driving East and then South. A young brain really helps!

It is now about six hours later and I am getting closer to Miami, luckily the same freeway I am on now goes straight there. I am finally over with cross country driving, that makes it about four thousand plus miles I have driven in the last two or three months. I find the address where John wants me to leave the car and get a motel room close by, not at our friends who I thought.

Now I will relax until I meet my young pilot tomorrow. I get to my room and call John to find out what time my young pilot is picking me up, about 11 am he tells me. Great! He is a really nice young man, and a good pilot from what I am told, cannot remember his name. His father works in one of the casinos where a good percentage of residents on the island work, I worked with him before I left. Bobby the pilot (I am calling him that as its better than no name at all), shows up early, about 10:30 am. I'm glad about that as I want to get this fiasco over with. We arrive at a small airport outside of Miami and he escorts me to the plane. "Oh my God, One Engine"! Hope my concern does not show too much.

He helps me up into the seat next to him and after a few back and forth pilot to tower conversations we are ready to take off. It was actually very smooth, I was surprised, but now we have open water for more than an hour. It could not have been more than ten or fifteen minutes and suddenly the sky was black and pelting rain. Next thing we encounter is thunder and lighting. I don't think I have to mention how scared I was. Looking down all I could see was black choppy water, I know there are sharks in it, not a nice thought. Bobby was amazing and very good at calming me down. I remember that this storm was over within a short time and we flew into blue sky, this kid is fantastic, I would fly with him again. Without a storm to fly through, looking down at this ocean is absolutely gorgeous. The colours look like something from a painting. Turquoise, green, and blue...really beautiful!

One thing that really is hard to deal with is the humidity. There are lots of little tricks that really help, like rice in the salt shaker, light bulbs on 24/7 in the closets, and cold showers six times a day!!!! If given the chance I would still live in the Bahamas for the rest of my life humidity included, but in order to be able to do that I would have to become a Bahamian or marry a Bahamian as these islands became independent in 1972. This is the reason I cannot look for a legitimate job. I do not have a work permit, and not much chance of getting one, but I do have an indefinite visa. I do not want to give up my British citizenship, and if I became a Bahamian citizen, I would have to do just that. Not so in the USA. What to do, what to do, what to do!

We are landing now, bit of a hairy flight, but I was never really scared of flying until now, at the age of 74, and still going across the Atlantic once a year if I can afford to. Have to see people I love. I think the big 747s are one of the safest planes made. I guess it is the size of these planes that overwhelms me.

Bobby and I go through the small building that deals with customs and immigration. I can always come as a visitor as I have the indefinite visa, lucky for me. I see John on the other side of the fence as we come out, and boy I am so happy to see him. He thanks young Bob and pays him whatever the arrangement was, then we drive back to the boat, John has been back on it for some time. Lonely boat right now my black Dane and the girls are gone. I did not know he moved out of the house but it makes sense, he does not need four bedrooms and have to pay double the rent that he pays to keep the boat in the marina.

We talk for a long time. He is still not sure about going back with his wife. The girls will be staying there and I think this is his dilemma right now. He misses them. At least the other dogs are still with him and that is a great comfort.

John is taking me to dinner tonight in the hotel where we once worked, lovely restaurant, super food and very nice music from a couple of musicians who play during the evening. Never been in this one before. This would be my introduction to hearts of palm, love them and got hooked. We had them as an appetiser with avocado, sliced tomatoes, and a nice vinaigrette. I still make this starter to this day, and I have added a little slice of red onion.

We are having a real gourmet meal tonight, nice change for me from burgers. Our entrée was Tornados Rossini, a small filet with pâté and mushrooms on top, and asparagus with Hollandaise sauce, very nice. Finished up with a good cognac and coffee. John does not drink very often, tonight he made an exception. Think he was very happy to see me, I am sure it got lonely after we were all gone, I am back but who knows for how long.

These were the years of marijuana and rock 'n roll, so needless to say we went back to the boat, listened to some nice music and went to bed together, it was beautiful, and it was only sex and rock and roll!. It would be the last and only time before I left again after the New Year a couple of months later. This guy was a ladies man. He sent me shopping about a week before New Year's Eve to buy myself a couple of dresses, he said we were going to dress up and enjoy ourselves for New Year's Eve, I believed him. I found two lovely dresses even though there were only one or two boutiques on the island that one could find nice clothes in. I bought a long black woollen dress with spaghetti straps and a slightly flared from the waist heavy bottom that really hung well, very flattering (by the way, I was 115 lbs., blonde, thirty-five, and very tanned, and still vain!). Who could ask for more? The second dress I bought was a long soft clingy pink jersey, crisscross straps across the back which was nearly non-existent, super looking. If you've still got it, flaunt it again. I knew that wherever John took me for New Year's Eve that Dave was bound to be in one place that we went, and I wanted his eyes to pop out of his head when he got a look at me, not nice but it's a woman thing, we all do it! Well New Year's Eve is here. John and I go to one of our local pubs, lots of happy people around. Only one thing wrong, not many of the casino workers are going to make it here, the casino is too busy. Guess Dave will miss me looking like a million dollars, doesn't matter anyway he has his lady.

It was a lovely evening. John had a couple of glasses of champagne with me, and I thanked him for all he was doing to help me. He would still be helping me for the next month or so, loved me but not in love with me. That is what he told me before I left the first time, and I was actually glad about that. No complicated situations are what I want, not sure why he had to come out with that statement, maybe he thought that I never heard him the first time and I had different feelings to what he had. Maybe if things were easier for me it would have been great to fall in love with a man like him, and maybe visa-versa. What a super guy, and here he was dealing with a wife who maybe just fell out of love, it happens, to the best of us. "C'est la vie". Life can be such a bitch! OK, get over it and carry on Limey.

24   Back to an Island I love

I am back on the road again, (Willie Nelson), is this "déjà vu" or what? I am trying not to think about what lies ahead. My long drive or my life. John has been in touch with somebody in Vegas who has lots of property, and he thinks maybe this man could give me a job in an athletic club that I heard he has interests in, teaching swimming. I am to meet him when I arrive, hope he will help me. I do finally arrive, and great news. My friend Michelle is living in town and she very kindly offers me a place on her living room couch. We do move into an apartment together further down the road, but for now I have to get a sponsor and get a job.

I call John's friend and we arrange to meet for breakfast. his friend Henry is getting on in years, but what a nice man. He tells me the plan that he has worked out for me. Evidently he has to advertise for a person to train people to swim, and it has to be put in the local paper in the classified ads. If he does not get any response or is unable to hire somebody, US citizens have priority, then I have a shot at it. Guess what? Immigration says an American can do this job even though no answers to his ad, and I have to sit back and wait. Thanks for trying, Henry.

A couple of weeks go by and I find a local bar, not a habit I have had going into a bar alone, but need it right now. The bartender was very handsome and sympathetic so this was going to be my local watering hole. He introduced me to the cocktail waitress. She and I hit it off straight away.

Over the next few years Carol and I became very close friends. This bar is visited by local politicians, University coaches, judges, lawyers and high-uppity-ups drinking and socialising there, and quite a few regular old Joes, they were the best! Carol talked to the owners about me working a few hours doing cocktails and they agreed and would pay me cash for a while as temporary labour. I was very happy to work any hours, any shifts, I suppose that helped. I was also a good waitress even though I say so myself.

25   And Then Along Came George

I started working a few hours a week on the grave shift (11 pm until 7 am). Not easy, but I worked with my favourite bartender, George. Could fall for him but he was married. Don't go after married men, very tacky! This job is going to get better and will shape my life for the next two years and then 37 years after that.

George and I worked very well together, we both know our drinks and we are great with people. Sense of humour and patience, that's what it takes.

Everything is good for the next few months, Michelle and I now have a two bedroom apartment, and I am cleaning for some of the guys who come in the bar who work in the casinos on the strip. They give me their door keys and pay me cash, which I have to declare later on my taxes. George and I start going to breakfast after our shift, some nights are extremely busy and very tiring. Breakfast at 8 am seems to be a good relaxer. We found a local place just off of the strip where the steak and eggs were to die for. It started off as really good friends. I just knew it would not stop there.

George now starts to confide in me and tell me that his life is not a happy one. How did I know this? Is this a line like a lot of men come up with or does he really mean it? We start to get very close over the next year and spend time together when he can get away.

In the meantime John has shown up and taken the car back, and cannot believe I have a boyfriend, he is guessing. Excuse me why not? You were going back with your wife and sent me off telling me to find a good life for myself. MEN! All the same. He leaves. We still stayed friends until his death about a year ago. George is having a bad time with his wife from what he tells me, they are not getting along. When he came to Vegas after retiring from the Air Force after nearly 25 years of service, he came alone and bought a house and set it up for his family, he told me when he brought the wife to town and took her to her new house she told him that she didn't like it. After all his work, pretty crappy!

Things went from bad to worse, and then I got dragged into the fray. I think she must have started to wonder why George kept being late getting home in the morning, and there were a few times after he played racquetball which he loved, that he would cut his games short and take me to dinner.

The first new years' eve in Vegas was nearly here and I found out that I had to work maybe a ten hour shift. No shit Sherlock! (Love these American expressions, they really describe a situation). George was going to get lucky, he would be off.

I can't believe it is nearly a year since I celebrated New Years' Eve with John, it has been a very eventful one.

A new girl has been hired in the bar and I have to take her under my wing and show her the ropes. She has never served drinks before and is rather nervous. I tell her "no big deal, it's a piece of cake". The secret I think, to being a good cocktail waitress is to learn what is in the drinks you are serving, and to have a good memory and a sense of humour. George has told me that he will try and pop in and have a drink with me on New Year's while I am working. Hope I can get time, and also hope nobody sees me having a drink. Not supposed to drink while working. I am sure one drink would be excused, strange rule for this town. All the workers in pubs in England are allowed to have a drink with the customers all the time! This 24/7 town, "Entertainment Capital of the World", hard to believe. I find out that Rachel, the new girl and I have to wear long dresses for work on the 31st. Guess it helps with the atmosphere, etc. and looks nice for New Year's Eve. About 10 pm we start to get really busy and Rachel is a little stressed because there are customers on her station that do not have much patience, some people when they are drinking can be demanding, and holiday times seem to be the worst. I give her a few hints and also a couple of good expressions that I use, it worked fine.

It is about 11 pm and not a sign of George yet. Suddenly he shows up with his wife and his brother and sister in law. I am not happy with this scene, especially when I see him dancing. Guess he really did not have much choice, so New Years' Eve was a big letdown for me, and my fault for getting involved in the first place.

The next few days at work with George were a little cold from my side, poor guy did everything he could to tell me how he was dragged into coming to our bar for New Years, even though he suggested may other establishments. It took about a week before we were friends again. I have been there and done that George, enough is enough, not sure if this is going anywhere.

As the months went by I felt much more relaxed as I had finally got my green card which meant I could work legally. George and I became much closer, and he confided in me more and more. It seemed that he was not very happy at all at home, and I understood after some of the things he had told me.

I had moved into an apartment on my own and sometimes George would come round for a meal with me. I introduced him to food he had never eaten before. Indian curry, roast lamb, which he loved not knowing it was lamb, and steak and kidney pie, which he also loved.

He was born in New Mexico in a small town (name not important), and his mother was Mexican, nice lady.

She taught me how to make dishes that George liked. It took me a while to get used to cooking that sort of food. I had never tasted things like menudo, tacos or burritos, but I practised until I made very good tasting Mexican food. George told me that my menudo was one of the best he had eaten. Great compliment from a man who had eaten this most of his life, and also I was from across the pond! I was very proud of myself for doing this, he is gone now but I still cook this food and think of him every time I eat it.

Getting back to 1977, I think it was about April and I had changed apartments. I moved into a one bedroom on two levels. It was a little bigger that my last one and closer to the pool, in the same complex by the way.

One morning, I remember it was about lunchtime there was a knock at the door. I opened it, there stood George! He had his racquetball bag in his hand and a look on his face that I will never forget. "Can I come in"? He said, "I got home from playing ball and all my clothes and stuff were out on the lawn in the front of the house, I guess I have been thrown out". I did not think of consequences coming from this so I said "of course you can come in". The poor man never looked so relieved. He put his bag down and sat in a chair. I went to the fridge and got him a beer. This had to be very traumatic for him, I know I had similar happenings, now it is happening to him, very stressful experience.

He emptied his pockets and put everything on the coffee table. It seemed his cash worth was about five dollars, amazing! After all the years with one woman and having four children, that's what it came down to. I told him not to worry everything would be OK and I would help him. Needless to say we both had a couple of cocktails each, and sat and talked for a long time.

The next few hours of stories from George pertaining to the last 20 years or so, made me feel for him. Not a really happy union I guessed. We both decided he should move in with me. He will be happy I will make sure of that! This is one of the nicest men I have met in my life.

The next day he went to his house and collected his clothes, etc. I am sure it was very hard for his children to understand what was going on, and there was no doubt I was the bad guy.

26 A New Roommate

George and I decided to move into a nice apartment in a better area, about a mile or so from the one we are in now. The new one has two bedrooms, nice living room and kitchen, and the furniture was very nice. Marble topped tables and drapes that matched the bedspreads. The building was round, and the pool was made in the same shape in the middle of the complex. Completely round, very unusual. This complex was adults only. Children could visit but not allowed to live there. This is when the nightmares for the next eight years started. If I had not loved that man I would have been gone in a hurry, but I think I thought he was worth going through it for.

We were out for a couple of hours one afternoon and when we arrived home we found George's two youngest kids on the floor in the hallway outside of our door, with two suitcases. His daughter, and his son. We assumed the ex had brought them over and left them there. What a good job we hadn't left town for a week or two. The poor kids had to stay overnight and then George took them back to their mother.

I finally met her a few months later, what an experience that was. A loud woman that was not very polite toward me, indescribable. I think I could imagine why George was miserable.

He went to a lawyer friend of ours to get a divorce proceeding started, and after about two hours he came back to the apartment and said "you better sit down". I said "What's wrong babe?" He then told me that our lawyer had found out that he had been divorced for years, unbeknownst to him. It seems he was divorced while he was out of the USA, in Europe somewhere while in the military. Not sure how a woman could do that to her husband and not even tell him,. But now at least this meant we could get married without dealing with all the ugly stuff.

Superman

My sister came over from England for a holiday, so George and I decided to get married while she was here. We had a lovely day, lots of friends, and George's brother and his wife. One of our friends held our little reception in his house, and even did the cooking for us. Italian! It was super. Stuffed clams, Lasagna, Ravioli's and Caesar salad, (which by the way is not Italian). A Mexican restaurant owner first came up with it, it was left over greens that he mixed things into for tourists visiting his cafe. (He should have got a patent on it). One of the girls I worked with made us a wedding cake, it turned out beautiful.

The bar that George and I had been working in had closed down, so we were working in different places now. I was lucky to get a job in a showroom in one of the hotels on the strip, and George got a job in another local bar. We were doing o.k. and what a good thing that was, as we had to start paying his ex-wife eight hundred dollars a month child support. George was getting a retirement cheque from the military, so that took care of the kids (hopefully, I used to think).

27 Another Nightmare Begins, Getting Married

Our marriage did not start off easy or peacefully, in fact we were hassled non-stop for a few years. We both cared enough about each other that we dealt with it and dealt with it. It was very hard and really stressful. I was called a whore, a shack-up job, and other words I don't even want to put on paper, by his ex., I could have retaliated, but I am not made that way, and George told me what goes around comes around, I did finally believe that, I still to this day have a copy of the divorce papers. George and I thought about the kids first, it was not their fault and with him being away a lot of the time I guess for a women alone it was hard to have a lot of discipline in the house. I felt very sad for these kids, the two older ones from what George told me, were always getting into some sort of trouble. . I heard things that curled my hair, but I got over it, even after the ex dumped her 8 year old son in Child Haven. (That is a place where kids are taken who do not have a home or someone to take care of them). What sort of mother could do that.? She obviously was very bitter. When we found out, George and I went there and picked his son up and took him home with us. By this time we had moved into a nice three bedroom mobile home, and my sister had taken over our apartment.

I sponsored her with immigration, after she said she wanted to stay. George helped me and everything worked out well. She found a good job, and further down the road got married and had two wonderful children.

Now we have George's son to deal with. It was hard for me, as his Mother had told him what a bad person I was. Excuse Me! She dumped him in a foster home type place, and he must have been really traumatised. For a long time I dealt with him, wiping poop on the shower doors, putting his fingers down his throat after he had eaten dinner so that he would throw up, and wetting the bed five nights a week so that I had sheets etc... to wash before I went to work. He even threw things at me that I gave him to eat for a snack, like apples for instance. I used to try and punish him by unplugging the TV when he would play up while his dad was at work, but he would just get up and move the heavy table that the TV was on and plug it back in. After dealing with this for about two or more weeks, I held up the plug in front of him one night and cut it off, then told him "plug it back in now Charlie". This started an hour of screaming and crying and trying to use the phone (which I also unplugged and took the phone and held on to it). He finally calmed down and I managed to get him to bed.

This child was only eight and had been dumped by his mother. I tried to imagine how he felt, but all I know is how terrible it had to be for him. It also made mine and George's life very stressed. I think that was the idea, cruel was the only word I could use when thinking of all this. It took a few months for me to win Charlie over, and finally things got a little more calm.

The first thing we got going was his weight. He weighed about one hundred and fifty pounds. I assumed this was a result of him being left alone at night while his Mother worked and young sis having to look after him, eating snacks, chips and drinking cokes would certainly do it!. His youngest sister got stuck with baby-sitting quite a few nights, poor girl had lots of chores too from what I learned later.

Charlie and I sat and talked for a long time on my days off, and we finally came up with a plan that he seemed to like. I suggested that I would make him lunch instead of him having money and getting crap from machines at school. I would give him five dollars every time he would lose five pounds. I started making him sugar-free Jello and healthy sandwiches with wheat bread, and once a week we would pig out and have cakes or doughnuts and good ice cream. The first five pounds he lost was a big celebration, he was so happy and we told him how proud of him we were. After fifteen pounds lost, Charlie and I went shopping. I bought him a nice pair of white Levi's and a couple of shirts that he picked out. He looked great, a very handsome kid.

Things were suddenly becoming much happier and so much less stressful. Our peace did not last long though. The first upset we had to deal with was Child Welfare showing up after someone (I am guessing who) had reported child abuse on Charlie. My God! If it was this woman, she is really sick in the head. Well after checking Charlie out, including him taking off all of his clothes, they apologised and left. Next, "CRUELLA" decided that Charlie should stay with her on her days off. George should have said no and put his foot down, but once again she got the better of him. Charlie went off with her for two days a week.

When he came back is was not the same kid. When he arrived back at the house she let him come to the front door on his own, didn't even walk up with him from the car. When I opened the door, his first words were "my Mom said my teeth are dirty". George brought him into the living room and sat him down and told him in no uncertain terms, if he cleaned his teeth that they would not be dirty. It took patience for a few hours to deal with him, but finally we got him calmed down. I then told George this has to stop.

This woman is making this kid's life and ours a misery. So far she has dumped him in a child refuge place, then she dumped him in

St. Jude's, of all places (without our knowledge again), and now even if she does not want him all the time, it seems that she is being very unkind to all of us! Maybe she should be dumped!! This situation went on and on for months and months, until we talked to a person at the child haven refuge, who steered us about the way to go.

28   Charlie Comes, Charlie Goes

Finally, Charlie went back to live with his mother. "God bless him" he needs it. His little game that we were playing with his weight problem went out of the window. During the next year or two, I had a lot of confrontations with the ex and Charlie and the other kids. I am still the Wicked Witch of the West. Charlie now weighs about 250 lbs. How sad! He is only eleven years old. He is going to get sick I can feel it. All the crap I've been putting up with, only putting up with it because of George, "we will overcome!" as they say.!

I was always in touch with my Mum and Dad, and sometimes felt very homesick. I told Mum she should come for a visit, I will pay the fare for her, Dad, and Patrick, my sister Ellen's boy, who is now being raised by my Mum and Dad. I believe his Father had emmigrated to Australia not long after Ellie died. I write back and forth to Mum, and come up with a date for the three of them to come over from England for a holiday. We all decide on December, about a week before Christmas. Can't wait! I know they will enjoy Las Vegas, to come to America will be a big thrill for them, and I know they will like George when they meet him. I have never told Mum anything about his ex-family, or what has been going on for two or three years, it will come out when I see them I'm sure. My sister Susie is getting excited. She has not seen our parents for a long time. I have waited nearly seven years. This will be a happy Christmas. My father has emphysema, so we arranged with the airline when I booked their tickets to have a wheelchair for him when departing London, and when they arrive in Las Vegas. Delta Airlines employees were phenomenal! I believe Mum and Dad were looked after very well for the whole trip, and this was before there were flights directly from London to Vegas. There were changes in one or two airports, hard to deal with when a person is not healthy and getting up in age. This was also the time when one could meet incoming friends or relatives at the gate, and then go with them to pick up their luggage. Times have certainly changed, now cannot even go for a cocktail with a loved one who is departing the airport. Safety first I guess.

Here they are! What a lovely sight to behold, the best parents any person could wish for. George and I walk up to meet them and I can tell Mum is beat. Dad is in the wheelchair, and is carrying a couple of bags, he looks beat to. George takes the bags from little Pat and then it is all hugging and kissing, and some tears, very draining but expected. We get everybody out of the airport and into our station wagon, great vehicle when one has company, and we make it home at last.

Tea, beer, and rum and coke are the first order of business. We all sit and talk for a long time. It's so great to have them here. Sue arrives next, more tears, and hugs and booze.

I show Mum around the place and I can see she is "gob smacked" (amazed) at seeing a washing machine and dryer, a water cooler with hot and cold, and other luxuries that most homes in America have. Mum was used to taking the washing to a Laundromat in England, and sometimes having to get a bus to do it, depending on where they lived at the time. Think I mentioned this before. Dave and I had most of these luxuries in the Bahamas.

It's about time for bed I know everyone is very tired it's a long journey from England to Vegas. Sue goes home and we put Patrick to bed. Mum and I have decided one more cuppa after Dad and George have gone. We must have sat and talked for more than an hour, about things past and present, lots to discuss over the next two weeks in-between taking the three of them out and about and showing them a wonderful Christmas.

We buy a lovely real fresh tree and Mum helps me decorate it, looks very nice. George and I do not have much furniture, paying eight hundred a month child support and three tickets from England did not leave much to spare. We had bar stools at the kitchen counter, a couch and a couple of chairs, no dining room table, meals will be eaten at the counter.

When we first moved into this huge three bedroom mobile home, we rented with an option to buy. We even rented our bedroom furniture from the owners. Lucky for us or we would be sleeping on the floor. When we first moved in we had a TV, a recliner which I came by from a friend, and luckily I had all the china and pots and pans, etc. We had moved from a very nice furnished apartment so it will take us a while to get everything we want or need! Poor George had nothing after twenty years or so with a family, but who cared. We had about three hundred in the bank after paying all the bills and the rent, and what we did next I'm sure most people will think us a little crazy, me especially. George in the chair, me on the floor (carpet, thank God) reading the paper, and I spotted an ad selling Bassett Hound puppies for seventy-five dollars each. I knew if I said "George, let's get one", he would go along with me, he did. We phoned the number in the ad for directions, sure, it had to be miles away, did not deter me though by Jove! Off we went. It took us about an hour to find the place, and then we were faced with about four eight week old Bassett hounds. I want all of them. Maybe I am thinking of Freeport, in fact I know I am. I had a Bassett hound, and now here I am in Vegas looking at a carbon copy of a pet I left behind. Maybe this is the reason I want one, no it really isn't. I love these dogs, in fact all dogs! We finally decide on a female with a big belly. Oh! She is so beautiful. We pay the man and head home.

We now have a TV, a recliner, rented bedroom furniture and a Bassett hound we have named Gussie (I think I named her). When we reached the house, George opens the front door and I put Gussie down on the carpet. This room is huge and empty, and the back wall is covered with mirrors, floor to ceiling. The dog runs at the mirrors when she sees her reflection, she runs into the mirrored wall at speed knocking herself flying. It looked very funny, but not for her. She wasn't hurt just shaken up. Guess now we have our work cut out training her. George and I work different shifts, so that really helped. Gussie would not be left alone for hours.

29 The Best Christmas

The dog was about one year old when Mum, Dad, and Patrick came for Christmas. Patrick took care of her while he was here, they got along great. Christmas Eve is here and Charlie is brought over, by whom I have no idea! Poor kid I feel for him. We have gifts for him under the tree and I know he wishes he could stay here. He is hanging out with Pat, company for both of them. Christmas morning and I am up very early to get everything taken care of. We are having a traditional English Christmas dinner, like we have had in England for most of our lives. Turkey with sage and onion stuffing, roasted potatoes lovely and crispy, roasted parsnips, Brussels sprouts, (baby ones of course), maybe carrots and to die for turkey gravy, followed by individual mince pies, Christmas pudding with thick cream, English custard or brandy butter, nothing can compare! Pretty obvious why most men fall asleep after Christmas dinner, us poor gals have to clean up all the mess, occupational hazard.

George has to pay a visit to his kids and ex before we have dinner, it is going to be like this for the next twenty eight years. Thanksgiving and Christmas are something he does not look forward to. Most of the time it seemed, there are always scenes. Arguing amongst each other, not like my family. I am so grateful that George and I don't live like that. Those kids never understood, and never will understand how I felt for them. The youngest daughter and I are the only ones who became close, and to this day we keep in touch.

"Love you Sheila! Thank you for appreciating everything I tried to do. Glad your brain worked, and your son has done so well, you should be very proud, I know your father would be if he were still here."

The holiday is over. Two weeks have flown by and Mum, Dad and Patrick are getting ready to leave. George and I have discussed with them packing up and coming to Las Vegas on a permanent basis. George and I can sponsor them and I am also a citizen now, became one two years ago. They are getting up in age and Pat is only 10, he will need somebody to look after him if anything happens to Mum and Dad, and his father went to Australia. Have no idea where he is or what he is doing.

30 A Big Transition From England

We say goodbye and make plans for their future, which George and I can make much easier for them. Dad is still working back in England I believe, and hard for him, even if it is part time. Mum is also doing the same, working in a nursing home a few hours a week, ENOUGH!

These two people deserve a little relaxation and fun time before they die. George and I start working on how we are going to help them make the transition from England to the USA. First thing they have to do is sell everything they own, well just about. The house is not a problem. It belongs to the local council (government). They have to get a permanent visa on their passports and finally say goodbye to any relatives we have left in England. My Dad has a brother and sister, and Mum has two sisters. It must be very hard for them making a big decision like this. I think they are mostly thinking about Patrick.

If they take him to America he will be safe and looked after, we will do our best. The weeks and months fly by and pretty soon another year and it is time for Mum, Dad and Pat to come back, only this time for good. By the time they arrive we will have a bit more furniture I hope. It's going to take a while even though George and I are both working five days a week.

Our Gussie is doing well, what a character she is. One afternoon on our day off, we made a rum-and-coke each and took them outside to sit on the porch steps. While we were talking, the drinks were sitting between us on the floor. Gussie drank one of them without us even seeing her, guess we were too engrossed in our conversation. She may have regretted it by her actions a little while later. Bless her. She fell over at least four or five times, got sick and finally passed out. Is this what we look like after a few toddies? Pretty ugly!

I have the spare bedrooms in order, and George has taken care of the backyard. Looks very neat, and our little lawn is growing very nicely, well Gussie thinks so.

All travel arrangements have been made and Mum writes to tell me everything is going well on their end. The house has been handed back to the local council, and now they are hoping to get together with the last of family for a final 'Bon Voyage'. Been there, done that! Not an easy thing to do, the only difference between Mum and Dad leaving England and me leaving, was the fact that they were getting up in age and also not financially able to return. I left when I was in my twenties, so I was able to work and save the fare back home. My parents were in their sixties and too old to be raising a young grandchild, this will be a relaxing few more years for them hopefully, and George and I can take over the job for them.

December is fast approaching and another Christmas is nearly here. Cannot believe a year has gone by so fast, mind you, I have had plenty to occupy my mind and my time.

The ex does not let us relax for too long. Nasty letters, sickening phone calls and verbal threats of what she is planning to do to make our lives more miserable. George and I are getting used to it now, it has been going on for over three years it seems part of our weekly soap opera. It would be nice if she would give us a break for the holidays. I think money might do the trick, as if eight hundred and more a month is not enough, George gives her more help, I know that, but it's fine with me if she would just give us a break! This woman cannot accept the fact that George had enough and left.

GET OVER IT! You and the kids are being taken care of. We have all had hardships and break ups to deal with, life goes on!

We have the dates worked out for Mum and Dad to travel. It will be about two weeks before Christmas. I get the tree up and put up a few decorations, have to make sure Gussie cannot reach any ornaments. They will be gone in a flash. Seems she will eat anything, I mean anything inside or outside, but what a beautiful dog she is. Pity humans cannot possess the love and loyalty of dogs. (repeating myself).

Cooking is now something I am doing a lot of, I am trying to get a few dishes made that I will be able to freeze and then have for the holidays, like stuffing, and apple sauce for pork, and mince pies, that will just need twenty minutes or so to cook in the oven.

We are obviously working on having an English style Christmas dinner again, but this time a large pork roast with crackling, (skin from the pork) which is fabulous when roasted. Have to order it that way here as the skin is usually cut off. We will have English custard with our mince pies this year, as well as brandy butter, yum, yum. My Mum is bringing the custard powder with her, we cannot get it in Vegas. The powder is mixed with very hot milk, stirred very fast, it then gets thick and creamy, with pies of any kind it's delicious.

I am married to a very good man, there are not too many men that would take on a wife's parents from another country and pay for them to get here. Also, they will all be living with us and it is going to be a challenge, but I am sure we will handle it. We have had a challenge from another source for a heck of a long time, so one more won't make much of a difference.

'Feliz Navidad'! My parents have landed at McCarran Airport and George and I are off to pick them up. It is the same scenario as it was a year ago. Dad in a wheelchair and poor Pat loaded down with bags, only more this time. Their whole lives in three or four suitcases and a couple of carry-ons, they are doing this so that Patrick will be looked after and have a home, I hope he will always remember this sacrifice these Grandparents are making for him. There were never two people as wonderful and caring as these. How lucky did I get? And I hope one day if this book goes public he will read it, along with his father.

Gussie goes nuts! She remembers everybody, what a happy reunion this is. First thing for me to do is make Mum a nice cup of tea, Dad is having a beer with George, me, a rum and coke.(lush)

George takes all the bags into the two bedrooms that are a little more inviting that a year ago. I managed to buy a couple of chest of drawers and more sheets, also a couple of bedspreads and rugs. Much more cozy and inviting. We'll get there eventually.

Our Christmas dinner is going to be eaten at the kitchen counter again, as we still don't have a dining table and chairs. We have bar stools and a couple of odd chairs that will suffice, so not to worry, dinner is going to be great.

Christmas Eve and it is very cold outside, colder than it usually is at this time of year, but I love it. What a nice change to put warm winter clothes on.

My mind has just wandered away from this story again and I am sitting here about to watch W. Somerset Maugham's 'The Razor's Edge', a movie released in 1946. I love old tearjerker movies, maybe getting old seems to make me want to watch them more, and now I find myself even getting teary eyed at some commercials!

OK, I'm back, coming up to 1980, New Years' Eve. George has bought a few fireworks, have no idea where he got them, didn't ask. I think they are for the kids, Pat, and Charlie who will be coming round for a couple of hours. I told George that it was against the law to have fireworks at the house, only July 4th is when they were allowed. He had not told the boys that he had fireworks, so they will not be any the wiser if we don't light them. There usually is good TV coverage of firework shows from around the world on New Years', so we are all going to settle down with some snacks and cocktails for the big people, sodas for the small ones, and enjoy the show.

How lucky are George and I to have some time off on New Years' Eve. It is not easy to get off on this day if one is a bartender in Vegas, it's not what you know, it's who you know! This applies to many things here, not just your job. Gourmet restaurants and showrooms also come into it, and big tips help tremendously if one would like a great meal and a good seat for a show. Things are different now that big corporations run most things. Shows are expensive compared to the 70s, and a gourmet room is very rarely comped anymore, so a hundred dollars per person is about average with drinks and tips.

The holidays are now over and we have to come down to earth and go back to work. The folks will not be left alone for too long as George works grave shift (eleven pm until 7 am), and I work day's and swing. Dad is helping out by getting veggies peeled for me, so that when I get home from the 8-4 shift dinner won't take so long to get ready. When I work 4 to 12 midnight, which is only a couple of shifts, George buys take-out. Things are working OK. Next thing to take care of is getting Patrick into a school. It's going to be a while as immigration comes first.

31   Snowing in Vegas

Weather is about to be a big problem for us. It is snowing! My father cannot believe it...in Vegas? I think we all found it rather strange. The snow began to settle and our roof started to leak in Mum and Dad's room, and the living room. Climbing up onto the roof seems in order to shovel off the snow. It's a good thing that we are renting this place, so repairs like leaky roofs are not our responsibility. We are actually renting with an option to buy. This is a good thing, as it lets us really find out what needs repairing and will the place be worth buying. George and I are on the roof with shovels and a shot of Black Velvet whiskey each, he talked me into it I don't like whisky. It is amazing how the snow settled that fast, and it is pretty cold up here, the Black Velvet did help, and I cannot believe I am up here I hate heights.

The roof is now cleaned off and hubby and I are now inside putting on some dry clothes. We let the owners know what is going on, and they tell us they will be coming to check things out.

A couple of days later they did show up and they will get our roof repaired. Thank you Lord, George and I do not have spare money for roof repairs, which can turn into an expensive job. We really don't need any more problems right now. Life has to get easier...

Please? We can now take the buckets from Mum and Dad's room, hope nothing else goes wrong.

I am back at work, five shifts a week. It is hard going, but doing it, need it, so get on with it. Cooking for five is not an easy task every night either. I am so lucky I get help.

Mum was scared of cooking in America. It was very different from what she had been used to most of her life. I tried to convince her that whatever she cooked would be great, but she still would not go for it. Preparing veggies for me and doing dishes was about it. I did not care about her not cooking anything. I love to cook so sometimes everyone had to wait for dinner.

Our first barbecue on the grill outside was a real winner. We did not have garden cook-outs in England, could have been because people did not have grills outside or one could never rely on the weather. I still love that little island where I was born and lived for many years, and sometimes I get very homesick. I think if I had lots of money, I would like to live there for six months a year, but I don't have and I can't, so what's the point of thinking about it?

The next two or three months were very tiring for me. Taking Dad to the doctors, for his emphysema, cooking, working five days and dealing with Godzilla (We all know by now who that could be.)

I found a very good internist for Dad who advised him to send to England for his medicine and inhalers as he could not prescribe anything quite as good. Amazing that a little country like that could have advanced drugs better than America. Dad decided not to have his brothers send medicine it would be too much for them to deal with. They too were getting up in age. The medicine etc. that the doctor gave Dad seemed to help with his breathing, and he assured us that if things got worse there would be other alternatives.

The roof is leaking again after a couple of days of rain, and this time in more places than before. George and I have had to call our landlords three or four times in a month, and suddenly we are having a problem getting this roof taken care of. We both have thoughts about this and decide to start looking for another place to live. I start looking in the local paper for houses to rent, and I finally find one that sounds big enough for all of us and within our budget. We are actually lucky that our lease is about to expire, otherwise that would be a big problem I think.

Mum comes with me to look at this house I found. It's a three bedroom, two bathroom, two-car garage, in a nice area. About sixteen hundred square feet. A nice big kitchen, horrible back garden all dirt, but no problem as far as I am concerned, I really don't have much time for gardening.

I meet with the owner, a woman in her late thirties. I am guessing she has money. She seems very pleasant and we come to an agreement on deposits and rent, and decide on a move-in date.

Moving has to be one of the worst jobs there are, especially in Las Vegas in the heat. My mother is a trooper she really helped me a lot. Poor Dad cannot do much because he has trouble breathing. We get moved in and I found one or two things that needed taking care of. The front door has two dead bolts, only one works, and the tile in the shower in the master bedroom has quite a bit of mould or algae on it. I mentioned it to the landlord, but I neglected to put it in writing. We would regret that down the road.

I cleaned the tile by standing in the shower and spraying bleach on the walls, silly thing to do without a mask, it nearly choked me to death. I replaced the dead bolts on the entry door, and I remember the owner coming round and telling me what a great job I was doing.

One afternoon her father came round, and asked if he could use the washer and dryer as his machine was not working in his house. His daughter, our landlord, evidently told him to come round and ask if he could use ours. Naturally we said OK. Thirty minutes after he started, the washing machine overflowed into the kitchen and part of the living room that had a sunken sitting area. It took us three or four hours to clean up all the water. Don't know what he did, but we had to pay for the drying and cleaning of the floor and carpet. That should have been a sign of things to come!

The next thing would be George discussing with this woman

how much she wants for the house at the end of our option to buy lease (another one like the last one). Hope this one may go easier than the last, but I'm not holding my breath. She gave George a figure that will suit us, so we agree and we on our way, I guess towards buying the house.

About a year gone and it seems that our plans are coming together. The lease is about to expire and George contacts 'Mrs. Anonymous' to find out about our payments and legal papers that need to be signed. Hello! Surprise! Surprise! She had made a decision, how surprising the price has gone up, take it or leave it. We cannot take it, too much for our budget to handle, so we have to give a month's notice. Why is this happening to us? We are good people and we take care of things. This (I have to say this) bitch has decided she will not give us our $350 Security deposit back either. Have no idea why, I have improved this place to no end, so I am taking her to small claims court. Not sure how to do this but I will find out.

I find out which office I have to go to downtown and get the papers I need to deal with this situation that has arisen, it seems the nicer we are the more crap we get thrown at us. I busted my balls cleaning and fixing things in this house, and this piece of nasty womanhood (second one I know now), is being so mean I cannot believe it.

Poor Mum and Dad, they are here to have a relaxing easy going life, this is not it, and George and I are not having a good time either. Our intimate life has gone right now, we don't seem to have the time or the inclination. I fill out the appropriate forms, and take them back and file for a hearing. We get a court date and Mum is insisting she comes with me for support. That will not be a bad thing I thought.

Courtrooms are scary places. I cannot believe what I am hearing from this woman, who told me six months ago how happy she was that I was taking such good care of her property. She was telling this judge, one in town that I had not heard of,(should have called our lawyer friend) how dirty our family was,(that was the second time

I have been told this, not sure where this keeps coming from?) and that she had to keep her eye on us. MY GOD! What is happening to my world? My Mother jumped up and started defending me, she was told to sit or be in contempt of court. My Mum had never disrespected any person in her whole life so she did not understand what she was being told. I had to convince her to sit down and listen to this "Cow" run us into the ground. We did not win, why would we? I am a bad dirty person and deserve to be punished, so we had to forfeit our $350 deposit and pay the court costs. This house was ten times cleaner and nicer than when we moved into it that's for sure. Why are there mean, miserable people in this world that just get pleasure from hurting others? Wow! Now we have to find another dwelling within a month. That will be number three.

32   Moving Again, And Dad Dies

Suddenly I feel like we are a family of gypsies. The next one we found turned out to be a place of trials, burglary and the saddest thing of all. (Bet you think I could be making all this up don't you)? It was much smaller than the other two places, but it was cozy, and the garden at the back was going to be my pride and joy. There was a nice little covered patio which we bought a table and chairs for. George got a lawn going, and I planted about six pink azalea bushes around the edge of the patio. We bought a small kids wading pool for the dog and things started to look good.

Wrong!!! Dad started to show signs of constrained breathing, so back to the doctor. He suggests that I take Dad to a local hospital once a week for the pulmonary breathing classes they held. Also we had to arrange to have a medical equipment company provide breathing apparatus for the house. This consisted of certain chemicals that Dad had to breathe in maybe four or five times a day. Poor man! From a strong person who worked two jobs all his life, to a shadow of what I remember. After a few months the inevitable happened. We had to get oxygen in. I found a hospital bed in the local classifieds, and George got a friend to help him go and pick it up. We got a bargain. It had everything Dad needed. Up and down buttons for the mattress, and easy controllable sides, just right for him. It is getting hard for George and me again. Mum and Dad don't have insurance so most of what dad needs has to be paid for. Guess what?

If I have to work another job to provide what he needs, I will, and my good husband will do the same, this man I married would give you his soul! I am now working 3pm to 11pm and George is permanent graveyard, 11pm to 7am.

I get dinner ready before I leave for work and somebody, not sure who, would finish it off. I know for sure it was not George He was not the chef in the family.

He made up for his lack of cooking skills in other ways. He started helping a friend with concrete work, putting up brick walls and patio slabs. Very hard work, especially in the heat, and still working behind the bar too. He must have been very tired when he got home in the mornings, and then off to dig trenches, strong man. We needed extra money, but I did not want him to work himself to death.

Dad's breathing was getting worse. He has only been living in Vegas for a year and a few months. I thought the dry air would really help him. I guess his lungs are too far gone. I came home from work one night about 11:30pm and found him on the couch really in distress, struggling to breath. Poor Mum did not know what to do. Emergency number in England is 999 and here it's 911. I did write it down for her in our phone book. I think she was too scared to call or forgot that she had it.

Health care in the USA is so completely different from England. Over there we call our doctor first, no matter what time of day and he takes it from there. Anyway I dialled 911 and an ambulance showed up. First thing they gave him oxygen. I could see by his face what a relief for him... I told the paramedics I would follow behind in my car. They told me they were taking him to one of our local hospitals then they took off, sirens screaming.

I arrived at the emergency room and Dad was on a gurney in the corridor. I found the person in charge and could not believe what I was hearing, talk about shock! I was informed that they could not treat him as he did not have any insurance or a green card. I have heard of people from the states going to England to have babies and get medical help as they could get it for free, or next to nothing. How disgusting? My Father is laying there dying and I was told he would have to be taken to the another Hospital? I guessed it was the hospital that anyone without insurance or money would go to get medical help, including homeless people and obviously foreigners who have not been cleared by immigration yet.

It is now about one am and Dad is transferred to the county hospital. Mum and I are allowed into the cubicle in the E.R. and now we wait for the Doctor. Thank the Lord for this hospital they are making my father comfortable at last. The poor man was really suffering. I realised I had not eaten since about noon and have worked an eight hour shift on my feet, getting tired now. I take a walk into the hallway to check on the Doctor and find myself waking up on a gurney. I was told by a nurse that I passed out. Told you I was tired! She suggested that I take Mum home as they will be quite a while before they admit Dad. I drove home and called the bar where I work and told the guy working to pass on a message telling the boss I would not be in tomorrow and I would call him later. Then I called George and filled him in. Time for a strong cup of tea. I know Mum needs one. The bed is going to feel good now at nearly 4am, and to sleep-in will not be an option.

I get up pretty early and call the hospital. Dad is finally in a room. I take Mum a cuppa and a cookie in bed and tell her we will get ready and go to see Dad. George is sleeping this morning, no concrete work. Good! We creep around getting ready so as not to wake him. Then we go.

The parking lot at this hospital is awful. A very, very busy place. Who would have guessed? Dad looks better than last time we saw him, but not breathing well even with the oxygen. One would think watching a person gasping for breath that it would stop them from smoking. Not me! Not now anyway, it is going to take a few years to bring me to my senses.

Dad smoked, but he also worked for a very large precious metals company in England, stoking furnaces I believe, and something to do with smelting gold and silver. He had two brothers who worked there and my ex-husband also worked there. Three of them finished up with emphysema. The fumes from the furnaces must have been very unhealthy. I think this company is still in business and is very profitable fifty or sixty years later. My ex died from emphysema at age 60, and my uncle at 57. Dad is 68 right now, but 69 does not seem to be in his future. I think now-a-days if people work for companies whose products or work environments etc., can cause health problems, they should at least get medical help paid for, especially in the U.S.

It has now been three or four days since Dad was admitted to the hospital and we have started getting phone calls from the nursing staff to tell us that it seems he will not make it through the night. So far we have had three and he is still hanging in there, but now moved into ICU. He is there for about ten days, then moved back to a regular ward. I am still not back to work. I will be surprised if I still have a job. Who cares? I will find another one.

Finally after a visit one morning to see Dad, the nurse in charge tells us that it will not be long now, Dad is fading fast. We make a final decision about visiting. Mum and I will go home now, shower and change, and bring back a bag with necessities and come back to stay in the visitor's lounge as long as it takes.

George is going to take care of Patrick at home, take-out is easy. The customers from the Lounge where I work are calling the house and inquiring about Dad. He has gotten to know a few people there when George would take him for a beer. He also played cribbage with a very good friend of ours who was also our best man when we got married. Super guy, now deceased, he died at a pretty young age of cancer. My Sister dated him for a while, I think they really got along, but I think his drinking got in the way, shame he was a really nice person.

Things are not getting any better at the hospital, it has been about three days that Mum and I have been on hard wooden couches in the visitor's lounge, and spending time in Dad's room on and off. We check in on Dad on the fourth day that we have been back, and notice that he is actually laying down sleeping. This man has not laid flat in a bed for years. One of the nurses tells us it is probably the strong medication they are giving him. What a wonderful thing to see, my Dad asleep laying down!

Time for us to go to the cafeteria while we can. We have a couple of coffees and a sandwich each, and I can see Mum wants to go back up to Dad's room. He is still sleeping after a few hours, so we settle down in the lounge and try to get some sleep ourselves, that's not easy on this furniture. Guess we both did sleep a little, as I am awakened by a nurse very early in the am to tell me that my Father has passed away. Thank you God for ending his suffering. Now I have to wake Mum and tell her.

She is very calm, and somehow I suddenly remembered that she has been watching him gasping for fifteen years or more. When two people have been together for over fifty years, I believe that they just want what's best for each other even if it is death!

We wait for the mortuary to arrive at the hospital and take Dad to the funeral home. I had started a payment plan for Mum and Dad for funeral expenses when they first arrived in the U.S.A, but did not think this would happen after a year of them arriving. I had to transfer the payments on Mum's plan to help with Dad's funeral. Then George and I had to get a loan for $5000 to cover some hospital bills, and what was left to pay on the funeral expenses after we transferred Mum's plan. Luckily we had a friend, who was a loan officer, so no hassles with borrowing that.

A few days later I went to finish the arrangements. The funeral home did a fabulous job on Dad. They made him look very, very nice. We had an open casket funeral and Mum made a decision which surprised us all. She did not want to come to the funeral. I can really understand how she felt. The one man she had been with all of her life since they went to school together was gone, and that was hard for her. Patrick stayed at home with her while we went to the funeral.

We all, George, my Sister and I told her it was very OK not to come if that was her wish. There was a nice turnout at the chapel, considering Dad had only lived in Las Vegas for a short time. A lot of people made an appearance. We went back to the house and a few friends brought food. Mum handled everything very well, amazing woman.

33　We Buy Our Own Place

The next thing my husband and I decided to do was to buy a place of our own if we could find something that was within our budget. I now start to look for a house, something we all like and will be happy with. We are tired of renovating other people's houses and getting nowhere, and on top of that, belittled. Looking through the real estate section of our local paper I come to mobile homes. I ask George what he thinks about that and he says "We have already lived in one, why not?"

I take Mum with me on my days off (I still have a job by the way), and we start looking at mobile homes, not too far from where we lived when the folks came over from England, not a bad area in 1981-82. We find a nice three bedroom, two-bath, well taken care of place, pretty large living room and kitchen.

George comes with me later to look at it, and we decide to make a deal with the owners. No roof problems with this house we checked it out. Now we have to get a loan, amazing! It was pretty easy and straight forward. Is something going our way for a change? I also have other business to take care of, finding a school for Patrick and then dealing with the Immigration department to get Mum and him green cards and make them legal residents. I wonder if anyone knows how tired I am!!!

When Dad was alive, he had made a trip to Los Angeles with George and a friend of ours who said he had a lawyer who could help them with immigration. We paid this so called Beverly Hills shyster over $800 to begin the paper work. That was at least nine months ago, and no word of any kind from him. I made phone call after phone call to no avail. I then decided to write to the Bar Association. I did get a reply to this inquiry, and was informed there would be an investigation.

One day while I was at work, the lawyers office called the house, and unfortunately Mum had dealt with the call as neither George nor I were there. They offered to pay back some of the eight hundred dollars and made Mum an offer for five hundred. She took it. I wish I had been there and talked to this bunch of creeps, but I guess five hundred was better than nothing. We did receive a cheque within a few days, amazing what a few letters to the right places can do.

So now I make arrangements to take Pat and Mum to our local Immigration office. I know when I became a citizen there was a lot of paperwork, and learning a small book with facts etc, etc… about America for a test to actually get citizenship. It will not be as hard to get green cards I'm sure. I registered Patrick in a local school and I know it will be hard for him for a while, not having any friends and coming from England, and having a funny accent. I am still told by my customers that I have a funny accent, and I have lived here for forty years, bloody hairy twits!!!!

We are working at getting him a bicycle which will give him a little freedom and independence. He is a friendly good looking kid (like his Mum) and it's not long before he settles into the American way of life. (I will come to regret that statement later).

34   Immigration, Adoption, and Les

We all go through the immigration experience and green cards are coming forthwith. Next on the agenda, George and I discuss adopting Patrick. My mother has taken care of him since my sister died, and his father has gone to live in Australia, so we figured he needed parents. We find a lawyer who is an expert at adoptions and he is willing to take payments. Yippee! Things seem to be getting a little easier for us two hard working people. The lawyer tells us that we have to post a notice in our local paper on our intentions, and in a paper in England. Also he has to get in touch with Pat's father's lawyer if he has one and can be found. Our lawyer does all of this and calls us to let us know that no-one has contested on either side of the ocean, so he proceeds with the legalities., I really hope Patricks father reads this one day.

We finally get notice to go before a judge who will decide yea or nay. The verdict is yea, we rush home to celebrate. Pat will be taken care of and now Mum does not have to worry. She has spoiled him no doubt about that, but that would be natural for anyone losing a Daughter and having a Grandson who only has Grandma and Granddad. I think Patrick seems to be happy about the whole thing.

He is now on the school football team, so Mum and I go to the games and support him, and he has his bike, so life is pretty good. In the meantime in between all of this going on, I have been in touch with my son who is now 21 and can come and go as he pleases. I tell him I will get him a ticket to come for a visit, not sure when but we will work on it. I have not seen my son in nearly ten years. That is a long, long time!

Nobody but nobody will ever know how traumatic it was for me when my ex got the custody of my son. I think that influenced me to go to the Bahamas and be with Dave. Things are different now, I can see him and he can see me, whenever we can afford the fare across the Atlantic. What a thing to stop us, money. It really is the root of all evil. When I had the money to send Leslie a ticket while I was in the Bahamas, his Father would not let him come to see me. Now when I can see him anytime, I don't have the money.

George and I have helped to keep lots of people since we got married and have also had to come up with unexpected sums that have put us in debt a few times. We are both busting our 'you know what' and more, but we both know it will get better one day.

I help Mum to get her pension (social security) sent from England, the only downfall is the exchange rate. When the dollar goes up the British pound goes down or vice versa, so Mum gets less pension.

A few months pass, and now I can help my son come for a visit. I ask the young guy I work for if I could have four days off, a workmate will cover for me. Then I will cover for him when Les leaves. The boss says yes, great! But another let down coming, his Father who actually owns the place decides I cannot have four days off, have no idea why when it is covered, so I am fired because I took the time off anyway hoping his Son would defend my actions. A piece of paper was in with my pay cheque to tell me that I was let go. I just do not understand people sometimes, and the nicer one is and the harder one works, the more one gets crapped on. Anyway, now I can enjoy a little relaxation, not too long we are not independently wealthy.

Leslies ticket is booked, cannot wait to see him. He has been playing with a band, or bands, since he was young, and has travelled to a few countries already. I remember he wanted a guitar when he was twelve, and his father and I went halves to buy him one, his dad not believing that this was something he really wanted to do in his life, play music. Eight years later he is even keener.

His flight to Vegas is in two parts, changing in Atlanta if I remember correctly, one of the busiest airports in the U.S. He is supposed to arrive early evening. Evening has come and no Les. About 10pm I started calling airlines to see what is going on and trying to find out where he is. I find out that his flight was delayed and he has been diverted to Dallas, Texas. This was a time before everybody had a cell phone, so I could not call him, only airline information which kept telling me the flight had been diverted, no why, how, or what time it would get to Vegas. Mum, George and I decided to go to bed about 12:30, Les had the phone number, and I was sure he would call when he arrived. There was nothing else we could do. Hope he has the address written down correctly. Men are very bad at asking directions, right? I have heard about men driving 2 or 3 hours in the wrong direction rather than asking the way. It's a man thing! There is a loud knocking on the front door, I jumped out of my skin and put the bedside lamp on. I look at the clock and see that it is 2:30am. Suddenly I get very scared. What has happened? Is Les OK? Is it the police? I grab my dressing gown and go to the front door, on the way meet Mum in the hall, George is behind both of us, in front may have been a better feeling, but he's there so that's all right. I shout out "Who's there?" and a little soft voice comes back "its me, Mum". I open the door as fast as I can and there he is, looking very pale and tired. Mum calls him by another name, who is a cousin of mine, guess she didn't recognize him. I tell Mum that it's Les your Grandson from England, and then she hugs and kisses him, that's her Grandson from England on the doorstep at 2:30 in the morning? it's ok Mum, he got lost!!!!

After the hugging and a little crying in the doorway I get my poor tired boy into the house and then the kitchen. Tea is in order again, to calm and heal frayed nerves. It does work! I'm sure of that.

Les needs to get to bed, we can hear about his adventure tomorrow. Morning comes around too fast for me. I cannot remember sleeping more than 2 or 3 hours. I am know getting breakfast for Pat before he goes to school. A woman's work is never done, seems to be a true statement for me whoever came up with that. I would like to meet him or her. I'm sure it was a her, don't you think?

Patrick is gone and I sit and have a cup of coffee on my own for a change, while waiting for everyone to get up. It is a nice hour to myself. Do not get too many of those.

Les is first up, amazing! But then he is only 21 and at that age one can bounce back in a hurry. Mum is nearing 70, and George is working two jobs, he is entitled to sleep as long as he wants to.

Les and I have lots to talk about. The flight he was on evidently was delayed and diverted. The poor kid was all over the country, and the cab was not too sure of our address, so it took time for that part of his journey as well, but he is here that is all that matters. We are going to give him a memorable two weeks.

While we are on our own, we have time to talk and discuss his life. His father has remarried ten years ago, and his new wife has four children, grown up now I guess. Les tells me that she is a nice person, and I think for the most part he has gotten along with his step-siblings.

It took nine years for his dad to give me a divorce, he did not want one, and unless it was agreed by both parties in those days, it would not pass. I remember it was during the week that my sister, Ellie died, June 1971, that I was at last granted a decree nisi. How could I ever forget that? I went to court and the lawyer for Jimmy said "It is not contested by the husband, therefore granted". Nine years, a long time. Why? I often wondered, what was the point? It really did not make a difference to my relationship with Dave though, he was not the marrying kind I knew that, and Jimmy really did not know what I was doing or who I was with, but I guess I would go on hoping that Dave would at least tell me that he loved me, I am suddenly a single woman. I had to wait another 35 years to hear him say that, but he finally said it, even if he had been drinking, it was nice to hear. Bit late maybe, but better late than never, it made me happy!! Some men are just not that way inclined. I guess George was the opposite, always told me every day, very loving man.

Les and I get to talk for at least a couple of hours before Mum gets up looking for her cuppa. I have not got her turned on to coffee in the morning yet, but she loves one around lunchtime made with half water and half milk. We have been having our coffee back in England that way as far as I can remember.

After coffee, tea, and breakfast I get Les and his stuff unpacked and hung up. He is sharing Patrick's room. I put his clothes that are creased in the gas dryer, ten minutes, right as rain. He cannot believe it. Nobody has a gas dryer in England, well no-one he knows. This is one thing I love, my washer and dryer. Wash, dry and wear in an hour. I am still sure that families where I came from are still drying sweaters and heavy clothing on the radiators that heat the house if they do not have a good dryer, what a pain in the neck that must be.

George has just gotten up. No concrete work at the moment, that's good, he is getting a break and a chance to get to know my son. They hit it off instantly. How great is that? But then it was the same thing with my Dad. George loved that man, and used to enjoy taking him for a beer to our local bar, that is where he made friends with a lot of people, very likeable man, Dave loved him to.

The next two weeks goes by quickly. We take Les to parties, some given by a wealthy couple we know. He is impressed by these people. Guess they are fun, but not what I would call classy rich, money does not make classy, he will learn that over the years. Time fly's when one is having fun and my son is suddenly about to leave. Wow! That visit went fast. I really hope it's not another ten years before I get to see him again.

Life is back to routine, and I now have to find a job. George tells me not to worry, he will take care of whatever needs taking care of. I do really appreciate him and how hard he works but I am going to do my share. Isn't it give and take?

I have made lots of friends and contacts since I first arrived here seven years ago. It does not take long before I have been offered a job, a small very busy bar near the Culinary hall. Should have known, behind the union hall, Hello! Busy, busy, and busy. Not only union workers, but construction workers for large companies graced me with their presence. There were also Mexicans who spoke very little English, and African Americans, a very varied smorgasbord of human beings. I am glad that bartending seemed to be my forte'. A sense of humour and a lot of patience was also in order. Five days a week in this bar was hard, I even had to change the kegs after rolling them from the main walk in cooler to a cold cabinet behind the bar, lucky for me I had plenty of guys to help me roll a keg down the bar into the other small cooler which was at the other end from the main one, a portable type keg holder.

I had a scary experience one morning when I was behind the bar, four cops burst through the door with guns drawn, they were big guns I remember, maybe rifles, I was not an expert. I had to raise my hands in the air and find my ID to let them know I was who I said I was. After the introductions and I was in the clear, we figured out what had happened. I had unknowingly set off the silent alarm that I was not aware of. When I started this job nobody told me about this hidden alert, and to this day it is still used in bars. Obviously this is not something I will share as it will give the bad guys a head start!

35 The Fabulous Mill

I was probably working in this place for about six or seven months, when one morning I had a phone call from a friend of ours named Cherie who was a real estate agent, commercial property mainly. She said "Sam, I have found a bar for sale that you and George could take over if you want to assume the debts". I told her I would talk to him and get details from her later. Hard to talk on the phone when I am working. I told George about it when I got home, and we decided it would be worth going into details with Cherie.

For the next month or so we found out what we needed to know to get into this bar. It was not going to be easy we both decided that, but I think we were go-getters as far as hard work was concerned, and so we suddenly were going to take over and run, and have fifty-one percent of a local bar. Let me explain this. In order for George and I to take over this bar, we would have to have partners or shareholders. George and I did not have the money to buy this place, and taking over the debt would be an opportunity for us to own, or part own a good business. We both have lots of friends. Im sure we can make a go of this place. Now the paperwork, lots and lots of paperwork.

The two friends that steered us into this bar, (one a real estate agent/broker, and the other a businessman who owned a furniture company), took care of getting us a lawyer (will talk about him later), and dealing with most of the paperwork we had to fill out and sign. Two bartenders who really do not know much about owning a bar only working in one, suddenly find themselves having to learn how to deal with liquor laws, taxes, slot machine companies and more and more. Well, we did it! The 'Mill' is ours.

I learned how to do payroll (nightmare), order liquor, and take care of making sure we never ran out of anything. I did pat myself on the back more than once or twice, as we never ran out of anything needed for this twenty-four hour a day home from home establishment.

Our opening night was something to be remembered. After friends had helped us clean the place and make it look like a cozy bar, I realised we had ten cases of Jeremiah Weed (cheap vodka based product), and only one or two cases of regular liquor (i.e.: vodka, gin, scotch, etc.), and very few cases of beer. There was not a thing I could do about this awful predicament. Everything was thrown at us in a hurry. OK let's just hope for the best and sell everything we have on hand, and have a wonderful night.

As far as I can remember, we did just that, and something happened that was really unbelievable. After George and I and friends had got the place looking like a warm inviting bar, we opened the front doors and hoped our friends and also a few new customers would show up to give us a boost. Well our friends from all over town did show up, and every one of them bought a bottle of liquor or a case of beer and donated it to us for the bar for our inauguration. We had a longtime friend helping us behind the bar (the days before the required TAM cards and this card and that card). If I remember correctly, a Sheriff Card and Health card was all that was required, and being as George and I and a few of our friends were already bartenders, NO PROBLEM. We had a fabulous opening night.

One customer who was also a friend, sent an enormous flower arrangement, and being as he was a wealthy man he made sure that the customers were well taken care of at his expense. He was also very good to the bartenders as far as tips went.

What a shame my father had died, he would have loved this place. Our first nights takings, included using some of the donated booze that our friends let us ring into the register (which was a gift)was nearly two thousand dollars. WHAT A GREAT NIGHT, WHAT A WONDERFUL START!

The next day would start seven years of hard, hard work, along with a lot of dedication. I was voted to run the place and only bartend when I was really needed. My first challenge was to learn how to do payroll and order liquor. I also had to be aware of whatever was needed to run the bar, like glasses, napkins, straws, fruit and anything from the bar supply company. This would also include cleaning and janitorial supplies.

Slot machines would be my next challenge, or should I say our next challenge. The previous owner(s) of the bar had a lease agreement with a slot machine company, and it was agreed by all that we should carry-on leasing from this company. The liquor licence and Gaming licence would be in George's name, which required him to go through background checks. He had served over twenty years in the Air Force, so this was a pretty easy avenue for him to go down, and he had heavy security clearance when he was stationed in New Mexico. It took a while, so in the meantime we worked with temporary permits. We ended up not applying for a Gaming licence, financially it was impossible, it entailed buying our own slot machines, and the licence was way beyond our reach. We are going to get rent from the slots we have, and take a percentage of the drop once a week. We knew nothing about gaming companies, but eventually we would find out there were supposedly a lot of underhanded things going on with the one we have.

I was left to make decisions on my own that would benefit the bar which I did, and we were suddenly a very busy, money making establishment. I got the kitchen started and kept the food at a reasonable price. I also introduced food not really associated with a bar, like Indian curry, which I made myself, liver and onions with garlic and tomatoes, and shepherd's pie also my contribution. We had all the usual bar stuff, the best chicken wings, and burgers, but we also had a great cook. This is the answer for most good menus. He was very versatile, and I believe at some point in his life he had worked in restaurants in San Francisco. George and I were very lucky to find him, and we were really happy with the bartenders that worked for us as well. They were all friends which made for a fun and hard-working place. They respected us and wanted the bar to be a success, as did me and George. I came up with some great ideas with help and encouragement from our customers, and our super crew that worked for us. The first was to throw a party for New Year's. I would cook and have a buffet free to the customers, which we placed on the shuffleboard table, which was covered with a huge, long board. I also rented a fountain that held champagne, but we decided to have Asti Spumante from 9pm on, also free. I also made a special request that everyone had to dress up. Nice dresses for the ladies, and jackets or tuxedos for the guys. Ties were not really needed. I managed to secure all the horns, hats, and stuff for New Year's to top it off. Our first New Year's party was a blow-out, and the band was outstanding. That is what New Years' Eve is all about.

Guess the word got around what a great bar we were. We started getting busier and busier. OK, what next? How about a shuffleboard team? There were a few guys really interested, so we got some friendly games going, and picked six people to make-up a team. I made it, not because I was the boss either. I was pretty good at it, surprise to me too! I got us signed up to a league which meant visiting other bars all over town. Great publicity. Amazing! Our team did pretty good, and our home games packed our bar. I thought a few free wings would help, yep! It did.

One of our bartenders was into golf, so we (him and I) worked out some plans to have a golf tournament. Terry was his name, and he turned out to be a great asset to George and I, as well as being a good bartender. He helped me with a few things that needed repairing, and managed to put his hand to a lot of things that needed totally replacing.

Then Terry and I got down to organising a golf tournament. It was bloody unbelievable how many people signed up. I think around a hundred or more. Terry did most of the putting teams together, etc. In fact we had a team picking night where we put all the contenders' names in hats. Teams A players, B players, C and D, and then we would pick one player from each hat. If it didn't quite work, (it would be an A and B with 2 C's or an A and 2 C's and a D, and so on and so on), it would actually take the playing of a tournament to work this out where it would be fair to all teams. There were players who supposedly were A's and turned out to be much less, and also with the other categories some better that we thought, and some worse, but it turned out to be a great day.

After a long day of golf, everybody went back to the 'Mill' where I had set up a buffet, getting food to the bar early in the morning before I played eighteen holes of golf. Now that was definitely what would be called a hard day. George, love him, helped me at the end of the day washing pots and pans etc… He too had played eighteen holes of golf. Like me (only a little worse), we were classified as hackers I guess, who cares? Great fun if one remembers it's just a game.

This was going to turn into a great three times a year event. Some of the liquor distributors and beer companies gave us things to be given for prizes. Novelties, a few bottles of booze, tee shirts etc. 'Those were the days my friend',(good title for a song).

We also had a couple of friends video one or two of the tournaments for us, amazing what people act like when they are being themselves not knowing they are on camera, some of the film was very funny. We did give prizes for the winning team and also as far as I remember a best player award. Great fun all around.

Thinking back, I remember that Super Bowl Sunday would be the busiest day we had every year, we even took reservations from bartenders and friends from other bars to save them seats, which entailed us to rent tables and chairs. The bar would start to fill up about 11am even if the game did not start until 3pm. Crazy! We had football boards that customers could bet on, and did not know until years later that the Gaming Commission did not allow that. Every bar in Vegas had football boards, a gambling town and one was not allowed to put money on a football game in a bar? I guess it was a licence thing, still not sure to this day, anyway we supplied food and drinks for the whole length of the game to people who had money on the boards, and they could bring one guest who was also fed and given drinks. I took care of the food (of course), and it was always a great spread. I made a buffet, hot and cold that we would spread out on the shuffleboard table that had been covered with table cloths, paper plates and containers for cutlery, I also had chafing dishes which meant the hot food was kept hot.

After the game had finished, we would have a drawing for 'loser's pool'. There were 28 winners (the way we would do the pool), so we would put all losers names in a hat and draw 10 names, those people would get their money back. The way we did this pool was very popular. Guess this was one of the reasons besides the camaraderie that we were so busy. I know for sure that our customers were taken care of, our bartenders were taken care of, and a good time was had by all. Another day that my husband and I busted our butts, but so rewarding.

36 Mother Loved Wedding Receptions

I remember Mum used to enjoy all these events, I always took her with me, people loved her and she made a lot of friends. Mum was not a drinker, grapefruit juice was usually the aperitif of the day. There were occasions that she would like a glass of sherry before dinner, and there were occasions (we will get to one or two of those shortly), that she went a little overboard not really meaning to. I think she was entitled beyond any doubt in my mind. Getting to the one or two of her being over-served mishaps. I think one of the worst for her and for me having to take care of the aftermath, was my sister Sue's wedding reception which was in our bar. Mum found a taste for Frangelico, a hazelnut liqueur usually sipped slowly from a small snifter like brandy. Forget that! Friends were buying her drinks, and the bloody hazelnut was being glugged from what I observed. I hurried over to the bar to let George know (he was helping out, as it was very busy) what was happening with Mum and whatever, nobody was to serve her anymore. My sister was marrying Terry, one of our bartenders who I mentioned earlier. They seemed to hit it off when they were introduced, and they finally tied the knot. Back to the reception and a Mother full of Frangelico, and who knows what else. It finally "DONE ER' IN"! My sis and I had to carry her, well just about, to our station wagon. George always liked station wagons. I think most of our 30 years of being together, we owned about 4 wagons, and none of them ever let us down,(getting off the subject), I am back to Mother. George was going to stay at the bar and make sure that everyone finished having a fun night, and Terry and Sue were OK.

Well I got home with Mum, a fiasco if ever I had one. I managed to get her from the car to the front door, luckily we had a bench outside next to our door, so I sat her there while I got the place open. Then I had to get her to her bedroom. This was not an easy feat but I got it under control, maybe secretly I am a sidekick for John Wayne, otherwise I have no idea how I did it. As I tried to get clothes off the top half she would lay down, then I would try her bottom half and she would sit up. It took a while, but WE DID IT! I was so proud of her. Mum was very sick but that was to be expected, the amazing thing was she did not wake up the next day with a bad headache, just a wee bit slower than usual. Told you how tough she was, glad it's in my genes!

A couple of years have gone by and the bar is doing well. My girlfriend Rachel from the old 'Dutchman' (a local pub that is no longer there.), is helping us out waitressing one or two shifts, it's great. Everybody who works here has known each other from other bars they have worked in, and we all get along really great. What is really good, is the fact that every person does their share, it is never left for one person to clean the bar or stock beer etc... I am very proud of these people, and graveyard shift take turns emptying and cleaning the beer coolers and ice bins behind the bar every week as it should be!

Every Sunday we serve free hotdogs all day. We have a hot dog machine in the kitchen that we put out in the bar, it holds the buns on one side and the hot dogs on the other, so very easy to let people serve themselves. The boys on graveyard make sure the tongs and plates are out, and onions are cut and the hotdog machine is on, and they take care of all the accompaniments for me, which means

I don't have to go in too early and take care of this setup. What a great staff we have, I wish we could have doubled their wages, they are worth it. We do pay them for vacation, and we give them $100 gift for Christmas, they work hard for it.

37 Baby Coming

The next big happening was something wonderful! My sister and Terry are having a baby. I am so happy for them. I did not think my sis would ever have kids. She is thirty seven years old. I think she thought the same. This is fantastic! Wish Dad was here. Sue's pregnancy is going well, I don't think she is having too many sick days or other problems, and at 37 this is really a good thing. My sister is very attractive and even more so now. Guess it's true, being pregnant can make a woman look very radiant and healthy.

Pretty soon eight months have gone by, and the birth of baby is getting close. About three or four days or more before Sue's due date, I remember asking her if she has felt the baby moving. She was not sure, she has already had a miscarriage over a year or so ago, and with our family history (mine mostly) we tend to worry. I told her "please go and let the doctor check you out just to be on the safe side."

38　Very Devastating News

The news I received via a phone call from Terry, was absolutely devastating. He was at a local hospital with Sue, who had been given tests including an ultrasound. The baby was dead!

This can't be. Our family went through this over twenty years earlier with me. Every family who has tragedy of some kind, I'm sure asks "Why Lord?" We never will know why, there has to be a reason. The worst part of this is Sue has to carry this dead baby until the doctor says it is ready to be taken away. I have never, ever heard of any decision like this in my life, or understood why. Is there an answer? If anybody ever finds out please let me know. My poor sister had to walk around with a dead little girl, I cannot remember if it was a week or longer, and actually don't want to. It takes a very strong woman to deal with what both Sue and I had, but life goes on and we both finish up with beautiful children that we can be very proud of.

Strange that I am writing this section on the 14th of December, 2012, and have just learned from the t. v that 20 children and seven teachers were killed in a small town in Connecticut by a twenty year old man with an automatic weapon who had snapped. These children were babies. I am so sad about this happening, and it is a great tragedy that could possibly have been avoided. Seems weird that I reached these pages about the time that this horrific act took place. A young disturbed man shooting his Mother and twenty-seven more people, including children between the ages of five and ten just days before Christmas. These parents have to be very strong. Not an easy thing to deal with. God bless all of them.

I know I wander occasionally, hope you can keep up with me. Now back to 1985. We are all dealing with our loss here. The bar is still doing very well in all aspects. I decided to try making a good Indian curry, and I put an ad in one of our local papers. I was amazed at the response, mostly Brits who missed their curry restaurants in England, and Vegas does not have one. A good Indian restaurant could make a fortune in this town. Next, fish and chips. I gave my cook a good batter recipe. No milk, egg whites, oil and warm water and a little salt and pepper. Guess what? The best fried cod and chips for miles around.

One lunch time I happened to come out of my little office, when two people were at a table eating our fish and chips. I went over, introduced myself and asked them if they were happy with their meal. They told me they were from Canada and staying on the Strip. They drove their rental car into a gas station near the hotel they were staying and happened to ask the attendant (we had those in '85) if he knew a good place to eat that was reasonable with good food. He recommended our bar, which was about a five or ten minute drive, and here they are. They were two of many visitors to town that returned to our Mill.

One couple in particular John and Christine, deceased long ago, but never forgotten, were an exceptional couple who found their way from the Strip to our place. It so happened the night they came in the door we were having a little monthly get together with a band. The band happened to be on a break and George was working behind the bar. I had been home and cooked a dinner for Mum, and then came back for a couple of hours to try and relax after my ten hour day, which sometimes turned into a twelve or fourteen one. Well, as these two elderly people came in the front door, George shouted "GET OUT, STAY OUT AND DON'T COME BACK". One of his favourite things to do. These two poor old tourists looked around behind them and then at George looking very worried, when shouted out again, "COME IN, JUST A JOKE, the bar buys your first drink". Well in they came and we made them feel at home. They had just left Florida and were moving to Vegas. and were very loyal customers until they passed away years later. Christine first in an Assisted Living Centre, and then John at the age of 92. A unique old couple, they were invited to all of our private and bar parties. They managed as George and I did, to make a lot of friends and drinking buddies. The saying George yelled at them is still heard from time to time in local bars. It caught on as a great intro to a new bar customer, from bartenders who were working and would pick a certain person or couple to yell at. Now we just say "AND STAY OUT!"

39 Last Move and Worth It

The new property George and I bought was wonderful, especially for having parties and dinners. We purchased a mobile home that actually looked like a cottage inside. I loved it. Living room dropped down inside the front door, fireplace, wonderful big long kitchen with a dining area at one end with windows that went nearly to the floor, another dining room off of the kitchen, two bedrooms, two bathrooms, small laundry room and the most beautiful feature of all was our garden. The lawn was about 2000 sq. ft. with raised planters at each end, a very large tree at one end of the lawn that gave some shade to the covered patio which was about 50 ft. long, and a lovely black pool that actually looked like a natural swimming hole in the mountains. When I say black, I mean dark grey and black concrete. There were large black volcanic lava rocks placed all along the back side, with a large Canary Island palm tree set into a small curve halfway up the pool. It was 50 ft. long and kept the water warm much longer that a standard white bottomed pool.

This was a party garden for sure. The patio had a fire pit on one end, George and I put in a bar with stools (from a local hotel, which were going to be dumped in the trash) the bar was ours, and a fridge. Mum bought us a gas barbecue that we had connected to our house line. We purchased folding chairs and a banquet table from a rental company that was going out of business, and good old Targey (Target) was where we managed to find smaller folding tables. It seemed when we had a party we never had less than twenty or so people. We had some wonderful times, great people, great food and lots of super holiday get-togethers.

Time is flying by. We have now been in the bar for over four years and unfortunately we have a rude awakening coming. George and I relied on two friends who supposedly knew what they were doing as far as selling real estate, commercial and otherwise, also educated in all the paperwork and all that went along with purchasing a property. (Also since deceased). I keep forgetting that most of my friends are the same age or older than me, these two died a long time ago, very young, both with cancer. Seems to be more prolific than ever now days. George and I were bartenders, we did not know the first thing about business. We just knew and learned more, on how to run and work a local bar. Suddenly a person who was a partner of the previous owner, who we thought had been paid on a promissory note that George and I signed, (which our professional friends told us was o.k), decided to sue us for the money we had already paid him. It was a total screw-up and my husband and I were the victims, after working 16 to 17hours a day for five years, we were dealt a blow. How this happened I will never know.

The next thing would be the coin company that had their machines in our bar, screwing us. They were accused of putting a chip into a machine that would prevent a royal flush (highest payout on poker) from being paid with five coins in, which is the maximum amount of coins that could be played on these machines. They allegedly did it all over town, and also allegedly, lots of places went bust on account of them as gaming removed all the machines from the locations they had them in. They took off to who knows where? and never spent time in jail from what we were told, not many could get away with this one!!!! But they bought our bar before they were accused and all this happened, we could not pay the jerk who had already been paid, so they stepped in and bought it. Who were we to know what was coming, we were given jobs, that was a life saver!

This happened after we were sued and lost and had to pay $47,000 that we didn't have to a low life. This person was so low, that he even went into our bar on the graveyard shift one night and offered our bartender $50 to get our bank account number from the office, lucky for us was Ray a very good friend and bartender and threw his ass out.(he died 2012). Miss him, he was only in his late 60's and a super friend. Our fabulous lawyer did not help. He was even arrested for smoking and possession of Marijuana, remember seeing it on T.V. certainly was not a help to us, so we finished up eventually losing the bar through a slip of a pen! At least our shareholders got their original stake back, not so for us. We had to get a lawyer to help us get our cars back that the scumbag who sued us had tried to have repossessed. George and I did not even have the pink slips, they were held by the bank. Not really sure how all this happened, but we had paid most of the debts back and it was finally over?

The 'Now finally it was over' suddenly turned into another nightmare. I had found a lump in my right breast a couple of months back and it seemed to be getting bigger. After having a hysterectomy that was pre-cancer and keeping it to myself five years earlier, I was needless to say, a little concerned.

40   Tumbling Down

I was, at the moment, working as the manager of the bar, under the new owner. I did not need anything bad right now, George and I already have had it bad, please don't let this be another disaster. I had been told by a doctor at the Air Force base hospital, that I have a cyst, not to worry. Well I am worried. After about six months I really am able to feel this lump through my clothing. I make an appointment and another doctor is present. After he examines me, he calls radiology and tells them he needs a mammogram ASAP. After he is very adamant about getting the procedure done now, I am there in about thirty minutes. The radiologist and the doctor came to talk to me after the exam. the doctor says, "Samantha I would like you to come in to the hospital for a biopsy." I remember it was a Thursday and the doctor said tomorrow would be good. Friday was my Mother's birthday, and I told the doctor it would have to be Monday, so that is what it would be. Funny, I was not really nervous about this upcoming procedure. I guess after all the months of exams and x-rays it seemed to be routine, not so I was going to find out.

George took me to the base hospital on Monday morning and I checked in. They scheduled me for the biopsy on Tuesday so Monday would be tests and after that eating I hoped, as the next day I may have to face something upsetting, which would kill my appetite no doubt. I am really trying to think positive and good, but not that easy to do, as long as other people don't see me looking worried, that will be the good thing.

Tuesday is here and off I go to surgery. What a wonderful feeling having anesthetic is, not a care in the world, until one starts waking up! Pain is the first thing to get my attention. I have a large dressing on my right breast on the side near my armpit. The whole day seems to be a bit of a blur. I do not remember a doctor, a nurse, or a visitor.

Wednesday morning is here and a different scenario is unfolding. George is here early in the morning and a nurse comes in to tell me the doctor wants to talk to me in his office. I can go in my dressing gown (robe)which is convenient, the doctor's office is just down the hall from my room.

We walk there and get into his office before him. He shows up about 10 minutes later and shakes George's hand. He then turns to me. "Samantha, I am very sorry to tell you that you have cancer." I remember going very cold and reaching for George's hand. I squeezed it so hard it's a wonder I did not break his fingers. It seemed like an eternity before I could speak, and then I said "So what are we going to do about it?" My doctor was from Asia, the nicest man. He said softly, "Samantha, I would strongly advise you to have your right breast removed, and at the same time we will remove lymph nodes and make sure it has not spread. If you would like to go home for a few hours today, I will give you a pass to get on and off of the base, and you can come back later this afternoon." Nicest thing being on a first name basis with my doctor.

He wanted me to make sure that I knew my decision would be the right one, and if I went home to be with George and Mum I could do it much better. We left the base in our pick-up truck, me in my dressing gown, and have not even cried yet. That soon changed when Mum opened the front door. The tears from all three of us started flowing prolifically. My mother was very distraught, as my sister had died of cancer eighteen years earlier. I pulled myself together and told both of them, "I am not going anywhere, so let's knock this off".

I found out later from my friends and the bartender, that George had been told by the doctor that I had cancer after my biopsy the day before I knew. He evidently locked himself in my office and cried for a long time, poor man. I was a little upset about that. Why was he told before me? He did not want me to ask why, so we dropped the subject.

We drove back to the base hospital and George left. I think it was early afternoon now, and a nurse came in and told me 'D' day would be tomorrow. She then asked me if I would like to scream or throw things. "Thank you, I think I have accepted this already." I said. It was nice of her to make me feel a bit better by asking that. Time seemed to stand still, but I knew it hadn't when my sis showed up. She left work when she found out and came straight to the base, as soon as we saw each other it was lots of crying.

We overcame that and went outside to a little patio where there was a table and chairs for visitors. We both lit a cigarette, I was not supposed to but what could be worse at this stage of the game? We could not sit there too long as this was August and the heat could get to one pretty fast, 100 degrees or more

Sue had bought me a new robe, a short one which I would put on before she left, felt good! Now I have to get my head together and get ready to deal with tomorrow, very traumatic. I seem to remember being given medication to help with relaxation and sleep, and it worked. I do remember it was a Thursday and I guess that would be hard to forget, and waking up in pain that meant it was over. What are these two plastic egg shaped things hanging from my chest? I soon found out, they are drainage receptacles. 'DUH'! These monstrosities have to be emptied every three or four hours from what I remember.

George and Mum were there the next day, and I asked Mum to call my son and let him know what was going on, just in case the big 'C' got the better of me, although I am convinced deep down that I won't let it.

A couple of days later Mum and George came to visit and I could tell that there was something bothering George. Mum tells me she could not get a hold of Leslie and so she called his Father, who told her that Les was out of the country playing at a concert in Germany I believe. Well, calling his Father evidently upset George, which was absolutely ridiculous, and he came to the hospital and took his animosity or whatever it was out on me. This was very cruel, and very unnecessary, taking into consideration what I am dealing with. I had not seen my ex in over 25 years. I managed to get out of the bed, Mum walked me down the corridor sobbing. As we passed the nurses station, one of them hurried over to me and asked what the problem was. I explained it was personal, and she told me that I certainly did not need this right now and I needed to get back to bed. I pulled myself together and went back to my room. I never spoke to George and he soon took Mum and left. I decided that I would not get upset like that again, I have to heal my body, and I don't need my mind in a tizzy dealing with stupid things.

I am being looked after by nurses, and two young male interns who I would assume are learning about surgical procedures. On about the fifth day I remember one of the boys came in and asked me if I would like a cup of tea, which I said I would. Before he turned to leave I said I had a joke to show him. I picked up my pad and pen on the nightstand and drew him a picture.

Making Lite Of It

"Do you know what this is?" I asked him. "No" he said. "It's two men walking a breast" I told him. When he stopped laughing he went to the door and turned around and said "Sam, you are bad" to which I replied, "Does this mean we are not bosom buddies anymore"? He was still laughing when he came back with my tea. I explained to him that I had to make light of this traumatic thing that has happened in my life. He understood and said I was very brave. I am not very brave, just dealing with what I have been dealt with.

It is now 12 days I have been here, and the doctor says it is time to remove the drainage bulbs. "OH My God", the pain taking out the first one was excruciating. From what I gather, the flesh around the tube attached to the bulb, had grown over it. I know I came about two feet off of the bed when the doctor pulled it out. The woman in the next bed shouted at him and was not very polite. He was very sorry he had no idea that this had happened. The next one would be in a couple of days and he promised me that I would be given something to help with the pain.

These tubes go quite a way into the chest cavity, they are not just poked in an inch or two. One thing I thought was, that I guess I am healing OK.

The next pulling out procedure was upon me. I was given a couple of pills, I'm guessing Valium, and within about twenty minutes after taking them, I really didn't care about any pulling out or whatever!. In came my doc, and within a short while it was over. I did develop a blood pressure problem though. I guess it plummeted to an unsafe low. The nurses were coming in about every ten minutes I think for quite a while it seemed. I did feel very out of my body if that sounds right, very strange experience.

After a long time or so it seemed, I began to feel much better. What a sensation that was, very weird feeling. I do know that my blood pressure most of my life was always low, but this time it was extra low 80 over 58 I was told, guess I could have been on the way out! Not so now-days, I have to take medication to keep it down, guess old age can change lots of things.

Fifteen days and I am now going home. Thank you lord. I was home for a few hours and had a couple of friends visit. More tears. Then I began to get a headache that turned into a very bad migraine. After a few hours of throwing up, George took me back to the hospital. I was very dehydrated and in pain. I was put back in and given intravenous fluid, just overnight did the trick. I do remember the doctor talking to me before I was discharged, about migraines which I had suffered from for years. He asked me if I drank coke, and I said yes. He suggested that I should cut it down or give it up altogether, as there was an ingredient in the soda that did not always agree with some people who suffered from these headaches.

I was released and sent home again, but this time more worn out. I did make a decision. I will not drink cola again. Even rum and coke was out, so socially I will have to find another cocktail. Yeah... plenty to choose from!

41   We Will Overcome

I have been home for about three weeks now, things are OK and I am healing nicely, although looking at myself is not easy. Getting out of the shower and seeing my reflection is gross, so I start to wear George's tee shirts in bed. I have not worn clothes in bed for years, but I feel so ugly. George tells me not to worry about it, but it is very hard for a woman to look at her body that was pretty nice at fifty, to this hacked, scarred sunken chest. What a shame that the time and the place where I had my breast removed, did not automatically put implants in, this would be something I will have to decide later down the road.

George and I are now both without a job! The bar is up for sale again and the owners of the coin company have disappeared, after a lot of intrigue. This is a very hard time for George and myself A mortgage and keeping our heads above water, also having Mum to worry about. Our adopted son was no help either. After collecting a rather large sum of money for a traffic accident he was involved in, he moved out. We tried very hard to give him everything he wanted, guess it wasn't enough

I have another problem about to descend on us. While Mum and I are in the car driving home one afternoon, a driver in a very large U-Haul truck, made an illegal turn from the centre lane into the right lane to drive into a gas station, and it just so happened that I was in the right lane driving past the opening, and so he drove into my large station wagon and the front of it got caught up under the side of his truck. This huge car Mum and I were in was dragged into the gas station parking lot. The police were called and he was given a ticket for a dangerous illegal turn. I still had sutures in my chest, and I pushed on the brake so hard that my right leg started hurting. This was a nine passenger wagon I am driving, a big monster. I knew I was not in the wrong, and after he got the ticket I got in touch with a lawyer. I had to go to a doctor and have treatment on my hip and knee. This went on for weeks, and to finish this episode, months later it went to arbitration and I was awarded $12,000.00. Seems I pick the wrong lawyers. Have no idea why or how he got away with that, but after paying the lawyer and doctor's bills I came out with nothing, so our next move George and I decided was to file bankruptcy. Not something we really wanted to do but it gave us some breathing room. We did not file a Chapter Seven. That would have eliminated every bill we had, instead we filed an eleven which meant people would be paid over a period of time. Life can really dish it out sometimes. Like my Dad always said "God give me strength".

Plodding on, we may have a chance of a job, both of us working in the same place. A woman who worked for us for a few months in our bar before all the drama, was trying to get a coin company to back her in securing a bar. This was one of the better coin companies in Vegas, and if they did, it would mean that their machines would be put in the place.

It worked, her and her husband were able to buy a large bar and she hired three of us including Ray, our friend that worked for George and I. We were all looking forward to being back at work. There were going to be a few big changes to this place, which would take all of us working hard to achieve. The building had been a bar before, but with not much success. The coin company had agreed to do improvements to the bar itself, making it very long and very attractive with brass and copper finishing's, then putting in their slot machines.

There were two floors which was a little unusual for a bar. The top floor consisted of an office and a large open area with tables and chairs, and a railing all the way around that overlooked the bar downstairs, a bit dodgy if one was really pissed (drunk in England). The restaurant side of the place downstairs was very spacious, and during the remodelling the old floor which was concrete, before it was covered with flooring, was going to be cut in certain places to rebuild the shape of the bar. There were tables and chairs that finished up covered in concrete dust as all the cutting was done inside, Hell of a mess!! These all had to be cleaned, a lot of work for George and I and even Mum and the rest of us to do. Mum wanted to come and help get the place ready to open and that was hard at her age. She was the age I am at now, and boy do I know how she felt! There was very little heat in this building, and so we worked with our coats on most of the time. Very, very hard work cleaning about a hundred or so tables and chairs covered in concrete dust.

I had just had reconstruction on my breast about two months before that, unfortunately didn't work, and it did not help that the place had no heat. It was hard going for a month or so cleaning this big bar, especially when one is right handed with half a chest, well that's what it felt like! We all pulled together, me, George and Ray thinking this would be our employment for a few years to come. WRONG!

I won't mention names but she knows who she is, the manager/owner that sat at the bar on opening night with a clipboard and a dress with a slit up one thigh. During the day her husband and I had cleaned toilets, put chairs and tables in place and lots more piddling stuff that needed doing. I had cleaned ovens, fridges, floors and furniture for over a month. I am now waitressing food, serving drinks, and helping out behind the bar. Our opening night was absolutely out of sight! All our friends and our loyal customers from 'The Mill' came to support us even though this place was a bit of a long drive for some of them. I am serving food which I hate to do but it had to be done, Madam Fu-Fu is still sitting at the bar with her legs crossed, alright for some!

A busy-busy night, going home very tired. Working five days a week starts again tomorrow. I also volunteer to pick up buns that are specially made for the burgers we are serving. They are enormous. One of these would feed three people, amazing how many we are selling. The bakery that provides us with the buns is about five minutes from my house so that's not a big deal, but the rest of the drive to work is a long way, even in those days without all the traffic it still took about thirty-five minutes.

The downstairs back room was decorated with old pictures and metal wall hangings. Ray brought in a very old treadle sewing machine that belonged to his grandmother, and George and I bought the metal décor for the walls. It was a very different looking bar and restaurant, one of a kind and rather unique. The only thing was the whole place was cold, temperature wise. I think it was heated with heat pumps, not the usual air conditioning and heating that the majority of homes and businesses had, and in February it can get very cold.

Everything was going well for a few months, then the bombshell. One lunchtime, George served a guy that used to hang around in a local bar about a mile away, and he did not have a very good reputation, anyway he told our manager that he ordered a vodka and cranberry juice and that my husband had served him vodka and grenadine, and by the way he had drank every drop. Excuse me! Who drinks a glass of grenadine (cherry flavoured syrup), thinking it may be cranberry juice? I guess some jerk trying to get a free drink!!!

Our manager, and supposedly a friend that our family had busted our balls for, even my poor old Mum who she was going to buy a bottle of Frangelico for, (glad she didn't) decided it was an excuse to fire George. How dare she! My man worked very hard for her, 110 percent. I think this may be her start to get rid of all of us, not sure why, maybe we are a threat as we are too popular with a lot of people. This woman is not liked especially with my close girlfriends. They all told me before I went to work there, don't go Sam, but I did anyway. Now I am seeing the light. Her husband is a really nice man, a bit too nice I think, he would not say boo to a goose!

After she fired George I wrote her a letter. I told her how wrong I thought she was and that I wanted her to send me a cheque for everything I had taken to that bar, especially kitchen equipment such as chafing dishes, knives, pans etc., I also told her not to expect me back to work after what she did, another cow,(that's 3 now).

Next thing, Ray called me and said he had been fired. Surprise, Surprise! Evidently one night on graveyard shift when he was working, there were customers enjoying the music on the juke box, but it was a bit too loud for 'Greta Garbo' as she was staying overnight with hubby in the office upstairs. Ray said she came out and told him to turn the music down as she and her husband were trying to sleep. "Madam you won a bar, that's not what happens in happy bars." A manager sleeping in an office is not usually an issue. This was a start of the decline I guess. Why would this bar succeed? I think one has to give in a certain amount to make customers happy. Obviously there are limits, but when one runs a bar one usually knows how far to let people go., and owners don't sleep there and moan about music on graveyard.! I received the money for the things I took to this place (she got a bargain), and now George and I have another episode in our lives to work out. What now Dr. Watson? It seems as though life or the powers that be is really sticking it to us. We work bloody hard, we are as honest as the day is long, and we keep getting the short straw! Things have to get better, and I think we are getting a little depressed with the trials we have to keep going through.

My wonderful girl friends have now gotten together to take me out to lunch and tell me exactly what they thought of this woman that we hired in our bar, and then she hired us in her bar, and the girls have learned expressions from me that came from England.

Polite ways of referring to a person without actually saying the word. For example, this woman according to a lot of our friends and using a polite English phrase was a "See you next Tuesday". I'm sure most people can work this one out. Four letter word that is very uncomplimentary to a woman. The girls were right. I should have taken note. We should have all taken notice. C'est la vie!

42 Lord Lift Us Up

It is September and I have been having trouble with this implant (number two). The surgeon who did the reconstruction tells me that it has to come to out. My tissue is not holding and the skin is breaking down.

This is another big upset for me. I checked into a local hospital, and on my second or third day after procedure I got to thinking about Dave. Not sure why, but I realised it was coming up to his 50th birthday. His was four days before mine. So I sent him a card that I got from the gift shop in the hospital. Cannot really remember what I said or how I got it mailed, I only know I sent it. When I got home from the hospital I found the phone number for the pub where Dave was working as owner, manager-lease holder?. It took a lot of telephoning to friends who still lived and worked in the Bahamas, but I finally got it. I am feeling very guilty right now, but I have not done anything wrong, just want to talk to someone that I have not seen and loved for years. It is possible to love two men at the same time? It's just a really different kind of love from one to the other. There is a love that is a very comfortable safe feeling, and the other kind is very heart wrenching and sexual. I have had, and maybe still have these two.

I have dialed the number and am waiting for a voice from the other end. What a wonderful voice he has, very distinctive and sexy, to me anyway. He cannot believe it is me, it takes him a few minutes to collect himself, and I can tell he has had a few cocktails. After not talking to each other for about eighteen years it is very surprising how easy it is to have a conversation. After talking and joking for a while I passed the phone to Mum, from the first time she met him she was always very fond of Dave. She talked and laughed for a few minutes and gave the phone back to me. I must end this call right now, I would hate to have George come home, I would never ever hurt this wonderful man I married. I said goodbye and I will be in touch.

I am not sure what made me do that, I guess I will never get that man out of my heart, and yet I rejected his proposal of marriage, maybe a wise decision on my part. I decided right then after putting the phone down, that I had to somehow save money and go to England to see my son and visit David. I am not sure where this extra money is going to come from, but if one wants something bad enough there is always a way.

Within the next couple of months, my man and I, after looking and looking, found employment. We were actually offered it from bar owners that we knew. Having a reputation for hard work and honesty has paid off for George and I now. The stress is getting reduced at last. I know Mum was very worried for both of us, now we can all relax.

A husband and wife that owned a couple of local bars in town has offered me a job in one of the older places that they owned. In fact my husband's brother works there and has worked there for a lot of years, busy little place. I believe it is frequented by workers who are in Unions.

George has been recommended for a job at a Best Western by a friend of his. He gets the job on the graveyard shift. All of a sudden our family is much more cheerful than we have been for quite a while. Having a little faith I guess, never hurts.

I start my day shift in this small little bar, and find that lunch hours are very busy with guys from the Union and Convention Centre. This bar does not have a kitchen, so I get permission to order precooked chicken wings, which I put into a very large slow cooker after I get to work at 8 a.m. They come frozen and it takes two to three hours to get them ready. They are actually very tasty and the sauce has a little bite to it, for precooked they are good and will be a great snack for these guys at lunchtime.

I also had to buy the cardboard containers to put them in.

Next thing I got going was salsa and tortilla chips from the bar supply, I used wooden bowls to put these snacks in. The wings went down a treat, and I know the chips and salsa were a big hit to. The business picked up to the extent that I needed help during the busy period, 11am until about 1pm. Most of these men, only had a 30 minute lunch break, so I had to haul ass as they say! The bar itself was a long one. George's brother helped me out, he was a really easy going guy, a couple of years younger than George and a much quieter man.

I think I worked in this little bar for about three months, when I got a phone call from the manager telling me that the owner would like to transfer me to one of their other bars. I don't believe it! They bought our old bar. I don't really have a choice if I want to keep my job I have to go, not a problem, this will be like going home for me. Many of my customers are upset that I am leaving. Chicken wings and salsa are leaving to I think! One thing I know, I am going to be seeing lots of old friends who still visit that bar. My hours are going to be cut down, but that is fine with me. I could use a break, and I know Mum will be happy that I am at home a bit more.

It's good we have our Rottweiler. Got him for George after Gussie died. He is really excellent company for mum when we are not there, and this dog is very protective and loving towards her. Our Rotty could be unpredictable when we had company, and so most of the time if we had parties we would shut him in the back bedroom. Better to be safe than sorry. He was one of the most intelligent dogs I had ever owned, and to me very loving.

I have now started work at our old bar. My first day is a very memorable one. How great to see old friends and customers from way back. I consider myself very lucky to have people that care enough to come and see me on my 'opening night' (day). It is not long before my female boss (owner) decides she would like me to work swing shift (3pm until 11pm). I think I mentioned this before, if I need the job I have to work whatever shift she wants. The only setback here is making dinner for George and Mum,(back to that again), before I leave for work every day. I guess I have to start making meals ahead that can be put in the microwave or oven, and the crockpot is going to come in really handy!

This later shift is going to be a bit of a challenge for me and family, but the money will be better as far as tips go. The later shift is busier and more people gamble on swing, making it a better shift for winners and tips for the bartender.

Everything is going great at home and work. I am enjoying working back in this bar, and swing shift is very busy. I have a girl working with me who is in charge of the kitchen, her cooking is great and she has an imagination which helps with our Monday Night Football games. She puts on a small buffet that only costs the bar about fifty dollars, but my ring is anywhere between five and seven hundred. I think she is a real asset, but I just work there so who am I to say. A couple of months later, she is gone and we have hot dogs from a crockpot. I don't need to say how the business went down in a hurry. I guess the buffet was too expensive!!!!

43   Fired And Hired

What day? What month? What year? I don't know! I was fired. I do remember I had tried to get a little get-together on my shift for a basketball game. Not any basketball game, a championship game. I had customers who wanted to bring snacks and appetisers to the bar, as UNLV (University of Las Vegas) was playing in the final four tournament and we were in THE FINAL. We were all into our University's basketball programme. This was going to be a championship game for the college, and the whole town was very excited. Bars were laying on big spreads and having parties. I was out buying food that I was going to cook and donate, and when I got home George told me that the manager had called and told him I had been fired. I had never been fired from a job in my whole life. I was devastated. George was such a comfort as I was crying and making a fool of myself. He said "Why don't we go to the "bar and have a drink? I was not sure if I had the courage to do that, but between Mum telling me she would be OK for a couple of hours and George wanting me to be tough and face my foe, off we went.

A bunch of my friends were there and upset to say the least. I was trying to make business much better, not taking over or running it, but I am thinking someone that I worked with mentioned to the owner before I could ask her if it was o.k., that people were going to bring in snacks for the Final Four game, and she decided that I was trying to run her business. If she would only have stopped and thought about how many people were going to show up for this local college feat it would have been a great night, and we did not have a kitchen that was open anymore. Anyway, as we sat there George and I, she came in and told the bartender to buy us a drink. I'm afraid my pride came through or got the better of me, whatever! I pushed the drink to one side and ordered another one for both of us. How can a person fire you, and buy you a drink a couple of hours later and not even speak to you? This is something that boggles my mind.

I think I believe in karma, and what happened within the next few months was very creepy and very sad. Eventually the bar was sold to a partner of sorts I believe, and God bless him he gave me a job three day shifts a week. I am back amongst who and what I know.

This is a young man who suddenly owns this place. He is very shrewd and very aware of where he is going. I can see that nobody is going to pull the wool over his eyes. Not always easy to work for, but if one takes it with a grain of salt it is fine.

The word comes through, my ex-boss is very sick. I think I know what she is suffering from, and being a survivor right now myself, I decide to pay her a visit at her house. I have a homemade blanket that is crocheted, and a book that I think she would enjoy reading. I do not have any animosity toward this woman, but I do feel what she is going through. Her eldest daughter answers the door and I go in. She is sitting at the kitchen table and I can tell she is happy to see me. She takes me outside to show me her back garden that she has fixed up with the help of a landscaper and her kids. It is very relaxing, lots of plants and greenery and running water in a little rock pool-scape. We never talk about the bar or my firing, only up-to-date things like house fixtures, garden and grandkids. Somehow I feel ok when I leave, even thinking that I feel this woman does not have long to go.

It is December '96, and I realise I have been in this bar that I call home for about fourteen years, except for a year and a half that I was gone elsewhere. Christmas is here and it is busy at work and at home. I am having Sue and her kids, and Jen and her babies (Patrick's e-x wife) along with her Mum and Dad, we have a nice gathering. I wish it could be a much happier get together. Husbands are not present, Dad's is gone, but I guess that's how life has to be. I would love my son to be here, it doesn't happen that often.

Christmas was very nice, and over in an instant. I cannot believe my Sister's kids are in their teens, beautiful, well behaved children, thanks to Sue.

In January I decided to pay another visit to my ex-boss. I heard through the grapevine she is not too good. I take Mum with me as we are going grocery shopping after we stop and see Penney. Her youngest daughter answers the door. What faces me when I went in was a great shock. I immediately turned around to make sure that Mum was still in the car, too late she was at the front door. I did not want her to see this awful scene. Penney was in a bed in the living room, laying in a foetal position and not weighing more than about eighty pounds I guessed. Mum took a few steps straight into the room and instantly back to the front door and sat on a bench that was close by. Her tears started flowing, I knew this would upset her, it upset me, but this brought back bad memories for her, remembering when her twenty-four year old daughter died this way. I went back to the bed and bent down and kissed Penney on the cheek. I'm not sure how I held my tears back. Guess I didn't want her to see that. She asked me to stay for a while and I had to lie and say I will be back later. I helped her daughter Sharon turn her in the bed, and told her to please call me and keep me updated. She told me her Mother really regretted firing me. "Water under the bridge", I said. "That is not important anymore". Mum and I drove away, both of us in shock at what we had witnessed. It was only three or four months ago that I had sat with Penney in her kitchen, taken her books and a blanket, and walked around her newly landscaped garden. What an awful disease cancer can be. Some of us get very lucky. I am one! Three or four hours after we left, Penney passed away. January 12, 1997.

There were many people at Penney's funeral and I remember that it was a very cold day. In fact I had a chance to wear a beautiful fur coat that George had bought me. Funerals are not something any of us really want to go to, and when a very sad song about missing ones mother is played and the whole chapel is in tears, it makes it ten times worse.

Most of the mourners went back to the bar, (used to be her bar and our bar). A few shots and cocktails take away the funeral blues, time to celebrate life!

I am guessing that the bars that this lady owned will be left to her children and maybe they will sell them. Owning and running bars is not easy, and I think her girls already have other professions. I am glad my Mother decided not to come to the funeral. She did not need to be upset any more.

This day is nearly over as far as funeral and cocktails go. George and I are going home to Mum, and I will cook us a nice dinner. I am happy I do not have to work tomorrow, that really takes the edge off of everything.

It is now about three months into 1997. George is still doing concrete work with a friend, then working the graveyard shift at the hotel.

44   Please Be Okay Hubby

One day I noticed when he came home about lunchtime from his outside work, his right hand kept shaking. When I asked him what was wrong with his arm or hand, he said he thought it was continually lifting concrete blocks. This went on for a couple of weeks or so and I thought it was time to do something about it. Without telling him, I got in touch with a friend of ours who worked for a neurologist. When I explained to her why I was calling, she made an appointment for him to see the doctor.

When George found out that I made him a doctor visit, he got really peed off with me. Aron calmed him down when we arrived a week later, and I was allowed to sit with him during the examination. This doctor had a great bedside manner which put George at ease. The next thing the doc said would make the ease disappear in a hurry. He wanted George to have an MRI on his brain. The MRI machine is a very large confining tube, and if a person is claustrophobic as George was, this procedure is going to be a terrifying experience for him. Aron assures him that the doctor will give him something to relax him ahead of the time. RIGHT! I am the one who has to give him these relaxing pills, obviously good old Valium, that's the one I dealt with. O.K. give him one a couple of hours before we leave the house and another when we get there.

Needless to say this man is a jelly roll, and the perfect wife is above and beyond the call of duty right now. Isn't that what wives are for?

The clinic we got to actually let me in the room with George during the MRI. I thought this was unheard of, obviously not. I got him out of there, in to the car, and home. Don't ask me how! This is a man weighing one hundred and ninety pounds, I am a tough little shit, I think I know that. I feel that this day I went out with an Orangutan, and came back with a golden lab retriever puppy!

To get the results from the MRI we have to go back to the doctor. Aron made us a quick return date about three days later. I remember George had to have a test at the doc's office whereby he put pads attached to wires on George's head. I think this machine transmitted brain functions of some kind, anyway after all the tests we have the results. My husband has Parkinson's, a disease caused by a certain chemical lacking in the brain which brings on tremors. The doctor told us all about it, and what to expect in the future. He seems to think that George has had this for a while, but he also thinks we have caught it in the early stages. This debilitating disorder caused by the lack of dopamine, affects the central nervous system.

We head to one of our favourite local bars, two heavy rum and cokes are in order for George, plus a beer, plus a martini. He always started off with three different drinks. That was his signature tune. I am used to it, but there are people who don't know him cannot believe this when they first see it. It is usually only the initial round, he settles down after that. Bloody good job! I have one martini, have a lot to deal with.

Today he has a very good excuse. We are not talking about it right now. I am sure after we get home it is going to hit him, and the booze too!

My next wifely task is to get the prescriptions filled, which I will do at the Air Force Base. Luckily we are both covered for health and prescriptions as George did over twenty years of service. Thanks babe, it saved us when I had all my problems.

45 England Relieved Me

I did not mention that I had visited England in early February, but it definitely kept me going through this rough patch now. I had a wonderful time with Les and also visiting Dave. I am not going to talk about that right now, I do know I did not want to leave and Dave did not want me to either, I would never leave George and mum, but that was sixteen years ago and a lot has happened since then.

Back to hubby's medications. Not very exciting for him, but I made sure that he would remember everything he had to take, by putting his pills in a box that held seven days-worth at a time. He also had high blood pressure, pills for that too, and little did we know, pretty soon his pill intake would be tripled.

A couple of months later on a routine checkup at the base hospital, the doctor discovered that George had suffered a heart attack. He thought maybe it happened in his sleep as he had no recollection of any symptoms. Now he has more medications and he has to make an appointment with a cardiologist. Oh happy day! I got him in to see a specialist within two weeks, which was unheard of. I think having my friend Aron (now deceased) working in the medical field helped tremendously. She knew doctors who knew doctors etc., etc.

I do know one thing, 'embrace every moment of life'. I am not one for praying, but I did pray quite a bit, "Please don't let George finish up in a wheelchair, not being able to walk and having to be fed". Someone heard me, and although I did not want to lose him he would not want to exist that way, and I would not want him to.

This story I am writing is not going to get any happier at the moment. Is this a soap opera or what!!!! The next thing I have to live through is losing my Mother. I have been thinking about the bar lately and the customers we had, including well-known figures. I told you what a great bar we had, seems like a hundred years ago. OK, how I miss my garden and pool, they were my solace, have not got to that episode yet, much further on. OK, back to where I was before my mind wandered again. I believe I was talking about the bar, and the fun, and people we met during our seven or more years. George and I had a little click that we socialised with, drank together, played golf together and went on trips out of town to play golf and drink and have a bloody great time together.

One of our favourite places was in Arizona. We stayed at a place that was supposedly owned by the mob years ago. It was a huge mansion turned into a hotel, with casitas at the rear of the property, tons of fruit trees, grapefruit, lemons and limes and also their own nine-hole golf course. One of the reasons we all loved the place, free golf!

46 Fun In Arizona

I remember one particular visit, when ten of us stayed for three days and the hotel gave us a really good deal. The first night after we arrived, a barbecue was laid out for us outside of the small pool bar. Super steaks, lots of cocktails, a great night! The next morning we all played golf. The girls played together and so did the guys. I don't think any of us were that good at it. Well maybe a couple of us, but it was fun. After golf it was cocktails at the pool bar, very small little place, and the bartender (we loved him) was about eighty years old. I remember one occasion when about four of us on one side of the bar ordered Bloody Mary's. It took him about fifteen minutes to get to us as he was serving two people on the other side, and he was not a fast mover, there were only about eight people in the place and that was including us.

We were easy people to deal with, and when we saw how much vodka he was putting into the chimney glasses he had ready, it was even easier to wait a bit longer. Well he got to the third glass and was pouring the vodka in to it with a shaky hand, when a person on the other side of the bar called him. Continuing to pour, he turns around to see what the guy needs, and is still pouring, the liquor coming out all over the place. I think one of us yelled, not sure who, to tell him what he was doing. Poor old man got really shook up, so we made sure we calmed him down and took care of him really well Vegas style! Our bar bill, then ten of us, was more than our rooms and food together. One thing though, that was one of the best Bloody Mary's any of us ever had. It was actually Absolut vodka with a splash of tomato juice. That drink was nearly our quota for cocktail hour, and dinner. Wow! Great to be young (well younger) and fearless!

Those fast and furious years were outstanding, and I think our crowning glory moment was an episode in this hotel that none of us will ever forget.

On one of our visits for a fun golf weekend, we were all supplied with a pair of glasses attached to a fake nose and moustache by a couple of friends that used to join us, from Utah, I believe. They were always part of our group. The disguises were a take-off of Groucho Marx, so one can imagine ten of us filing into the dining room on a Saturday evening with these things on our faces. I was actually amazed that we were allowed in. Guess in those days the hotel was more accommodating to crazy crowds from Vegas who spent lots of money.

Entering the dining room, a couple of the men went to the bar that was at the back behind all the tables and separated by large indoor palm trees, and pretty soon there were four or five of our men at the bar. The girls were left to be seated at tables and given menus, etc. All this time still looking like Groucho, we were aware that most of the other guests and diners looked as though they had stepped out of a Lawrence Welk Show! Lots of flowing organza dresses, and the average age had to be seventy-five or there about. Obviously we were all the talk of the dining room, and I would say, the hotel. We gave the faces a break through dinner, but after the meal was over and we were all well into the cocktails, Groucho appeared again on all of us.

The band was very good, and the music changed, maybe to accommodate our crazy crowd. What was really unbelievable was most of these older people that looked as though they were from the forties, finished up wearing our fake Groucho Marx faces. What a riot! They all loved it, and I think most of them had not had fun like that in years.

Some of us girls started dancing with the old men, and our guys did the same with the ladies. What an unforgettable night, fabulous!

Sunday morning, hangovers, headaches, and our own faces that were not too happy looking. Checkout time is about an hour away, that will give those of us who would like a Bloody Mary time to have one, and if our old friend is working behind the bar, then one is about all we will get or need!

This trip was one of the most fun-filled few days, I will never forget it. One final thing that I will also always remember was my wonderful, easy going, very giving husband, buying a round of drinks for all the people in the small bar at the airport in Phoenix on our way home. Even the bartender was not sure if it was a joke, our credit card took a bashing. Oh Well! It was only money and it will be paid back eventually. Love him for who and what he is.

I am now back to the present moment before more memories got a hold of me. My late forties and early fifties were something unique.

The years flew by. Mum was getting much harder to look after, her mind was going in a hurry. I have a very close girlfriend who would come and sit with Mum so that George and I could go out for a couple of hours. My Mother loved this woman, which really made it easier for us. Maggie would make her tea and watch TV shows that Mum liked, not easy to look after a person with really bad dementia, but this friend of mine was like Florence Nightingale, still is.

This was also the time when George's Parkinson's was taking a hold. The shaking was much more noticeable. It was a good thing that we had started his medication not long after the onset of this awful disease. It did suppress the shaking quite a bit.

47 Millennium

We were approaching the year 2000, 'The Millennium', amazing! I am still doing my shifts at our bar. I call it 'Our Bar' because to me it will always be **our bar**. George is still holding it together at the Best Western. I think he likes working there and his co-workers that I met are all very friendly, hard working people.

New Years' Eve! In Vegas, New Years is a wild party place at local bars and on the Strip. Hubby and I were off for this very special date in history, but we are not planning to do anything except stay at home with Mum and toast the Millennium with her.

The firework display from the hotels at midnight was very disappointing I thought, considering it was such a special date on the calendar. I would have thought it would have been spectacular, and not being prejudice, but London put on a show to beat all shows. Les sent me a video, it was really unbelievable! Fireworks from all sides of the river Thames, fireworks from the giant Ferris wheel (The Eye) and it must have gone on for at least forty-five minutes. Mum, George, and myself had a glass or two of champers while we watched the festivities on TV from all around the world, some fabulous shows.

Over the next few months Mum's mind got worse and worse. Her doctor suggested she should have a scan of the brain to see if she had Alzheimer's. The results showed that she had water surrounding the brain which was giving her very bad dementia. As the year came to an end it became very hard to watch her and listen to her struggle with names and words. The poor woman became depressed when she could not remember things. I tried to tell her it did not matter, but as I get to 75 years old, I know how she felt. Another year just flew by, guess they get faster with age!!

The year 2000 is about over now, and I am planning a nice Christmas dinner with Sue and the kids, now teenagers! Cannot believe it, and Patrick's ex and his kids and in-laws. I wish I had lots of money I could help all of them. Sad to say he has not taken care of his kids. His mother would roll over in her grave if she knew how he turned out, got in with the wrong people I guess. What a sad thing, good looking talented boy, what a waste of his life. Nothing George and I can do anymore, we tried our best. I am just glad my Mother does not know what he is doing, and not doing. We do not even know where he is.

Our Christmas was wonderful. I cooked beef Wellingtons, they turned out great, lots of veggies too, cannot really remember what I did for dessert, sure it went well, there were clean plates all around.

Next year will be Dave's sixtieth birthday, I am going to try and save and get to England in September, and I will get to see my son at the same time.

We are now coming into the hot weather and there are people who like 105 degrees, even after thirty-nine years of living in Las Vegas I still did not like it. What a good thing the humidity is nearly absent most of the time, but I suppose this is one of the reasons people have flocked here for years. I believe the population at the present time is around two million.

I have managed to save my fare to England, not sure how, and I think booking a couple of months early saves quite a bit. Going home in the summer months, April through September costs more but it's worth the extra. September is a beautiful time of year in England. If one gets lucky the weather can be perfect. I will be flying into New York from Vegas on the 9ᵗʰ of September on American Airlines, changing planes and hanging around for two hours in other airports is a pain in the butt, guess I have no choice.

I am on my way. Les is picking me up at Heathrow airport and driving me down to Dave's house on the English Channel no less. A beautiful little village sitting right on the ocean. France is visible from the beach when the weather is clear. It is about twenty-five miles across to Calais. Les is dropping me off and coming back on the eleventh and staying at a hotel a couple of miles away with his wife Rebecca. They will come to the pub on the twelfth for Dave's sixtieth party.

It is wonderful to see friends that I have made over the last ten years, and staying with Dave is fun and relaxing. We may sleep in the same bed, but those days of sexual intimacy have been over ever since I started coming back, long over I'm afraid. I think too much alcohol might have finished Dave sex life. We have known each other now for nearly forty years, well thirty-nine, and I think we will be soul mates forever, the sex is not important anymore, and I have a husband who I really care about. This may sound awful, but George will never know or be hurt by my visits over here. Dave is not a very romantic or sexual person, and does not give a lot of signs that he might love me, never tells me, in fact I think he only ever said it twice in all these years and both times I think he had been drinking. George on the other hand tells me all the time and I know he really means it. He is a very loving sexy man. I really believe a woman or man can love two people at the same time, (repeating myself again, can't help it, getting old!) but it is a different sort of love. One very powerful and painful, and the other very easy and calming. Why do most women go for the painful one? I was so lucky I was with a man that really loved me for nearly thirty years. There is one thing that boggles my mind about sex, I see it on TV all the time. "If you have an erection lasting four hours or more, see a doctor". HELLO! Whoever has that? Not any man I ever knew. Must be a bloody powerful pill!!!

189

The day before the party a girlfriend comes to pick me up at Dave's and takes me into town for lunch. I met her in the pub a few years earlier. She works for Dave managing the place and seems to be doing a good job. We had a nice lunch in a local pub in town, a couple of drinks and nice conversation before heading back to the house.

As we were pulling up near the front door, a couple, also friends I had met over the years, flagged us down, so we pulled over and they told me that the Pentagon was being attacked. "Sure" I said. Then Jason, the guy said "Sam, go in the house it's on the TV." He was very serious looking, so I jumped out of the car and ran in the front door. Dave was watching the TV and what I was seeing was very hard to take in, it was like a movie, the Twin Towers coming down, the Pentagon on fire, and reports that a plane had been hijacked and was still in the air. This was 9/11 2001, my God! What is happening? My girlfriend left, and Dave and I sat watching these horrifying events take place. We finally saw the taped news pictures (don't forget England is eight hours ahead of the U.S.A), and saw the planes fly into the twin towers, along with the plenty of other awful pictures. The rest of our day was very subdued, definitely a night for drinking with friends, and Les and Becca who drove to the pub and joined us.

The party organised for the next day, (Dave'sbirthday) was supposed to be a surprise, So while he was playing golf, a bunch of us were going to get the pub decked out and take care of the food. Not sure if he knows about this shindig, but if he does he is doing a good job of pretending he doesn't.

Les and Rebecca came down from the hotel and Joyce the manager had everything under control. We decorated with banners and balloons, and Joyce had the kids in the kitchen working on the buffet food. I think it took us about three hours to finish, and one lucky thing the pub was not open to the public in the afternoon. In 2001 the hours of the pubs were still a little restricted. It would open at six pm, but I think Joyce has made arrangements to close to the public about eight, and put a sign on the door reading "Private Party".

I went back into the house about five pm and got myself into the shower. Les and Becca have gone back to the hotel to get ready. Dave comes home a little while later and I find out he is aware of the goings on, not to worry it will be great!

48   9/11, Missed New York By Two Days

The images on TV are still horrendous and to think I flew into New York two days before the terrorists struck. I had a few weeping moments since yesterday, especially when I saw the Royal family in St. Paul's Cathedral singing the American National Anthem. It always gets me, but now much worse I have a special birthday party to go to, I need to shape up. It is time to get dressed and ready for this party. I bought a dress to wear for tonight, bright pink, and I had big drop earrings in gold and thong sandals. The dress is long and straight and can be worn slightly off the shoulder which is what I did. I have a nice tan and at sixty-three I think I am looking pretty good. My breast reconstruction (another episode) lets me wear this dress without a bra, HEAVEN!

Dave has a couple of friends that have driven down from the West coast, and they are going to spend the night. Pauline and her boyfriend Ron are good fun, she worked in the pub for Dave a few years back, what a great thing to still be friends. That is how life should be for everyone, shame it does not happen.

Dave and I made it into the pub about eight thirty, it was packed with his friends and mine. People who had known him for twenty-five years, all waiting to party hardy. I noticed when we walked in after the yelling and the cheering died down and Dave acknowledged people, there was a woman sitting at the bar that I knew deep down really fancied him. I had met her on a previous trip, nice person very friendly, and I remembered her grabbing him in front of me and trying to put a lip lock on him, a little embarrassing for him and me, Could have been the booze I guess. This night it was a peck on the cheek. I suppose Dave never pursued her advances, but he still considered her a friend, that is one nice thing about the man. He was a ladies man no doubt about it! I don't know for sure because I only got to visit once a year maybe, and his life was nothing to do with me, but she tried hard I will give her that. Great party! It definitely took away the 9/11 events even if just for a few hours.

49   Dave's 60th

At seven am, yes seven am, Dave, two friends Pauline and Ron and I, went out onto the beach and released all of the party balloons. It looked beautiful. I finally gave in and went to bed. Dave was left there on his own. I am guessing it had to be about eight-thirty in the morning, it was all a blur, and time for the cleaners to come in to the pub I was thinking when I was awakened by the phone ringing next to the bed. It was another friend inviting the two of us to go for breakfast. Are you joking? That's what I thought before I responded to his voice, not really sure if it was a dream. After I came to my senses and realised after looking at the clock on Dave's bedside table, that I had only been asleep for about three hours, and where was he? His side is empty. I give Pete my apologies about not going for breakfast and then I jumped up and put on my dressing gown. Dave is not downstairs, don't tell me!!!!

I run down the back alley, about twenty yards to the back gate of the pub garden, through there into the back door and into the bar. My eyes were not deceiving me now. There he was with a brandy snifter in his hand looking 'oh so happy'. The manager and one of my friends, Nancy who works behind the bar, were standing with Dave laughing. He was very entertaining when he was drinking. Nancy asked me if I would like a coffee. "I would love one" I said.

Then I said to her "I guess the cleaners are just finished", when I saw two women sitting at the end of the bar, the cleaners had been long gone she told me, then she said "Sam, the pub is open, look over the other side, we have customers." Oh my! I am standing there in my dressing gown, hair not combed, face not washed. What on earth must these people be thinking? I know Robbins doesn't care, the state he is in. Too late for me to rush out now, everybody has seen me. 'That is Dave's friend from America!' I can hear it now to this day.

I finished my coffee and once again left the new 60 year old at the bar, and went back to the house to have a 'cat's lick' (small wash all over), then I put on a little romper suit that I had brought with me for sunbathing in. I got lucky, it was about eighty degrees and gorgeous, so I got a lounge chair and went into Dave's back garden to have thirty minutes in the sun. He finally came in the back gate, scary sight! I just left him alone and he staggered through the back door and into the kitchen. I had about an hour in the sun and then went into the house. Dave was laid out on the couch in the living room. Out for the count! I told you earlier that we had a couple staying overnight, the girl used to work for Dave and I got to be very friendly with her and her boyfriend. I think years earlier he had a big crush on this girl, but I think a relationship with someone twenty five years younger than yourself and also works for you, probably not a good venture, anyway I got on great with her. As I was going into the bathroom she came down the stairs and we had a little chat about 'Don Juan' then she went back upstairs to the bedroom. About an hour later Dave appeared in the kitchen, I could not believe it. He decided that he was going to pull my romper suit down as I was leaning against the kitchen counter, he did, and just at that moment Pauline was coming back down the stairs, very embarrassing for me. I shouted out before she got to the bottom, "Sorry Paul, I am standing here nearly naked". "It's OK", she shouted back, "you look beautiful". I guess a new boob and a tan helped make it a good picture from her point of view.

After convincing Dave to go and lay down again and let me put my clothes back on, Pauline and I arranged to have a lunchtime pub visit, like we really needed one! We pop in the gate down the alley and the place was busy, many friends from the night before also still drinking. I suppose this party is still going. I told them stories about how I left David in the men's room asleep about 8 am, the coffee in my dressing gown in front of customers, then the romper incident, we were all laughing about the fact that he wanted Pauline to help him lift me onto the kitchen counter, it's amazing what booze can do to a person, Dave's antics this morning kept us all laughing for quite a while.

Pauline and I had a couple of half pints of bitter, and then thought if the guys wanted to, it would be nice to go for a curry in the evening. That's if the men were in shape to go. We went back to the house and took turns to have a shower, that way we would be able to get ready later without four of us having to use all of the hot water. Time for a nap me thinks, good idea Paul thought, and we both know this is going to be another long day.

I came down to the living room and decided to call Les before he drove back to London. He told me him and Becca had a fun night and he would be down again to pick me up in about a week. When I leave Dave's I stay with Les and Rebecca for a few days. I told him I would take the train back, which I had done in the past, and he said "no" he would come and get me. I actually enjoy the two hours on the train, coastal scenery, countryside, farm houses, etc. makes a very pleasant ride. Also, a railway employee comes around with a trolley with tea and coffee, alcoholic beverages, and I think snacks. Obviously one has to pay for this service, but at five pm in the afternoon on a train, it's great to have an aperitif before dinner later.

I usually arrive in East London on the train, Waterloo Station to be exact, and my beautiful Son is always there to pick me up. On this visit to England, I will be driven back, either way is great I am happy to be home for a couple of weeks. I do get homesick even after being away all these years.

Nearly time to leave Dave, maybe for another year or longer, who knows? He takes me to dinner the night before I leave, to a little Italian restaurant in Dover where he took me when I first came back in 1991. I love this place, it has about ten tables total, and is very cozy and looks really authentic Italy. The two young waiters are Italian, one of them is the son of the owners, and the Mother actually still does a lot of the cooking, which is superb!

Dave and I have escargots, followed by shrimp scampi, a wonderful cold dry white wine, and a coffee and brandy to finish. I do love this place, soooo relaxing, but makes me a little melancholy knowing I am leaving tomorrow. 'Not on a Jet Plane yet'. One song I like alot, not sure why I have to make myself sad?

It takes me a couple of months after getting back to my American home to get back into the routine again. My sis has looked after Mum while I have been in England. 9/11 shook everyone up. I think I remember Sue telling me that the Vegas Strip closed down. I know she got sent home from the shop where she works. I would think the whole of America was in a state of shock. I know everybody where I was wanted revenge for this horrendous act, immediately!

Les checks the airline I am with when I get back to London. Not sure if I am going to be able to fly out on the date I have on my ticket. The airlines on both sides of the Atlantic are all grounded right now, meaning thousands of people will be stranded, and when they do start to fly again I'm sure it will be a big mess. I hope I am not going to have to be delayed too long. I am getting low on spending money, and I have to get back to work. I think having my flight booked at least three months in advance, I am sure I have some sort of priority on my return flight when this mess is sorted out.

Les finds out my outward bound will be the same day, just later by maybe a couple of hours. We have to keep checking every day for the next three or four to make sure.

Next on the agenda will be an Indian restaurant. I cannot go back to Vegas without having a good prawn curry and Pilau rice, accompanied by *popudums* (very flat thin crispy thing, looks like a tortilla but much thinner), it is usually fried very fast in a little oil. There are a couple of Indian restaurants in Las Vegas, George and I have eaten in one of them, but somehow did not taste as good as the one I go to in London. It is pretty close to where Les and Becca live in Dulwich, so we can walk there, which also gives us a chance to have a few wines as we are not driving.

On the Saturday before I leave, Les takes me to Covent Garden, which is a huge complex of little shops, boutiques, restaurants, pubs and street entertainers. Years ago, Covent Garden was nothing but green grocery and vegetable markets, also fresh fruit. I think it was about 1980 that it was converted to what it is present day. There is a lot of history associated with this place, and Wikipedia on the computer will give one information. The modern technology and what a person can learn from it is mind boggling, (not sure if boggling is a word, but I use it all the time).

There are stalls that sell souvenirs, and I always try to take something back for friends, key rings, English candy, or cookies. I do miss my English cookies, the ones I cannot buy in the States, probably a good job, I would put more weight on!

Leslie's treat for dinner on my last night, I think the three of us are going to a little French restaurant, again walking distance from the flat. Yippee! More wine for all. We have a very nice meal, except for the *tatin* (tart for dessert) it was a little soggy, no problem! I don't think any chef can make one like Pepin!

After we walked back home, Les and I had a nice long chat, we always do when I am there. I wish he would have had children. He would have been a great Father. I guess Rebecca did not want that, it seemed while she was with Les anyway. She had an abortion about a year or two ago, cannot remember exactly when, her choice I did not want to know the details, I was over there and they were both having dinner in Dave's pub. I joined them for a drink before we celebrated New Year's Eve later. Les asked me, "Mum, would it bother you if you didn't become a Grandmother"?

I think I picked up on this question immediately. I replied "Of course not. Is Becca pregnant?" obviously yes. I then gave them my advice and my opinion. "OK guys! Having a baby is one of the most wonderful things ever, but you are suddenly responsible for another person's life for a long time to come, you really have to want this and give it your all, and more. It means giving up a lot of freedom and expense that you don't have now, but to have a son or daughter is indescribable, no words can describe!" Les and Rebecca were divorced some time later.

Losing the custody of my son took a big chunk from my heart, it never did grow back, and also losing a daughter, and at age forty having to release another baby because of health problems, it takes much, much strength to deal with. There are many times I sit and think about this, and sadness creeps over me, but at nearly seventy six I suppose I have been a good and caring person, and I have certainly loved and been loved.

Some people never get this opportunity. My speech to Rebbeca and Leslie did not make any sort of impact. I think Les wanted it, she didn't, he cried in front of me, devastating for me. I then got up and went back in to Dave's house and told him what I have just dealt with. He tells me "Sam, it's their life babe, whatever they decide you cannot influence them". Of course he was right.

Time to celebrate another year coming in. I do not remember what year that was. Time flies when one is having fun!

50 Reality Again

Home, back to work and reality. I am very lucky that I have a family who takes care of each other so that I can go away for a couple of weeks. January 2002, Mum is going downhill fast. At the beginning of February she has a couple of small strokes and she is unable to feed herself. I call for help from one of our many Vegas institutions for the elderly, and tell them that I believe my mother needs hospitalisation. I called my Sister at one point as I thought mum was dying, Sue left work and rushed to the house but Mum seemed to pull through, just did not recognise either one of us for a while.

A nice lady arrives and goes into the bedroom where Mum is. She checks her out and tells me that Mum can be sent to a local hospice. Her age eighty nine, takes priority over everything. She will get taken care of more than I or George can do. We are both working and we do not want her to be left at any time. I have to tell Mum when this lady has left, that she has to go to the hospital. She does not really understand what is going on. Pretty soon the ambulance arrives and I tell her that she is going to see her doctor and I will be right behind her in the car. That seemed to help calm her a little.

I get to the place they took her about twenty minutes later. She was already in a room and in bed, which was very encouraging to me. I wanted to be very sure that she was going to be looked after.

My Mum had never been in a hospital or home of any kind in her whole life, except the emergency room in England once when she broke her arm.

I felt very, very guilty about her being here. I had always promised her that she would NEVER have to go into a nursing home, and it looks as if it might be inevitable. Her mind is gone maybe ninety percent of the time, and I cannot look after her and go to work, plus take care of George. I left a couple of hours later and went home. It is heartbreaking for me to have to leave her there, but it is the best thing for her.

I think she was there for about a week, and then they transferred her to a local nursing home in town. It was a very nice clean and friendly place, pretty large, with outside areas for the residents to sit and relax. For those who could manage on their own, there was a huge dining room where relatives were allowed to sit with their loved ones during meal times, and help them to eat their food. Mum was not able to handle eating on her own very well, so when I did not get there the staff helped her. Most of the food she had was about the same as baby food, blended and pureed veggies and fruit juice.

It would only be two weeks later that I had a phone call at about 8:30 pm to tell me my Mother had passed away. Somehow I was expecting it as I had been there earlier in the day, and Sue had also been there with her Son a couple of hours after me, she had to have expected it as well. We both met there about an hour later and went in to say goodbye to our wonderful Mother.

She would have been ninety years old the coming August. It is a very odd feeling for George and I to be on our own and have the house to ourselves after twenty three years. Mum's funeral was very nice but George did not handle it well, he cried quite a bit. . Lots of people that had met her through her years in Vegas attended. We all went back to the bar (still our bar), and then the house after the funeral, I have a nasty feeling I am always going to be in and out of this bar. Oh well, Que Sera, Sera.

51   Mum Gone

I might as well get all the depressing parts of mine and George's lives out of the way. The time is soon coming that I can see he has to stop working and driving. The shaking is worse, and we find out he has cataracts, so the next thing is the eyes have to be taken care of. After the cataracts are taken out the ophthalmologist will put new lens in both of his eyes. I am going to be a caregiver for another month full time. As hard as this man has worked he will be taken care of by me, if it's twenty four hours a day.

Meanwhile we are having a nice relaxing couple of weeks before the surgery, going out to dinner in the gourmet room in one of our local casinos. Super little place, very intimate, great food and a woman playing a baby grand piano, she was awesome! George and I would have oysters on the half shell, share a Caesar salad and then have a surf and turf, lobster and filet mignon which we also shared. One steak between us, and maybe one lobster tail each. It's amazing how getting old affects one's appetite. We used to eat much more than we do now, and not even dessert anymore, maybe a coffee and a liquor, and that's it. Lucky for us we get a comp occasionally, couldn't afford to eat like that very often.

The eyes are healing nicely, next its back surgery and finally convincing George he has to give up working, shame now he can see well, he really cannot drive as the shaking is progressing. He was very happy that his back pain has gone, and he can see so well he thinks I have repainted one of our bathrooms white. It was already white, but I guess it looks so much brighter with the new lens in his eyes.

He gets himself prepared to call the hotel and tell them he has to quit. Seventy-four is a good age to be working even if one is healthy. (Think I know about that!!). We make arrangements to go and pick up his final paycheque. The owner's Son meets us at the bar at lunch time, and shakes George's hand telling him he is sorry to see him go. That did it, George started crying, it was awful. Then I cried with him, seeing a man cry is one of the worst things for me.

We had a couple of cocktails and drove home. A physical therapist is coming to the house two or three times a week, and I had a handrail put on the cool decking at the three feet end of the pool, so that George could walk in the shallow water and get exercise. Our pool being dark kept the heat a lot longer than a regular white cement one, which helps him into warm water easier, it was beautiful pool I really still do miss it.

It was April Fools' Day and I got a phone call from my boss on my day off telling me not to come to work tomorrow. I thought at first it was a joke being April first. No joke! He is replacing me with a young bartender from a bar close by who is going to work five shifts, I was only doing three. He did tell me he was sorry and that he would compensate me with a month's pay. This came out of the blue, and after working for him for six years a bit of a shocker. I had worked in this place except for about a year and a half, a total of nearly eighteen years. Now what will George and I do?

As per usual, he tells me not to worry about anything, we will overcome. We have just lowered our monthly income by about fifteen hundred dollars which was what George made. Maybe more some months depending on the tips he made. It was not easy to lower ones monthly spending in one go, it takes working out, and now my money coming in is also GONE!

How fortunate it was that I knew so many people in or associated with the bar business, this is one of the things that has kept us above water. Within a couple of weeks I had been offered a job in one of the very old bars in town. Who cares how old it is? I have a job. It won't make up George's money, but it will save mine hopefully!

One thing that really saved us from a big melt-down was George's air force retirement. We decided to refinance our home, but before we can do that we have to make it into real property. At the moment, it is considered a mobile home. One would never know, it's like a little cottage inside, anyway it means we have to put it on a concrete foundation which will cost us a few thousand, but we cannot refinance unless this is done. The loan for the refinancing will also include the foundation work. Our monthly mortgage will be at a lower interest rate and our payment will be less.

The only trouble is it seems as if we are starting from scratch. Oh well there are people much worse off than us. I have survived cancer for over ten years now which is supposed to be a good sign. Don't need any more things to worry about. We have a nice house and a beautiful back garden with a lovely lawn and a huge pool. We are lucky in a lot of respects, if I could cure George life would be perfect I think.

I am working three days of swing shift, three until eleven p.m. I have lots of friends that are loyal and come to visit me at this new location. This bar has been here forever, at least thirty or more years, maybe more. It is a little run down, but who cares if I have a busy shift?

I relieve a lady who is over eighty years old. She runs behind the bar, she drinks shots of vodka, and insists that I have one with her when I start work. As long as I have a sip of the shot she pours me, then she is happy.

Now I have to hope some of my friends can make a later shift. They are all used to seeing me during the day. I think most of us get used to going to our favourite bar and going to a different one takes an effort. When I worked in the 'Mill 'now under a different name, (used to be our bar), I knew who would be in, what day, what time, like all the guys from our local school district, not teachers, maintenance specialists I guess one would call them.

About six of them used to come in on Wednesday afternoons. The bar was close to their main building, very convenient eh? Nice bunch of fellows. I still see a couple of them to this day twenty years later. In fact I think one of them is going to help me with this manuscript, maybe typing it for me. He did, and he is gone. I hate to keep losing friends, but it is inevitable I'm afraid.

Now, let me talk about this little old scruffy bar where I am now working. Peggy(who died years ago) the old lady I relieve, who drinks shots quite a bit, is a super person to work with and we hit it off straight away. I have picked up customers from other local bars in the area and also have visits from friends I met when I first came to Vegas, astonishing! My son always tells me that people love my jokes and my English humour that is why I am busy most of the time wherever I work. I think I was meant to be a bartender, but I would have loved to have become a professional singer. I still go to karaoke occasionally in a local bar or casino even at seventy-six. Am I a ham? Noooooo!!

There are a few rough characters that come into this bar. I have to learn how to deal with them without causing a riot. I did not have this problem where I just came from and it really does take a mental and physical strain on a person. My sister will not even venture in the bar to see me when I am working. I guess she mixes with a different sort of clientele to me, and her and I are a lot different as far as that goes. I can mix with the lowest if I have to, but I don't think Sue can, then again why should she if she doesn't have to?

I know I can go to the best gourmet restaurant and know which fork and which glass to use and also know how to order, and so I don't worry about having to mix with low life people when I am at work. This is the way I chose to go and I accept it. I have also met some people who are down and out through no fault of their own and got along very well with them. One of my weaknesses is giving and lending money when I have it, and buying drinks for people from my tips. I have been telling myself for years to stop but I still do it. My hubby is made the same way. I suppose it may come back to us one day. My sister actually does it too, for me a lot of the time, gives and gives. She knows there are times when I need help and she is always there bless her.

There are two, or three couples that come in the afternoons where I am working now and I usually pour a nice shot for them, it's called a buttery nipple, Baileys and Butterscotch in a very cold shot glass and we all have one together every week. It always turns into more than one for them and then the fun begins. Everybody gets happy, and I do try and make sure everybody is okay to drive, and if not I will get them a cab and pay for it. Unfortunately I don't seem to know anyone who doesn't drink who could be a designated driver. That sounds awful doesn't it?

George is not used to sitting at home at night especially on his own, and I do not get home until about twelve midnight. So I came up with a plan and need to discuss it with him. "George, let's get a dog" I said. This would be our third one. I was not sure about his reaction but I told him it would be great company for him while I was at work. He sat and thought about it for quite a while. He then said, "Okay let's do it." We discussed it on Saturday when I was off. We decided we would go to the animal shelter on Monday, and see if we could save a dog that would love to live with us and we would love him, (or her).

52   And Then There Is George #2

Monday morning and it is pouring with rain. This is going to turn into a day I won't forget. It is Washington's Birthday which is a public holiday, but the animal shelter is open so we are on our way after they open, and still raining very hard. I am really looking forward to having a pet again. George and I have had a Bassett hound and a Rottweiler and it's been a while since we lost our Rotty. He was one of the most intelligent dogs I have ever had, but as with many large dogs he got hip dysplasia and so we put him out of his misery. We had him for twelve years.

We get there and walk into the lobby. I tell the ladies at the desk we want to see the dogs. George is on his walker so it takes a few minutes for us to get to the back where the cages are. I cannot believe how many dogs are here in cages. Some have three dogs in each, how sad! We start checking out the dogs. Seems like a lot of pit bulls here, guess these poor things have a bad reputation. George and I are big dog people but we do not want a pit bull. Something gentle is what we are after. Suddenly there he is, this beautiful Golden Lab Retriever.

We find our way back to the lobby and sit down, George gets tired very quickly. He is now seventy-four and not a fit person. I walk back with him get him safely seated and he tells me to go back and check out the Lab. I go back in and find the cage he is in. There are two Chihuahuas in with him, and as I get close he looks up at me. He had me at, 'looking up at me'.

I started reading his paperwork which all of the dogs have attached to the front of their cages. He is eight years old, abandoned, and he has been here for three or more weeks. Euthanasia is due in about one week according to the paper I am reading. When I finally get to the bottom of the page and I have read his history I am suddenly flabbergasted. I rush out to the lobby to tell George what I have read. "Guess what?" I say. "His name is George". He then tells me to get him the bleep-bleep out of there. I hurry to the desk and tell them we want to adopt George the lab.

I am so excited. I cannot believe I now will have two Georges. . I do the paperwork at the desk, make a donation and get my copies. Then the lady takes a short thick blue rope with a make shift collar on the end of it and gives it to me. We walk to the back and she shows me to a small room and says, "Wait here Samantha", I will go and fetch him."

I heard him before he got to the door of the room I was in. Talk about hearing an excited dog it was amazing how loud he was. I suppose he had a feeling he was going to be out of there. What a beautiful creature. How could anyone abandon him? After he was in the room with me, he was jumping, leaping, barking and rolling around, fabulous! When I finally got him calmed down we had kisses and hugs. Then I took him out to the lobby to meet my hubby George. I think that was an instant friendship. All of a sudden as I was signing the last paper to let us know he had a chip under the skin, and had also had all the shots he needed, he started barking and he would not stop. I think George was assuming as I was, the dog is just barking for no reason and he was being a pain in the butt. I tried to hurry and get him out of the door, and as I opened it I noticed a cage with a big brown rabbit in it. I think that was what he was yelling about! We get to the car and it is still pelting with rain. I open the back hatch which lets down, (we have a Chevrolet Blazer

SUV) and I am thinking how to get the dog in the back before I help George who is still standing in the rain, into the front, when all of a sudden the dog leaps into the back of our SUV as though he has done it forever, made it easy for me. I now get my husband into the passenger seat and get into the driver's side and off we go. My hubby seems to be very happy with this trip. On the way home he rolls his window down when we get to a red light. Next to us is a car with kids in it. He shouts at them telling them we just got a dog and they all wave, (still raining)!

We pull into our driveway and I get hubby out first with his walker and take him inside the front gate and under the patio cover. Our back garden was not visible until one opened the front gate and then a little piece of heaven was staring you in the face. A huge two thousand square foot lawn, one end a three step planter, another planter inside the gate, a fifty foot covered patio, and our beautiful very large pool that was finished with dark cement which made it look natural. It also held the warm water a lot longer after the summer months were over. (Still raining)!

When I got the dog out of the car, I took the collar and attached rope leash off and he followed me into the garden. I don't think I have ever seen a dog run and roll like he did. George looked at me and said, "That is one happy dog," still raining very hard and the dog is on his back in the middle of the lawn, legs in the air rolling from side to side. What a lovely thing to see, he is saved! I suppose now I have to start trying to ignore my lovely clean house from getting dirty. I told George #1 to watch George # 2 while I went into the house for old towels that I could dry him off with. The animal shelter gave me a small amount of food until I could get to the store and stock up, obviously with treats, marrow bones (fresh) and a decent dry dog food. I came out with the towels and managed to get him rubbed down. I am sure by now my animal is hungry, (and the dog!).

It has been a long fun filled eventful day and we all need feeding. This plan of mine to get a pet is going to work. I can see that my hubby is not looking so down, he has a pal. Now, even though the dog is supposedly house trained I have to make sure he is, and so I let him out at least three times before we go to bed. He follows us into the bedroom and lies down in the corner. I must get him a bed or a large blanket. I am already in love with this creature. It has finally stopped raining but it is February and it is winter and we are happy to have rain in the desert. The next morning I get up very early to make sure the dog goes out. Oops! He had already made a caca in front of the door. I show him what he has done. He knows it's wrong, but I am not going to get mad with him, he at least went to the door and it's his first night. I clean up and then we go into the garden. George finds the pool, straight in no hesitation. The water cannot be more than fifty degrees if that, but this is a Lab Retriever. I guess they love the water however cold it is.

He eventually finds the steps at the shallow end and after a few minutes of swimming he comes out. I let him do his shaking and rubbing himself on the grass, and I manage to get into the front door while he is not looking and find towels again. This is a big job getting him dried off. I have to work today at three p.m. so I have to get things organised before I leave. George # 2 will have to have makeshift bowls for his food and water until I can get to the pet shop, I'm sure he won't care as long as he is fed. He follows me into the house after his rub down, obviously feeling good. I give him a biscuit, the ones from the shelter. It cannot be too bad as he gobbles it up. I will get his food ready and my husband will take care of it later in the day. I am going to cook George a meal before I leave and he will be able to eat too. Wish we were well off. I could stay home and take care of everything. Don't think I will hold my breath on that issue.

I believe that there are people who are meant to have money, and some are not! It is impossible to save much on my small pay cheque and George's Air Force cheque, but we manage and all our bills are paid. I find it hard to believe that we still have a mortgage, but over the years the cards have been stacked against us. It doesn't matter we are quite happy with what we have. Summer is approaching pretty fast. I hate the heat and don't care if it is dry. Still hate it. There is a nice side however. George and I have parties and great barbecues in our back garden. It is usually twenty or more people and great fun and great food. Our friends always bring a bottle of their choosing and if we go to their place we do the same. Life is good really. I am pretty content with it. We have had many special occasions in this garden. My two Son's weddings were on the same day, when I had nice small tables across the lawn, also decorations hanging from the patio and the trees. Then there was the rain, thunder, and lightning which wiped out my tables across the lawn, along with my blue and white paper wedding bells, and drove all our guests at least fifty of them under the patio. It did not stop for a long time, so eventually we brought out our bar from the house and set it up under the patio, this is before we had the permanent one. Glad we had one, it turned out really great! I think the storm that blew through here even lightning striking our patio roof added excitement to this day. Now it's turned into one sweaty party and nobody cares. It is July. Jump into the pool. Nobody cares!!!!

All our friends have now met our new four-legged family member George. Everybody loves him. How could anyone not? He is the most gentle and loving dog, and very obedient. That's a big thing with large dogs, they have to do as they are told more so than a small one. He does not seem to have a flaw. Two thousand and three and it is a late summer. Summer? It seems like summer most of the year here. A cool October or November will be very welcome.

53 Was It Something I Said

December, oh no! Here we go again. I suddenly feel as though I have the plague. I get a phone call from my manager at the bar. Guess what? "Sam I have to let you go." "Why?" I ask. "I'm not sure, but I think the owner wants to put some guy in here, I think a friend of his maybe, he has shares in the place," John replied. "I cannot believe it John. I do my job. I have three busy shifts. How can he do this to me after nearly two years"? John says, "I don't know Sam, I am so sorry." "John, it's not your fault", "I'll miss you", he says. This seems to be a recurring thing with me. I am not going to let it depress me though, I know I can find something and it does not take long either.

One of my customers was the manager at a bar down the street from the one I was in. I believe she probably took care of more than one bar. Anyway, I think she has put in a good word for me with the owners of the bars she manages, and amazingly I know both of these men who own them. I met them when George and I were in the 'Mill.' I think they bought their first bar together before we left there in the eighties. It was about two weeks later that I had to go for an interview in one of their bars, along with a few more women who seemed much younger than me, a little nerve-racking to say the least. Our good friend Ray, who worked for George and I, came with me for support and I'm sure for a lunch time cocktail. Ray passed away in 2012. He was a good friend and a great worker.

I sat and watched a few prospects come in and out. Suddenly I was the last one left. I had filled out the required application and I thought maybe I was not even going to get interviewed, but then James and Arthur the owners, came out from the back office with Sylvia the manager. They came to the bar where I was sitting with Ray. The three of them sat down next to us. I seem to remember James asking me a few questions and then Sylvia said, "Can you start tomorrow"? It just blew me away! I couldn't believe how lucky I was, I have a job already and I will be working for people that I have known for many years.

54   Seems I Found Home

I obviously said, "Yes" to Sylvia when she asked me if I could start tomorrow. That was the seventeenth of December 2003. This will be the start of a long and interesting journey for the next ten or more years of my life. I started working three day shifts a week which was enough for me. I am 65 and getting a little tired.

I started working in London when I was just past fifteen. It's been a long haul. This bar I am in now is unique as far as local bars go...a real smorgasbord! There are customers that I have been introduced to by other patrons as maybe ladies of the evening, and most of them I get along fine with.

This place is not situated in the nicest of areas from what I have heard listening to bar talk. There are druggies, homeless and a lot of unsavoury characters, somehow it does not bother me at all, I think my husband and my Sister worry about it more than I do. If I mind my own business and treat people right, I am sure it will be okay. Where do I start? I have worked with one of the other bartenders for a few hours to learn the ropes etcetera, and the way the money has to be handled, and now I am ready to be thrown to the lions!

My first morning alone I arrive about half an hour early just to get organised. I hate the idea of rushing in the door and straight behind the bar. I like to take my time, have a coffee and see who is in the place. I relieve the guy who works the graveyard shift (Twelve midnight until eight a.m.) and he is really excited to see someone who shows up early, guess we are buddies already.

Steve and I become very close for the next two years. I count the money and he seems happy with me, so he sits at the bar and has an off shift beer. At eight a.m. there are not many customers so him and I get to talk and get to know each other.

The first person he introduces me to is his good friend Pam. She has been doing her running routine and comes into the bar when she is done. I like her. She is pretty easy to talk to and this is the start of a long friendship. I then meet Kelly, a girl (I call her girl as she is 40 years younger than me) who runs this place, assistant manager and bartender who works five days a week? I think she tends bar, two or three days, and manages the rest of the week. I have already come to the conclusion I don't envy anyone managing this bar and I have only just started.

Two thousand and four and boy have I met some characters during the few weeks I have worked here., Alex who is about my age, loves golf as I do. Ken, round about my son's age, loves to drink, Fred hard to deal with moody bugger, and Paul, who wouldn't say "boo" to a goose. These were the first regulars I met. I managed to deal with all of them. ALL since deceased except Ken, who stopped drinking years ago. Still seem him occasionally.

Bartending is an art and not everyone could do this. It takes patience, understanding, and maybe compassion in some ways. These guys made my shifts, whether drunk, sober, nasty, or nice, they became good customers. Three out of four of these men like a little gamble. One or two of them are not what I would call good losers. I have to try and let their outbursts go over my head. It would not be good for the bar if I ask them to cool it, unless of course it gets out of hand.

There are lots of gamblers who really express themselves when they lose money. It's gambling whether one wins or not! Sometimes the language leaves nothing to be desired, but I worked in a casino and served men from New York, Chicago and other big cities that lost thousands in a few hours, so I had heard plenty of swearing over the years.

Actually there were other habits that some of them who came to the Bahamas had that were disgusting to me. One big player in particular that used to come to the casino would stub out the cigar he had finished with on the carpet. This small casino was beautiful, with thick dark gold carpet and big crystal chandeliers. The flocked wallpaper stood out matching the carpet, and here we have a man without respect for any of this, dropping his nasty stub of a cigar on the carpet and treading on it. And he will never be asked to leave, why? Probably because he is wealthy and spends thousands every time he comes here? What a shame we don't have classes to teach people a little class, money cannot buy it that's for sure!

I have now brought George to the bar I am now working in and introduced him to my manager Kelly and most of the customers that come in on my shifts of course. He hits it off with everybody. He is a very likeable man and he loves to laugh and have fun. This is a big bar and when it gets very busy one has to 'haul ass'! As they say, good exercise though helps with the arthritis. The only bad thing is one does not sit down for eight hours, and that is if one is a decent bartender. I cannot remember ever sitting down while I was working, no wonder my bloody knees are going!

I have introduced my manager Kelly and lots of my customers to English humour. It was easier than I thought. My humour can often sound sarcastic. It is not meant to be that way. I guess because it is dry, not corny like the American. I think U.S. humour is more like slapstick.

At sixty-five I thought I had heard and seen it all. I had met one or two young women in the islands that were allegedly high class ladies of the evening. I was educated pretty fast after getting the job in the casino. These girls were very classy, had clothes to die for, full length sable coats, gowns and jewellery that I will never be able to afford in my lifetime. I started off wondering why they would be in the lounge for an hour, out of the lounge for two hours, and so on and so on. I was told after I thought I knew what they were doing, that they made lots of money. I really was naive. WHAT! I suddenly realised that I was sitting on a gold mine, but what a shame the entrance has been blocked. WOW! I could have been rich, (or maybe died of aids).

Anyway getting back to the bar I am in now, the girls that work near this place, not suppose to I hear, (no disrespect to any of them if that is how their life has to be) probably do the deed, or one of the deeds for a few dollars I heard. I feel very bad for some of them, I believe some do not have a choice in their life. Obviously having these women in and out of here sometimes brings the men in and does help me tip wise. One or two of the girls are very good to me. They gamble, and if they win they make sure I am taken care of.

Working for tips can be very hard some days. Some people are great and some are very cheap. This is not quite like a casino. One big player I have is Ken. He is a great tipper, but I have to keep him sober long enough to get one and if he wins of course.

Then there's Alex, patience is needed with him, also Fred, he may be worse, but Alex is older and him and I share our love of golf together. If there has been a tournament on over the weekend when I am off, I know we will discuss it on Tuesday when I am back. His favourite thing to yell at me is "bloody Brits", that is only if an Englishman actually wins, or gets a place.

This year is the Ryder cup, can't wait, it is only played every two years, I think around the end of September or the first part of October. It is early in the year so I have a few more months to put up with Alex's insults, in fun of course. I am going back momentarily to 2002 which I have commented on previously to George's eye surgery. He is still driving at this time, and sometimes he will take the car on my days off and go for a beer in our favourite local bar. Those are the days I get very nervous about. His eyes are not good and he even tells me that it gets a little blurry when the sun goes down. Well

I knew it. The next thing is eye surgery. He has cataracts that have to be removed and the doctor is going to put new lens in his eyes.

We schedule the procedure for a Monday so that I can take him and bring him home and the only setback we have is putting the drops in. I did not mention that we have to do one eye at a time and about three weeks before the next one. I worked it out to the drops in the morning before I leave for work for three days, then more when I first get home and then before we go to bed. Not sure why I brought the eye chapter up again, just seemed stuck in my mind, so skip reading this part if you want!

George has a problem with the drops as the Parkinson's makes him shake and putting drops in his eye is very difficult for him. He has three children that live in town about fifteen minutes away. Are they around to help him? Yeah, right. His son does come around now and then and take care of his feet for me. The Diabetes does tend to affect feet!

The eldest girl we never see, and the middle one only comes around when she needs something, usually to borrow money, or somewhere to stay when she has nowhere else to go, which has happened a lot over the last twenty-seven years.

Poor George, she is his daughter and his blood. How can he say no? I have gone along with her needing and given and given, clothes, sheets, towels, fake Christmas trees, china name it. She has had everything I can give. Now it stops my man, her Father needs help and where is she? The youngest and the best is in Florida, and I know if she was here her Dad would be taken care of when I was not there.

Evidently, I am the bad guy still, according to the other two. I am so happy that I had and still have a loving family that gets along. George's family do not seem to be very easy that way. They don't even have time for each other. Seems they are always at loggerheads!. This is why he always tells me, "I do not want to go round at Thanksgiving, or Christmas, I can't stand the bickering." Can you imagine? These are his children, I think Charlie is the exception. Every year for a long time he has spent a few hours at holiday times with them and was so happy to get back home where he could relax and be happy.

I have just had a bad week, money wise. We have 15 slots in the bar and a few of them have to be reset with a key after someone is paid out. I have not been used to doing this where I previously worked, so one morning when a guy tells me he has won ninety dollars I check the machine and it says ninety dollars. I pay him and find out later in the day, that the shift before me paid this out already to some other person, but neglected to reset the machine so this a'hole got me, no pay cheque this week!

Did not tell George I will get around it somehow. Have done it before when we were short of money, will do it again. Life is short, Sam keep smiling honeybunch!

It is amazing how busy this bar gets. I sometimes have quite a crowd by eleven a.m. and considering it is the middle of the week that is great for me. There are a few (excuse the expression) slime balls that have to be dealt with. They are people who have no respect for themselves, or anybody, or anything. I'm pretty sure it's drugs, but they do not want help, or to help themselves.

After a while one loses patience with these creeps. One morning the graveyard guy Steve, having no one in the bar took a toilet break, sometimes one has to go. As he was coming back one of the so-called creeps I mentioned was jumping back across the bar. He had stolen a bundle of money from behind the bar and was on his way out.

Steve hurried and tried to catch him, but he had bad lungs and could not breathe too well, so he couldn't make it. He had to make up the money from his pay cheque. Never did this jerk get caught.

Kelly, my manager, did point out a few people that she told me to take notice of. She was very alert as far as that went. I always thought she did a good job running this so called den of iniquity, not easy, harder than the one I took care of. Thankful for that.

The next thing I am doing is taking care of the bar supply ordering. The girl who works when I am off is not really taking care of it well. She is ordering stuff we don't need and missing things we do need. Guess the day shift has to do this job. The bartenders where George and I were did not have to deal with this, I did it. Just being behind a bar for over eight hours is enough. Anyway I took it over and got on with it. I am still doing it ten years later.

George is still driving here and now in his old pick-up. He likes to have a drink with me when I get off shift. He has made a few friends here and Kelly and him get along like a house on fire. He tells her my jokes (his rendition), which is a lot different, but Kelly thinks he is very funny.

He gets along with Fred, amazing how men seem to hit it off easier than women can. I am thinking their conversations are a lot different to ours, sports, military service and beer. I think that's about it, but we have to love you, take you or leave you and plenty of times none of the above!

I do remember one thing that George would do that everybody got a kick out of. A program I am watching on TV reminded me of this. It was an impersonation of, (no disrespect again) Stevie Wonder. He would put on a pair of dark glasses and move his head from side to side and tap both hands on the bar as though playing the piano. It was very amusing.

55   July 4th Party

It is approaching July and I always love to have a party in our back garden so I am getting a fourth of July bash organised. It falls on a Sunday which will be very convenient. Most of our friends are free on Sundays. So far this year we have had a Memorial Day, some birthdays and now we are going to have a great Independence day. I hope it won't be too hot as I want to get the grill going.

One consolation is this huge pool we have. A couple of the guys always help me with the grill, cooking steaks etc. One was Rachel's hubby Stuart. He just seemed to love cooking on the barby! He always did a great job, rare, medium and well done. Name it, you've got it.

There were a few gatherings that I cooked other things, for example, I did a gumbo one time and it turned out super. I had a compliment from a friend who was from New Orleans on the dish. Now that was a compliment!

Another get together I did paella. That too was a nice change from steak, ribs, or chicken. Having these get togethers like George and I have is work, mostly for me, but I love it and I have girlfriends that bring in the dishes and clean them off when we are done. I love to have real plates not paper. Okay, I'm crazy, but it seems to taste better on china. Whatever it is, I usually tell everyone to come about noon to one p.m., and we are all pooped, or a little inebriated by four or five. Lately it seems that nobody wants to leave. There are still the tough ones hanging in about eight p.m. I have no problem with this. I love my friends and by the way, we don't do fireworks!

This particular July fourth we had about twenty-five people coming so I guess paper plates are in order. I don't have that many dinner plates. The pool water is about eighty-six degrees. My dog is loving it. I have tried to keep him out of it today, but I think that is impossible and I know he is going to be encouraged when everybody shows up.

George sleeps a lot lately and today I can get everything done while he is out of the way. He is in the small bedroom now which helps me to get more rest as my three shifts can be very tiring. Nine hours on one's feet at sixty-five years old. I am glad I was athletic all my life, in fact, last week I swam fifty lengths of our pool which if fifty feet long. I figured it out that I swam nearly half a mile, wasn't easy, that's when I seemed to have more breath than I do now.

I have one large banquet table and three small fold-up tables that I have to get out of the shed. The large one is very heavy and I have to drag it from the shed to the patio, putting it away is no problem though as I get help from all sides.

I just absolutely love doing this. I love people and I suppose that is why I am still bartending after all these years. Once everyone gets here, we all get drinks and I have to have a couple before I bring the food out. The only trouble is, every time I pour myself a vodka and tonic, I put it down, go in the house to get cutlery, condiments etc., and when I get back I cannot remember where I left it. I think I have wasted much vodka doing that.

I know I can rely on my really close girlfriend Emily to pour drinks for me. She is also a bartender and when her and hubby, Lee arrive she takes up her seat behind the bar. I have four stools in the front and four at the back, that's eight people sitting.

Emily makes her seat at the back permanent as she will not go in the pool and a good excuse is, she is making drinks. Her and I have been through the same nightmare, a mastectomy, hers left side, mine right. I used to tell her, "If we sit next to each other very close, we have a perfect pair? It would cheer her up, but she was like me, what's done is done and we are both still here.(the big C came back and took her in 2007) Loved that girl!

This party has been super, the steaks were great, the garlic bread was good, salad and spuds terrific! George has been lying in our big bamboo chair most of the time today. I cannot remember what this chair is called, but I do know he loved how comfortable it was for him. The cushion was as big as the chair, round on a base. I know there is a name, but it escapes me.

This man is so relaxed when we have these get-togethers. One would not know that he has been through the mill as we say in England.

Dusk approaching and fireworks are going off all over town. Time to put my dog in the house. I am pretty sure the noise will scare him and I don't want to take that chance. It is about eleven p.m. now, everybody gone and I am loading the dishwasher for the third and final time. The trash is in the bins in the yard. The large table is back in the shed and I am off in the morning I will take care of anything that needs putting away from outside then.

George is already in dream land which gives me another alone time to relax and do my thing. I sit and have a cigarette and pour a small drink, and I will remember where I put it this time as I wait for the dishwasher to finish. Aaaaah, peace, just me and my dog!

There is something very rewarding about having a great organised party that everybody loved. I think Labour Day is on the way. Let's do it again. What the heck! Monday morning, empty the washer, clean up the back yard and steel brush on the grill. The pool has had lots of bodies in it which really helps to keep it clean as the water is moving into the filter, more than if it was still.

George is not up yet, nearly noon, but no problem. That is how it is now. He is in bed for twelve hours at a time, hopefully when he gets up he will walk up and down with his walker on the cool decking and then into the pool at the three foot end. I had a bar put on the decking for him to hold onto if he wants to get into the pool. Walking in the warm water seems to really do him good and if I am not there the bar makes it much safer for him. Then George has George. They love each other.

Back in the saloon, it's Tuesday already, ugh! "I wonder what the poor people are doing?" a quote from my dad. He usually made this comment when we were having Sunday lunch in England, roast pork, or a leg of lamb with all the trimmings. My mum's Sunday roast was the best!

Alex is in early for his black coffee, it's Paul's day off, he wanders in and I know this is his day for getting "pissed" (drunk in England), but he does not drive and lives next door, same as Ken so I really don't worry if getting drunk and staggering twenty-five feet is what they want to do. Ken gets a machine he likes and starts his gambling. After a couple of hours on the vodka he has to succumb to the machine and the vodka and so I have to see him safely out of the back door and across the parking lot to his apartment.

Alex lives in the next block to Ken, a different owner for these places. There are roughly twenty small apartments behind the bar and I have about fifteen people from these places coming in on my shifts, about eight of those are good for the bar and myself as far as tips go and playing the machines. The rest of them the bar would not miss.

One good thing about serving locals is if they are heavy gamblers and they cash out a decent amount, or hit a royal flush on poker then most of the time a bartender can be sure of a good tip. A jackpot on video poker playing five quarters at a time is usually a thousand dollars which means if the player tips ten percent that's a hundred dollars. Not a frequent occurrence though, and we have to pay tax on our tips!

Labour Day party is not going to happen this year. George is agreeing with me, too much too soon. I think we will do Halloween this year. It's George's birthday a couple of days before and I think dressing up for Halloween will be great. I remember when we were working in the Mill and I arranged a Halloween party one year with a band, and gave prizes for the best costume. I had a friend who did dressmaking and she made me a little Orphan Annie outfit. I had a little dress with a pinafore, long pantaloons with a frill round the bottom, white ankle socks and flat black shoes. She also made me a wig from yellow wool and put two long braids on it. The whole outfit was very cute. I lent it to a friend a few years later and never got it back.

George was not the costume kind of guy, but he had an apron that a friend made him, a little risqué, but funny. Everybody loved it. There were two hidden pockets in the front and it tied around the waist. One pocket held a small cloth penis, the other pocket held a large cloth penis. George would take the small one out and tell everybody that it was for small parties and the big penis, obviously for big parties.

This was his Halloween outfit! What made it fun was the fact that the two dicks were hidden so when a person would ask George what was with the apron? he would spring one of his surprises on them!

Our customers were fun people and quite a few showed up in costume. Ray was Jason from Friday the 13th. We had the "Refrigerator" the football player and a Bee which was very good and the usual pirates and witches, etc.

Four, or five of us had a vote and gave first prize of a hundred dollars to a witch, (she wasn't really a bad girl). Her make up must have taken a long time to put on, it was incredible. In fact, no one knew who she was until we announced her as the winner. She then took off her hat, wig and fake nose and by Jove, one of our regulars. Well done! I think we gave second to a friend who came as the "refrigerator" who played for the Chicago bears I believe. Todd had a real jersey, painted himself black and was plenty big enough to pull it off. He too, did a great job.

We are nearly approaching the end of September. I have added another year to my life, now as old as the famous highway route 66, only I am not so well known. It is amazing how the time flies when one gets older.

Hard to believe I have worked in this bar now for ten months already. My friend and fellow bartender Steve, is getting more and more out of breath. He has a very bad lung disease and is still smoking & so am I unfortunately. One thing scares me, he is on oxygen and he brings the tank to the bar with him when he is working and he will take an occasional break and light a cigarette and take oxygen at the same time. I think a few of us are waiting for the big boom! Finally one of the guys who was in every morning told him he needed to stop doing that as it was very dangerous. Thank the lord he listened and stopped doing it. It is amazing how smokers can watch a person choking and having trouble breathing, but it does not stop them from lighting another one. Poor Steve, I fear he is going to suffer the same fate as my Dad.

October and I am on the computer, still not really sure at what I'm doing, it's working though so I am not fixing it if you get my meaning. I have ordered a Cleopatra costume for our Halloween party. I figured a long black wig would be fun. Also, the big bangles and glitzy jewellery, very different for me. I am not one for excessive baubles.

56 Ugly Cleopatra

The 31st is on a Sunday. We are going to hold the party on Saturday, gives us all time to recuperate. My outfit arrived about a week before the party. It was pretty good for the price I paid. Long, white, straight tunic type dress with a slit up to the knee on both sides, a huge separate gold collar that went out to my shoulders like a small cape, a gold head band and a few small accessories that finished the whole thing off.

I look really gross in a black wig, but I am looking forward to this soiree. The heat should be gone by then. October is usually a nice time of year, perfect for outside parties.

Nobody who is dressing up has told us what they are wearing so it's going to be a nice surprise. I have bought baby back ribs and corn and I am going to cook jacket potatoes in the oven. It's easier than on the grill when there will be about twelve of us. They can be kept warm in foil after they are cooked, as I am going to do with the corn. I will cook it in a large pot, put it in the oven with the spuds and then there will not be too much to care for.

I usually do ribs in a foil covered pan in a slow oven and then put them on the grill outside with a nice basting sauce, yum, yum! My ribs have always come out wonderful.

That is one good thing about living in Las Vegas. One can always rely on the weather for organising an outside party.

George and I have been to dinner for his 74th birthday to our favourite small gourmet room in a local casino. This little restaurant was outstanding, called "Diamond Lil's". The menu was very easy to deal with. Great appetisers such as escargot, fresh oysters, shrimp cocktails and a couple of other things. Main entrée could be lobster, filet mignon, prime rib, large, or small scampi and a few other tasty dishes. George and I sometimes had a comp from the casino which made ordering much easier as the cheque would be covered.

We always tipped our waiter twenty per cent, or more, usually more. I'm sure you have thought how did they get comps? Easy answer to that. I use to gamble and what I spent certainly paid for quite a few gourmet dinners. I obviously stopped a long time ago. True story! One never wins in the long run. Really big players in a gambling town never pay for anything, rooms, meals, anything they want, but I'm sure they lose thousands to get this attention.

Back to Halloween and a day of fun, food and relaxation. The pool water is still warm about eighty degrees and I have cleaned it a couple of days ago. I learned to do most things one has to know about taking care of a pool such as back washing, cleaning the filter and vacuuming. It has saved us a lot of money over the years.

One thing I don't do is mess with the chemicals. We have a pool company that comes once a week to test the PH balance and put in the chlorine. This pool is beautiful when it is clean and when the sun shines on the dark coloured and shaded areas it really makes it sparkle.

We are starting our bash today about one p.m. I have the tables and chairs set up and the veggies cooked and wrapped. The ribs just need to be slightly charred and basted on the grill.

The first ones to arrive were our good friends Emily and Lee, not in costume. Then the next two, Aron and hubby Ronny who were dressed as clowns and very good ones might I add. Rachel and Stuart came as a very fancy pretty witch and a pirate. We finished up with three clowns, and a pair of bikers both in leather gear. An Elvira, famous for spooky movie intros on TV, and me, Cleopatra. I think I fooled a few of our friends who came a little later. The black wig did the trick but as soon as I opened my mouth the accent gave me away. Never could keep my mouth shut!

The party's over (good name for a song), it will be a while before we have another one as Thanksgiving and Christmas are on the way and that is for family. I know I have to work Thanksgiving as it falls on a Thursday every year and I work on Thursdays. We have a pot luck at the bar so I usually cook something and take it to work with me. Then when I get off shift I go home and cook some more. There are a few people who participate in the pot luck and the dinner for the holiday turns out pretty nice. Then of course, there are those that just eat and would never dream of bringing, or donating a thing. I only get annoyed when they get greedy and eat three or four helpings and then try to take a couple of platefuls out of the back door. I guess there are those that give and those that take.

George and I have been doing Christmas at our house for a long time now and I love it. Me thinks this year won't be too much different. I find it hard to believe Sue's kids are grown-up already. Melissa is now a beautiful nineteen year old and studying to be a pharmacist, Peter is seventeen, just a normal teenager having fun, and Patrick's kids, Joann and Chris are great thanks to their mum and grandparents.

One day Patrick may regret the way he has treated them. I hope when they grow up they might forgive him. I have not yet, maybe before I die, if I ever see him. After all his grandmother did for him when my sister (his mother) died. He could not even go to see his nan in the nursing home when she was dying. I guess he had more important things to do. If he had called and said he needed money for bus fare, or could one of us pick him up it would have been taken care of.

Another year over. Two thousand and five, a year that will change my whole life, not exactly what I was expecting in my older years. It started off basically the same old crap. Work, go home and work, and then go back to work. I have to interrupt my writing to say that Prince William and Kate have had a baby boy, July 22, 2013, third in line to the British throne I remember the T.V. announcing POOR KATE? Eight pounds six ounces, POOR SAM, eight pounds, twelve ounces in 1959. "Take a big breath and deal with it," they told me!

Back to the book and life at the saloon, long way since then, Leslie is now forty-six, hard to believe. He has not had the pleasure of visiting this bar yet. He was very familiar with the Mill, and an Office bar, and mixed with lots of our friends who I might add, took a great liking to him. I am glad he takes after me. He can mix with anyone even if he really does not want to! I am sure all the years of playing in a band and travelling to different parts of the world helped with that.

I have had a few celebrities in our house. A visit from band members from the group "Spandau Ballet", Jeff, Leslie's best friend who is a super keyboard player and did gigs with big celebs. I will maybe mention Jeff later down the road, anyway George and I had fun with these lads. Went to dinner with them and had Jeff playing the piano for mum at a party we had in the house.

We are back to, "as the world turns" in the saloon. Even though it has been a long time, Alex has not forgiven me for Europe winning the Ryder Cup last year. I love it when that happens. I am an American citizen, but I am still a limey at heart, although my favourite golfer is Phil Michelson.

Ken has now switched from vodka to tequila, not sure why. I think a customer told him that tequila is much better for you, wow! It takes my breath away. Unfortunately, the bar has an off sale liquor licence which means he can take a bottle home with him, yippee, and if tequila is better for him than vodka, I guess he will be increasing his consumption.

We seem to be going through a few bartenders in the last couple of months, or so. I know I have had to train a couple, not that I am

God's gift to bartenders, but I guess I have been doing it for so long that the boss feels I will teach someone properly. The last bartender to quit was my relief. She did the dirty on me. The day shift was eight a.m. until four p.m. I always got to work at least thirty or forty minutes early as I like to take my time counting money and having a coffee. I could also take note of who was in the bar so when it was my time to get off work I had usually been there for nine hours. It was my choice to go in early, but I always expected to be relieved on time and the time to take a person off shift was supposed to be fifteen minutes to the hour.

I should be so lucky! This one particular girl I mentioned did something one does not do when working in a bar in Vegas that is open 24/7. She was swing shift; four until midnight. One afternoon I was waiting for her to come in and take me off shift. It got to four-thirty and I thought she was just late. Then it was five p.m., no phone call yet. It got to around five fifteen so I decided to call a manager. I finished up working until six, or there about, until a relief was found. This was a no call, no show, one of the worst things for one bartender to do to another. I have worked double shifts and sometimes three weeks without a day off, but I cannot do it now at my age and I have George #1 to look after.

I am not sure what happened to this girl. It seemed that no one knew where she went. I think she was married to an English guy and I think he worked in Caesar's Palace, heard she left him too. I hope the next one that is hired is a little more responsible and conscientious. It seems to me that us older ones take care of business more than some of these youngsters.

I am having fun with my customers at the moment, teaching them English words (slang ones) and the meaning after the translation in America. They are loving some of these weird expressions and sayings we have. I think the favourite with all of them is "wanker." Not very complimentary. I think the meaning loses a lot in translation, but it certainly describes a jerk, or jack off as they say in the U.S.A. Some of the other words were, knackered, (meaning worn out, or very tired), clobbered, (meaning to hit someone pretty hard) and a piece of crumpet. I will leave that one for the guys to figure out.

There are so many more words I could try to explain, but it would take me two more pages of writing. I really try to have fun when I am working. That's why people go to bars, to have a drink, and relax, but some days are very stressful in this bar, especially when some of the so called addicts come in hyped up and in wild moods, I still try to keep smiling.

Then there are the what some of my customers call working girls. Some days these girls don't make money which makes it hard on me as they are not happy campers and I dip into my tokes a few times to buy drinks, or play music on the jukebox. I know the boss does not like it when I do this, but it does help to keep people in the bar and maybe help the girls get a companion, so to speak.

57 George gave Up Work more Problems For Him

This year seems to be flying by, suddenly it's summer. I leave work on a Thursday and go home and pick George up and take him to one of our local bars where our friends who we go to Arizona with hang out. What a shame none of us really get together any more. I think although we are all friends, some of us can afford to go places and some of us can't, but we still have drinks together when we meet locally.

My sixty-seventh birthday is approaching. Nobody knows how tired I am, but I have to keep going. George is having back problems, not sure if it is something serious, I do know he is in pain. His local M.D. has referred him to a clinic that will give him shots, from what I gather three is the limit. Bloody long drive to get them, way over on the West side of town.

Surprise, surprise after two months of shots in his back and the clinic ten miles each way, shots no workee. Now, we have to go to a spine specialist. I am sure you can guess what is coming next. Back surgery, from an earlier episode.

George is terrified which is understandable, but then I told him to stop and think about the back surgery I had, it was brilliant! The only setback will be who is going to vacuum the carpet in the house? Guess I will be back doing it, no big deal. I will bend my knees.

We set up the appointment and then visit the surgeon, very nice man, that helps, a good bedside manner.

The day is here. I spend a couple of hours checking George in and he seems to be much calmer than I thought he would be. Great! The next morning is his D-Day and they will call me when he comes out of surgery. This man has had enough. I have had my share, but I think he has had more. I need to keep upbeat and make him smile whenever it is possible, or necessary. We will be together whatever comes. We have made it through twenty-nine years and some of those were very hard, especially the early ones. Now, we both need a break. We are not really getting it. Guess one has to take whatever one is dished out with.

Things could be worse. We are not living in a cardboard box in a tunnel downtown Vegas. The hospital calls me and I am on my way. The parking at this place is horrendous. It is a county hospital so that explains a lot. I think I drove around for at least fifteen minutes looking for a space to park. George was doing fine. Most of his pain was gone, only the pain from the surgery seemed obvious. I made him comfy and did not stay too long. He did not need company even me. I visited for the next three days and I guess from his attitude and demeanour he is happy he had this procedure. I am happy for him too.

I have to get back to work and I have instructed the nurses who are looking after him to please make sure I am called at work if the doctor is going to release him before my next day off. It is about six, or seven days George has been in the hospital and suddenly I have a problem it seems. One of his daughters has taken it upon herself to inform the staff at the ward where her father is, that she can sign his release and take him home. Excuse me! While I am at work and suppose to not know anything about this? I am very pissed off at the nurse in charge for allowing this to happen. It seems that the eldest one is going to pick him up in her car and the two of them, her and the younger one are suddenly in charge. I don't think so! These girls could have called me. I spoke to the nurse and let her know how upset I was that this was being allowed. These two never visit him at home, never call him when he sits all day on his own and where were they after he got home from having a stroke? Suddenly, they are in charge? Not while I am still alive. If they were doing me a favour they should have called me.

If George had a caring family that would have visited all these past years it would have been different, but they only called when they wanted help with something. One of them spent many days and weeks in our house with her boyfriend when they had no money and nowhere to go. George was always sorry that he had to put me through their problems. I did put up with it many times, for him, not for them. I really tried my best to help, I gave this girl plenty of help over the years, lots of miscellaneous stuff and left off baby clothes from my sister. I think I even gave her clothes that I paid a pretty penny for, that I purchased when I lived in England. They finished up in black garbage bags in our shed with a bunch more of her belongings, and I'm the bad guy? This was not my idea of a loving helpful family.

The youngest daughter got married and moved to the East coast, very wise move. She was the best one of the bunch. I am now getting off of work and rushing home to see what is going on. I have called my sister to meet me there for support. They were there already and I knew when I pulled into my driveway that this was going to be a fiasco.

The eldest one (no names on these two) was trying to help George out of her car and the other one made a beeline for my sister, insulting her and being very hostile. This scene was nothing new to me, that's all I had ever seen with these people. Great white sharks and grizzly bears are more friendly than this. I did not steal their father. He was eager to leave, and I happened to be the one he chose, who gave him the next thirty years of peace and a relaxing life. After a screaming match in the driveway and George getting very upset, I managed to get him away from these two and into the house.

He had told me years earlier some of the things he had to deal with. . Poor man has now had his share of stress. This is the end of it. No more George. I am going to make sure of it.

The biggest shock of all for him and me was when he went to a well-known lawyer friend of ours to get a divorce when we wanted to get married. I remember him coming home to our apartment and saying, "You better sit down." I said, "Now what?" Our friend found out from going through paper work, etc. that George was not married and had not been for the last few years. I still have the divorce papers to this day. From what I was told, his wife divorced him while he was out of the country with the military. I guess he could not contest it if he was not in the country. Anyway, I will not go any further with this subject as it could be very hurtful to my favourite step daughter. George and I could, and did, get married without a hassle!

Back to the present moment. My job is to get George comfortable and tomorrow morning I have phone calls to make to set up his physical therapy. A good thing is they come to the house. I suppose doing twenty years, or so in the military is worth something! I am now going to thank Sue for having to listen to a bad mouth and then after she got home she has two teenagers to cook for. I am going to get George and myself a nice meal. Pretty sure it will be better than hospital food. I have some homemade menudo in the fridge that I did for him to eat when he came home. It took me months of practice making menudo to perfect it how George liked it. I wondered how a person could eat that stuff, but after getting it about right, I added pig's feet to the tripe and oregano from the garden, good chili powder from New Mexico, garlic, must not forget the garlic, and after cooking the pig's feet separately from the tripe for about one and a half hours, I would put the two together until both of these ingredients were well cooked.

George said I made better menudo than some Mexicans he knew. Great compliment for me and I found I enjoyed a bowl with the hominy added. I also made good green chili with pork. George's mother taught me that one. I have never really mastered tortillas. Made good tamales (pain in the ass they are), but I figured tortillas are so cheap to buy in the store why bother?

I have been in touch with the therapy people. They are going to come on my days off which means I don't have to worry about getting someone in to deal with this. The pain George had before surgery has basically gone and he was soooo happy, me too, for him. I remember what that pain was like. Anyone who is very scared of back surgery take note! Obviously what type of surgery and the surgeon, makes a difference, guess George and I got very lucky with both sides of the coin.

The two physical therapists who take turns coming to the house are very professional and the exercises George has to do are really helping him. Our pool had been a godsend to him as well. Walking up and down in the warm water has helped his Parkinson's and his back. It took me a while to convince him to do that, but I think he now enjoys it, and putting the handrail on the deck was a great idea. He feels much safer getting in and out of the water.

Number sixty-seven for me has gone and now George is on his way to seventy-five. Getting the dog was one of the best things we did. He is so good for George company wise. I think it has stopped him from getting depressed. His son Charlie, has been to the house a few times and taken care of George's feet. They are awful and need a lot of attention. The diabetes is taking a hold now.

I'm glad one of his kids is here for him. That has cheered him up immensely. What a sad thing when a man has busted his balls all of his life and when it is time to relax and enjoy ones final years he is dished out with all these debilitating problems. He is like me. He does not harp on it, gets on with whatever comes. I could not have found a better man, or husband, even though I am also in love with a man who is five thousand miles away for the last forty-three years George has to come first and I do love the man, just in a different way. I keep in touch with Dave on the computer. It is some sort of solace for me in the midst of everything going on here.

58   George 75

George's seventy-fifth birthday and we are going to dinner at our local casino near the house. The small gourmet room that we loved has been closed for a long time now, so we go to another restaurant there that serves oysters on the half shell, one of George's favourite things. I am not as impressed with this place as I was with the gourmet room, but the oysters are definitely a draw to come here.

I remember a few years back, Leslie was here, and a couple of friends from England were also visiting. We all went to this restaurant that George and I are in now and I seem to remember we all ate oysters, but Les and George ate more than any of us and George ate more than Les. I believe he finished up eating three dozen. Nancy and Ben were flabbergasted, no surprise to me!

I am sure that was during my gambling days and I had a comp for our meal. Those comps were great, but with the money I spent we could have all flown to Hawaii for dinner. Those days are long gone now, bloody good job!

After dinner we went to a local bar not far from home. This is a place we have spent many an hour in and I spent many a dollar playing poker. The manager Randy works behind the bar weekends, nicest man one could meet and he has worked here for a very long time. George loves this little place and a lot of our old friends still come in. A lovely meal and a few drinks later in the bar, we are going home. I have to deal with getting George in and out of the car and getting his walker in and out of the back and making sure he is secure. He is a good size guy and I have already dealt with picking him up once when he fell in the bedroom, nearly killed me! I had a few years of lifting mum up in the bath-tub, the old back is hanging in there glad to say.

Thanksgiving is upon us again, it is true! The older one gets the quicker time goes. The family will be here which I always look forward to. Not sure if turkey will be the meat (or fowl) of choice and I know whatever I cook everybody loves it. I am going to cook roast potatoes for the bar. I am sure they have enough meat so spuds will be welcomed. My life is full. I do not have time to get bored like some of these people who come in the bar. It is what one makes it and one has to answer for one's own decisions! I do cook a turkey after all.

I suppose over the years I made mistakes, but I cannot go back and rectify them. I just have to try not to make any more. George made a big decision this year for Thanksgiving. He is not going to visit the family. I know it took a lot for him to decide that, but he has just got over back surgery and a stroke a few months ago, he needs to relax, not deal with people arguing which seems inevitable when he goes there. That must have been a hard decision for him to make. I am so happy he is not going, but this is a temporary thing. I am sure he will want to make an appearance over Christmas and New Year, after all, it is his family!

Our weather at this time of year is fabulous, much cooled down from the summer's 105's, or more. This is time for boots and lightweight sweaters, great for us gals who feel that we look better in winter clothes, some of us do for sure, I am one of them. Even with exercise the arms need lots of work and belly fat has not quite made and obvious appearance. Don't worry my girlfriends, it will show up. At least most women don't get a beer belly that can be really ugly!

The worst thing for me in the winter is raking the leaves on the lawn. We have a giant tree at the pool end which sheds every single leaf and the pool gets a huge share. Lifting wet leaves with a net is a very hard and tiring dirty job, but somebody has to do it. George helps me by getting trash bags ready and tying them when they are full.

He finds it hard to move them anymore as he cannot walk well without the help of his walker so I have to drag the bags to the curb which is about 50 feet in front of the house, the smoking gets to me to now. One day I am going to stop. I cannot do it at the moment. It is keeping me calm and anybody who smokes knows how hard it is to give it up.

George and I have decided this year we will have a nice big New Year's Eve dinner. It falls on a Saturday and most of our friends do not stay up too late on New Year's Eve anymore. Our days of midnight celebrations and drinking until two a.m. are coming to an end. A nice dinner with wine and a few cocktails with good friends is the way to go now. I have it planned and I am going out on a limb! There will be 16 of us including me and George. I think the menu is going to be escargot for a starter, then a roast prime rib with lots of veggies and not sure about dessert yet. I want something easy after cooking a large amount for sixteen of us.

Christmas is over with and I am off to the commissary at the air force base to pick up the food for our new year's dinner. Some will think I am crazy cooking for sixteen people, but I love it. I also, have to find a nice gift for my friend Emily whose birthday is on January 1st. She will be celebrating her sixtieth and I am sure we will all help her do it on Saturday night the 31st!

I take the groceries home, check on my two George's, unpack the shopping, have a quick cuppa then go out to find a birthday present for Emily. I went to a local mall and found something in a hurry. A very nice plain snake like necklace, gold tone, classy looking. I know she will like this, I would.

59 Worst New Year's Eve Of My Life

I have my three days to work before the holiday weekend and George has told me that his youngest daughter and her husband and son are coming in from the East coast for a new years' celebration. Not sure how long they will be here, but I know I will get to see them. I think I did mention earlier that Sheila is my favourite out of this family.

Friday the 30th of December, George's family, the other two daughters and Sheila's son and hubby are taking him to dinner. I declined to go because I have a lot of food preparation for tomorrow to take care of, but I know it will be easier for him if I am not there. Who needs to eat dinner and not be able to relax? I am not a relaxing person, never have been, and that would really make me uptight.

I spent Friday keeping myself busy cleaning the house and did what washing we had. That way I would be free of all of that stuff for the weekend. The girls and company came to the house on Saturday to pick their father up about six thirty p.m. It was great to see Sheila and Ross, (her hubby) and son, Wayne. It had been a long while.

George mentioned, "Did you see ---"? he was referring to the middle daughter, (I will not give her a name). I replied, "Yes, I did," and I believe I said, "Hello" that's all I could muster. That girl never treated me with much respect after all the help I gave her and I have nothing more to say to her.

I know for a daughter she could have made her dad's life alot easier. Always asking for help of some kind. He was such a giving man. What could he do? It was his child!

Off they all went to an outback I think, that was one of our local restaurants, had an Australian theme to it, good food and draft beer.

I began to get the vegetables cleaned and peeled for tomorrow. It will save me rushing in the morning. I also made the butter for the escargots, do not have enough snail dishes for the snails, nor tongs and forks so I am going to put six each in small dishes with forks on a larger plate with garlic bread. I have seasoned the meat, it looks wonderful.

George finally comes home about 10 p.m. They drop him off without coming in. He tells me everything was cool and it was quite pleasant, What a nice change. We both sit for an hour and have a vodka and tonic together. Then I help him into the bedroom. While he was out I changed his sheets.

The time is now close to midnight and I have tons to do tomorrow so I get George into bed and ask him if he is okay and comfortable. Everything is fine, now I will go to bed. He is much better sleeping on his own and actually so am I. He wakes up during the night and puts the TV on, working graveyard for years did this I guess. I get into my bed and settle down. About an hour later, I hear George calling me. I get up and go into his room and he is very perturbed. We got him to bed without his diaper on and he has peed on his clean sheets.

I totally forgot the underwear and George never reminded me. I pretended to be upset, but then I told him it was okay and made a joke of it and made him laugh. I got him out of bed and washed him, and then I took off the sheets and got another set. Unfortunately, the mattress protector was also wet so I took that off and told him, "I will take care of that in the morning. You now have your panties on so you are safe." I kissed him goodnight and make sure he was comfortable then I went back to bed.

I remember waking up about five a.m. and seeing the light on in George's room. I figured he was watching the T.V. so I went back to sleep for an hour, or so.

I did not know that when I kissed him goodnight around one a.m. that it would be the last time I would see him alive.

This page is the hardest I have had to write, and I need a quiet room, no TV, nothing to make my mind avoid of what I have to remember.

It is seven a.m., Saturday the 31st of December 2005, New Year's eve. I noticed on my way to the kitchen that the light was still on in George's room. I opened the door very slowly so as not to wake him and I reached in and turned off the light. He looked very comfortable, lying on his back with one leg hanging over the side of the bed.

I shut the door and make my way to the kitchen for my morning tea and cookie. To sit on my own with my tea and the dog outside at our bar is so relaxing. No one to bother me and half an hour of not doing a thing, Heavenly!

Well, heaven for thirty minutes is over. Time to organise things for tonight's dinner, but wait a moment, it is only about seven thirty, the pool water is still nice, warm enough for me even in December, think I will have a swim. I know George will be in with me, hard to keep him out. Labs really are water dogs. Water is about 75 degrees, beautiful.

Now I will start on the stuff I need to do. I think I may blanch a few vegetables, that way it will be quicker with the cooking later. The large banquet table that we have will be perfect for all these people. I am going to put it in our living room.

We have plenty of fold-up chairs that we have had for years for the parties we have held so seating is no problem. The only thing that is bothering me is the fact that I have to get all this stuff from the shed and the table is very heavy. I think I will call Mark, him and his wife are friends of ours and they are coming tonight for dinner. (Mark, another good friend gone)

I give him a call and he will be here later to help me with the table. I can drag it so far, but it's about six feet long and to get it from the shed to the house would be too much for me. I do give in occasionally when I know I am beaten.

Luckily, I have a fridge outside on the patio and when I don't have room left in the one in the kitchen I can take prepared things and put them outside. I put 6 Escargot each in 16 small dishes, (I have 16 small dishes, got lucky there) and cover them with the butter I prepared. These can be put in the outside fridge. I decided to cook the vegetables and then I can transfer them to dishes that I can put in the microwave. The potatoes have to be par-boiled before I roast them. The meat will be last, as it won't take long.

Most of us like medium rare so when its time I will start cooking it on high heat. Maybe twenty minutes to brown and then I turn it down for about one and a half hours. I check the clock and I think I will call Mark to come and help me with the table and chairs. I go and unlock the shed and take out the chairs. They need washing off and drying. The hose does a good job and after I get them done, I put them on the lawn in the sun.

Now, I only need help carrying the table into the house. Mark shows up and we get the job done. George is still sleeping so I will get the table set with cutlery and napkins and three sets of salt and pepper one each end, and one in the middle. I will bring the chairs in after I dry them off. I have a nice table cloth that I have put on and the whole thing looks very nice. I also have a little greenery on the table which finishes it off perfectly.

Next thing I have to do, (glad I remembered), is to put the wine and champagne in the fridge outside and still have a space for a few beers.

Now, I think I will go and wake George up and get him showered etc., and clean up the bed. I went into the bathroom that has an adjoining door into his room so that I would not wake him in a hurry. I opened the middle door and looked in. I knew straight away that my husband was DEAD.

I froze in the doorway. He was still laying in the same position as he was at seven a.m. I could not move. I just stood and stared at him, then I got hysterical. I ran to the phone and called my sister at work, crying and screaming. She told me to dial 911 and she would be here as soon as she could.

I dialed 911. The operator told me to go and see if I could lift his arm and then come back and tell her. I went back into the bedroom and tried to lift his right arm. It was not easy to do, not only was I sobbing, but his arm was getting stiff. I went back on the phone and relayed what I felt to the operator. She told me that the paramedics and police would be on the way.

It seemed like an eternity before Sue came and the paramedics showed up just after. My sis was my saviour at this time. Still is. She took my phone book and started calling people. The first one was Mark, who had only left an hour or so ago, then all of our friends who were supposed to come to dinner. I was in a daze, still not believing this.

I am not sure how long it was before the house started filling up with people. First the police department, then some of our friends as well as dinner guests, unbelievable. I am doing a lot of crying at the moment. Sue is still calling more friends and George's family. Then she called Les. I could not speak to him right now and it might be a while before I compose myself.

The coroner was the next person I saw come in. He introduced himself and then we had a private conversation at the back of the dining room. I had to give him all the medication that George had been taking and he checked everything out. He was the nicest man. He said that he was pretty sure that George had suffered a heart attack and passed away instantly. He also said that he thought that he had died where he wanted to be, I really believed that as well. George you did not finish up in a wheelchair being fed my love!!!

By this time many more of our friends had shown up and one or two more that were not coming to dinner that evening. I was not the only one crying this day. I finally straightened myself up and dealt with whatever was needed at this moment.

It was about three hours before they took George out of the house. My sis and I and a couple of friends went to the coroner's car and before they took him we all laid our hands on the cover he was in. Nearly 30 years with this man, hard saying goodbye.

We went back into the house and my sister, bless her, is still manning the phone. All of the friends who were coming to dinner have decided they would like to stay. I think the time alluded me, it is more than six hours since I found George, hard to believe.

Two of the guys, here for dinner, have taken over the kitchen. They are cooking the beef for me and I take charge of the veggies and starter. It is really fantastic that we are all going to sit down to dinner and eat and drink as though George were still here. Finally about eight p.m. we are all sitting and the first thing we do is drink a toast to my husband. It is fantastic that our friends decided to do this. It helped me get through this day much easier. Thank you all, I love you.

60   Saying Goodbye To My Husband

My next overwhelming task is going to be George's funeral. He has a plot at the Veteran's Cemetery, we did take care of that. He told me he wanted to be cremated, (He did not want the worms eating him).

I think one has to be cremated to be buried in the Vet's cemetery. I want to have a service for him so that all his friends and family can say goodbye. George did not want a fussy funeral or an open casket, or a viewing. He told me plenty of times that he did not want anyone to see him dead in a coffin. I was honouring his wishes until his eldest daughter pleaded with me to let the family view him and say their goodbyes. I thought the decent thing to do was to let them have a private viewing, after all it was their father.

Les called me and asked if he should come to the funeral. I told him no. It is a long journey and expensive for a few days. He can come later maybe when I am not so miserable and I have had time to get over this. My sister and I went to the mortuary and I planned for the service a week later. I am going to play two tapes of songs that I like. One is my son singing the John Lennon song, "Love" and the other was Josh Groban singing, "A Breath Away." The air force will be presenting me with the flag. Not looking forward to that part.

Sue has stayed with me for a couple of days after George died and now we have all the arrangements made she is going back home. I am so happy I have the dog. He kept me calm.

Friday is here and as I drive up the long driveway to the chapel at the mortuary, I am really trying very hard not to cry. I know it will come eventually, but I want to get inside and speak to friends first. As I get out of the car, Sue and the kids pull up. I am very glad to be going in with my family.

I cannot believe how many people are coming in, some I have not seen in a long time.

George's ex-wife and kids show up and I direct them to where they can see their dad. I then go into the chapel and Sue follows me to the front with Peter and Melissa. George's daughter I love is going to sit with us and her son and hubby. On the end we have two very close friends Aron and her husband Ronny.

The place is filling up with long-time friends and people George knew. There are about one hundred in here already.

Next thing that I am having to deal with is George's loud daughter, yelling "Where is my mother going to sit?" I think, in a very controlled voice, I put her in her place. "Your mother can sit anywhere she wants to and don't start with your crap!" They sat in the second row behind me and that was the last I heard during the whole service. I remember one year when his ex wife got very sick, I sent George to her house with flowers from my garden, and pate that I made, he did not want to go but I made a point of telling him, that is your children's mother. Her and I got along much easier after that, she actually called and thanked me. Guess the loud one never knew that story!

I was surprised how many friends got up and said a few words. Then it was my turn. Not sure how I got through that little speech. I made a couple of jokes and kept it light that was the answer. Then we got to the flag ceremony and the trumpet player. That did it for me. I had been so brave until then.

I had let everyone know that we would be having a wake at one of the Office bars and I would like it very much if everyone could attend. A couple of my friends helped me to take some of the flowers back to the bar. They were beautiful arrangements and could not just leave all of them at the mortuary.

The bar was packed and just inside the door there was an easel set up with pictures on it. Our friends (mine and George's) had really gone out of their way to make this a memorable day.

The first thing I did after getting the flowers in place was to talk to George's ex-wife. I told her I was going to keep the flag and I offered her a brass statue of the Virgin Mary that The funeral home had given to me, she took it. I later down the road, gave the flag to my favourite daughter's son.

I asked her if I could get her something to eat from the buffet that the bar had put on for me. She declined telling me her eldest daughter would get her something. I just had to deal with this very chilly atmosphere from her and her kids, except for the youngest two. I even seemed to get the cold shoulder from George's brother's wife. I don't think I can explain how these people are.

George's brother was great. I always got along with him. His kids always seemed friendly towards me. I can't deal with any of them today. My husband has died. I do not need negative unfriendly people! I guess I am the bitch who broke up the family. It certainly did not need help from me, that's for sure!!

The Office, aka Mill and our bar, put on a beautiful buffet for me and would not accept payment of any kind. I did manage to buy the house a few drinks and take care of the bartenders. That was important to me. They worked very hard and it was not a small gathering. After going around the room and saying, "hello" and thanking people for coming, crying and hugging friends, it's time for me to plant my bum down and have a strong cocktail. I really could use one.

This has been a long, very hard, sad day. When one has been with a person for nearly thirty years it takes a lot to comprehend that he, or she has gone forever. A few of my workmates showed up which made me feel good, so I sat with them for a while and downed a couple of shots of George's favourite tequila.

Finally, time for me to go home. I have a dog to worry about and he has been left long enough. I would imagine that it is going to be strange for him too, without George.

The weather is getting very cool now which means dog and I will not be going in the pool much longer. Well he might I'm sure. Do dogs worry about cold water? I wouldn't think so, George certainly doesn't seem to. The next morning was very strange. Just me and the dog. No bed to check, no meds to sort out and next when I feel up to it, all of George's clothes, etc.

I am going to take his shirts and tees to work with me. I know there are some of my customers who would be very grateful for them. I am then going to send everything else to big brothers and big sisters of Nevada. They do love donations and they pick them up.

I have to also deal with the bed. I am going to throw the mattress away and give the bed to a friend. Not easy taking care of all this. I have to stop myself from getting a little down and depressed. Makes one think too much.

Next morning the dog has to go in the garden, so I let him out and then get my tea and a couple of cookies. I stopped saying biscuits years ago, (petrol too), and join him on the patio. It's January and he is in the pool, old towels needed asap, crazy dog! But beautiful!

I have to be back at work in two days. I have been off for two weeks now without pay of course so I have to get the bills paid. George had some life insurance that will keep me going for a while and his social security cheque which is only $680.00, has gone into our account, but alas, social security has informed me that because he died on a holiday, or as they put it, a weekend of the 31st of December and the cheque went in early they would be taking it back. Great! I have sent at least seven cheques off and this means they will bounce. We do not have much spare money in the bank and George's air force retirement comes to the house in his name. I cannot touch that so I have seven cheques at twenty-three dollars per cheque penalty and still have the bills to pay on top of the bank charges, Oh Lord!

Now, I have two weeks, or more without a pay cheque and about a thousand to come up with for bills and bank charges. The mortgage is also due six hundred dollars, or more. What do I do? Pray and figure it out. I am going to my boss to see if I can borrow enough to cover my expenses until George's insurance comes through. I have about four thousand to pay the funeral home. I know they will wait, that helps.

My boss lends me enough to cover the most pressing bills. Great to work for people like that, but they have known me for over twenty years and they know I am honourable. As soon as the insurance comes in, I will be able to cover everything.

61 No Air Force Pension

I have another big shock coming very shortly. I have to go to the air force base to renew my I.D. card and fill out some paperwork. After renewing my I.D. card, I had to have a conversation with, I believe a colonel. He informed me very gently that my husband had not, I said NOT, signed the paperwork when we were first married for me to receive his retirement if he passed away before me. It also would have been $40 or $50 a month taken from his pension which was not taken care of and from what I understood he could of done this within the first year. I think that was the time limit given.

How wonderful! After nearly thirty years with this man, I am obviously not going to be taken care of.

The very nice colonel told me that if I would like to move to Florida, I could live in the widow's villages in Destin, or close to there I believe. "George, why did you do this to me"? I am sure it was not intentional, (You really were a procrastinator) and I know how much you loved me, you told me every chance you got. Guess I have to forgive you and get on with my life and keep working.

I thought very seriously about moving to Florida. I could live in the air force widow's villages and cheaper than I can in Nevada. Also, it is near those beautiful white beaches and a big air force base which is good for me as far as medical help and commissary for groceries. I got all the paperwork together and filled out the necessary forms and had them signed. All I have to do is send them off. There is a fly in the ointment, my sister Sue does not want me to go. She tells me I am too old at nearly seventy to go and start anew somewhere else.

She finally convinced me and all this took place after I decided to sell the house. A very hard decision, but I think the upkeep with repairs and all the landscaping and pool I took care of, had to be given up. I was taking care of most of it myself and to have it done by a professional company would cost me a fortune every month.

I have climbed the palm trees on the lawn with a chainsaw that weighed about ten pounds or more, and I have mowed the lawn all two thousand square feet of it. I have vacuumed and backwashed the pool, planted, weeded and done more gardening back and front that I want to think about. I have shovelled rock in the back to cover dirt and I finally had to get help on that one.

I have climbed onto the roof to blow leaves off and clean out the gutters, (I hate heights) so I think I have done enough and this is one big reason I am going to sell this property. It will be a very sad day for me, I love this place! I am going to really miss my pool and my privacy and the only thing I have to do is find a place that takes large dogs.

I have already seen an apartment that is very nice and I will be able to take George, but I found out it is over nine hundred dollars a month and that is without utilities so I am thinking eleven hundred dollars, cannot do that and I am not putting my dog down so I have to keep looking.

62   Selling My Little Piece Of Heaven

My house is up for sale, never thought I would have to give up this place. It's like a sanctuary to me. I can hide here and have total peace. "George, what did you not do for me babe? And why? There are suddenly plenty of potential buyers for this place. Why wouldn't there be? It is beautiful.

I spent some of George's insurance and made a few upgrades. I put a new stove top and double ovens, always wanted new ones. Guess I won't get the benefit from them. Added new curtains in the kitchen, white sheers that tie in the middle and a nice valance, or pelmet as we say in England, in a heavier material. It looks great. What a shame I have to make it look more attractive and I won't be living in it.

The next thing I did was to replace the glass tiles on the side walls in the kitchen, and one whole wall inside the front door. The glass was very attractive and it brought in more light. I found a company that would put glass sheets instead of tiles. It looked super when they finished, not cheap there either.

One last thing was to take up the old indoor/outdoor carpet on the patio. Amazing! Underneath the carpet were red bricks. I am thinking I will leave it like this and get the bricks sprayed with a brick red paint and a matte finish. It should look really super. A couple of friends from the bar I work at have offered to help me for a reasonable price so that will be the next project.

In the meantime I am still looking for a place to live. An idea has come to me if I make enough on the sale of the house I may think about buying a mobile home in a senior park. I have to pay off the mortgage first as we still owe quite a bit after we refinanced There is a park close by. I think I will take a gander (look around it). Sue comes with me to check out a couple of homes in this nice park. I will have to pay rent for the space, but I think it will be much cheaper than eleven hundred dollars a month and I will own the home, that means my dog will be safe. We looked at three, or four and I found one that had been empty and up for sale for a while, now I have to get mine sold so that I can make an offer on it.

All the improvements I wanted to do have been taken care of. The patio looks super with the bricks sprayed. A friend made the bar a little bigger by putting a new top on it and now I have to get a good real estate agent.

After a few showings with two or three companies I found Alexia. She was very good at her job and seemed to be bringing more and more potential buyers. The garden was looking lovely at this time of year, around March. My spring bulbs were in bloom, daffodils, hyacinth and my all-time favourite, freesias. These flowers, especially the hyacinth and freesias, smell really gorgeous. When the back gate was opened and one would walk in the garden, patio and pool were breathtaking and owning this lot is going to help with the sale.

George has been gone for over a year now and I have had offers from friends to move in with me and help with the bills. Ray being one of them. Maybe I am crazy, but I would rather sell this place than have roommates. My mother was living with us for about twenty-three years. George and I also had his kids for a while, then Patrick for ten years, so I think I would like to be on my own. Maybe that sounds a bit selfish, so what! I think I have earned some time for me!

There have been a few couples that really want the place, but they are having trouble getting financed.

I have had one nice month at least lately. I went back to England for Christmas and New Year, 2006 and had a wonderful time. Les came down to Dave's and we had Christmas dinner in the pub after it closed late afternoon, with six friends from the little village where Dave lives.

Had a great New Year's Eve with people I had met in the pub years ago. I took a bottle of tequila with me from Vegas and at midnight I had a shot for my husband, he loved his tequila. A couple of the kids behind the bar then joined me even though they had never drank tequila, or met George. Dave was really happy I educated his bartenders, my tequila was gone by the next morning

I had a girlfriend stay in my house and look after the dog for me. She was very happy to do it as she took her small dog with her and I gave her two hundred dollars. It helped me out and it helped her as she was not working. I was a little upset when I got back because I had asked her to empty the leaves from the pool basket and she forgot to do it, which meant I had tons of work to do on the pool when I got home. I guess some people don't look after another person's property as though it were their own. Anyway, it was all in a day's work for me and I soon had everything ship shape.

Now, three months have gone by and I am in the middle of a stressful period trying to sell the house. My agent has suddenly found a couple that are really serious about buying and after meeting them I am feeling very positive. They put in an offer and after discussing it with Alexia I accepted it. It will be enough to pay off the mortgage that we had to refinance when George had to give up work, and there will be enough for me to buy a mobile home in the park down the street, also I will be able to buy new furniture after twenty-five years.

I have neighbours and friends that want to buy my present furniture which is in very good condition so now I am also going to arrange a yard sale. It will be a huge yard sale. I have tons of stuff to get rid of, but first I have to put money down on the other home I have looked at.

63 A Clever Thief Gets Me, Twice

There are a couple of things I have to talk about with the estate agent for the new place before I make a commitment. I go and take one more look at the new place and sis comes with me. One thing I need is a fridge in the kitchen so I talk to the other agent who is selling the place and discover that she owns it, I then tell her that I think the price can be lowered as I need to buy a fridge and there are a couple of other things needing attention, she agrees and so we have a deal. I also think I will feel safer in a gated park that one has to have a clicker to enter.

The reason for mentioning the gated park is, because about six weeks after George died, someone I had known for over ten years and worked with behind a bar, even teaching him how to bartend, knocked on my door one Sunday morning and said he needed a favour. Boy, did I finish up doing him a favour! I invited him in and said, "Nice to see you. (no names on this one). How are you?" He then told me that he was going through a divorce and that he could not get any of his clothes from his house, as his wife had thrown him out.

Naturally, I sat and listened to his story and felt very bad for him. He said how sorry he was to hear that George had died. We all knew each other for a long time. I poured us a drink and told him he could wear George's robe and I would wash his clothes for him. he was a young good looking guy about George's size, so getting into a couple of tee-shirts and the robe was no problem.

We sat around talking and he said, "I did some concrete work for Diane and she wrote me a cheque." She was someone I had also known for many years. He could not get to the bank to cash the check until Monday so I told him he could sleep on my couch for the night, as he had nowhere to go and no money.

We then got into a conversation about my driveway. The concrete under the carport was in need of repair and he said he would take a look at it for me. That is something he used to do for a living, slabs, block walls, etc., etc. I had been given an estimate from a couple of guys who came in the bar that did that sort of work. They told me over two thousand.

We went out to the driveway and he had a look at the part of the concrete that was crumbling away. He said, "Let me use the phone in the morning and I think I can get that done for half of the price you have been given." "That would be great," I said. I need every penny I can save.

I then told him about how George never signed me up for his air force retirement. He was another one who could not believe it. After this conversation, I then started my CHARITY work!!! We went in the house and I gave him money to go and buy cigarettes for both of us, also enough to get us some take away dinner of some kind. We decided on Chinese. I told him to take the spare key from the small rack on the wall and take my SUV. Off he went.

He came back about an hour later with very nice food and two packs of cigarettes.

We had dinner, watched TV and then I made up the pull out bed in the living room for him. Monday morning he made a couple of calls while I made coffee and toast, (and I realise now that he really did not make the calls, it was all a pretence) and I was really taken in.

He acted as though he was talking to a concrete company that I guess he had worked for in the past and got a quote on whatever he needed to do the driveway.

When he put the phone down he said, "guess what Sam"?, I can get that done for you for about Thirteen hundred dollars." "Wow, that's wonderful!" I said. "Okay, can you set it up for me then?" "Sure,". "I will call the company back and we will take care of it for you. I will need a deposit before they will deliver the cement and I am going to the bank now to cash this cheque I have from Diane, so if you want to write me a cheque for about four hundred dollars we will get this job started."

I wrote a cheque and gave it to him and told him to take the car. When he got back I said, ", you can stay here for a few days if you want until my driveway is done and then I will pay you for doing it and you will be able to deal with your problems much better."

He was very happy about that. I did notice that he kept sniffing and I thought he had a cold, so I gave him a box of Kleenex that I had in the bedroom.!. Yeah! If I would have known. It is not more than three days that I find out what this so-called-friend has in store for me.

I have to go to work the next morning Tuesday, so he is staying in the house, which is fine. He tells me when I get home that the cement is supposed to be delivered on Wednesday. I am at work on Wednesday and he calls to tell me that he does not feel well and he has cancelled the delivery of the cement until Thursday. I tell him that's fine, not to worry, just feel better.

I get home and cook us some dinner and I am very sympathetic to the fact that he does not feel good.

The next morning Thursday, I leave for work and just after lunchtime about twelve thirty p.m. he shows up where I work and tells me the driveway has been taken care of. "Great", I said. He tells me not to drive on that side for a couple of days at least.

Now, I go to my purse in the back room and write a cheque for nine hundred dollars which I cash at the bar so that I can give him the rest of the money. I then put him a small pizza in the machine that we have behind the bar and pay for it.

He thanks me and says that he has to get cigarettes from the machine before he leaves. The machine takes change so I told him I would give him quarters, but he tells me he has plenty. If I had a brain I would have wondered where did he get all the quarters? I will let you know shortly. He eats a couple slices of pizza, gets his cigarettes and maybe about an hour later, says he has to get going. I shake his hand and say, "Thanks babe for helping me out. I finish my shift and I sit down at four fifteen p.m. to have an after-shift drink. I stay maybe for half an hour and get up and leave.

When I get out to the parking lot my car is nowhere to be seen, gone! I stand for a few minutes horrified. This is not possible. I do not put two and two together, that comes later.

I go back into the bar and burst into tears. What more bad things are going to be coming my way? I call my sister and she tells me she is on her way to come and get me. My dear husband has only been gone a couple of months and now this. Sue shows up and she drives me home. It is now, as we pull into the carport, very obvious what I have been the object of. A huge scam and lies all of which I believed. The driveway was not cemented and when we went into the house, my spare car key was gone off of the rack and my change jar that I had been saving was empty in the bedroom. I was in shock, big time!

I just could not believe that a person I thought a friend would have done this to me. I had called the police from the bar before I left so I am expecting them at the house.

I had previously met some of his family who came from the East coast somewhere. I called his father and told him what was going on. He said, "Sam, I am so sorry, didn't you know?" We think he is on drugs and we think he has stolen some of his mother's jewellery and taken some of her cheques and forged her signature. I am still finding this just bloody unbelievable!

The police finally show up about four hours later. He had left town by now, (I know). I give them all the particulars and his name and they inform me that they already have his name. I believe there were warrants, or a warrant. Then one of the detectives tells me that if I did not see him drive off in my car I may not be able to prove it was him. This was even more unbelievable to me. He has just done me out of thirteen hundred dollars or more, and my spare car key is missing. What more would point to him being guilty?

One lucky thing,(if I can say lucky), I do not have to work in the morning so I can deal with my insurance and get a rental car. I hope one day I can get this story published and I will buy him a copy if I can find him, and tell him that my husband had an expression for people like him. It was, "LOWER THAN WHALE SHIT," in fact, you are even lower than that!

The next episode of this saga told me that I do NOT have a brain, or my actions make it seem that I don't have one. Maybe deep down I didn't want anybody to go to jail. Let me explain this and after I have, I will get this stressful period over with.

I suddenly remember a funny thing that happened in the Bahamas and I will definitely go back to that a bit later.

About three weeks after slime ball stole my car, a good friend of his that I had met a long time ago, came into the bar one morning while I was working and after listening to me rant and rave he said, He knew where my car was.

According to him he thought he knew that three guys had it and he said he thought he could get it back for me. If I could come up with a hundred dollars.

Like I said, my brain just did not put two and two together (again!!) He said, "He could probably get the car and bring it to my house about eleven p.m. that night." Did I stop and wonder how? No! This was definitely one of my blonde periods!

I just told him I would have a hundred for him when I got my car. What I should have done was to call the police and let them sit and wait for him. That would have been the best thing to do, but as I mentioned I was not thinking straight and I wanted so much to have my car back. I have kicked myself every day since I went along with this deal.

Anyway, he showed up about eleven thirty p.m. in my SUV and I gave him the money. He took off walking up the dark street and I watched until he was out of sight. I never wondered until an hour, or so later how did he drive the car here? how stupid and naïve or gullible am i? He is in cahoots with his friend of many years.

The next morning I go out and inspect my car. My CDs are gone and new clothes that needed alterations were gone, also my gloves and a blanket from the back of the car. The passenger seat adjuster was broken off which means the seat cannot be put up or back, but I have "Bessie" (my name I call my car) back.

I find mail in the glove box for an address in Arizona. I took it to a local police sub-station. Never heard a word on that.

Then the icing on the cake. About three weeks have passed after getting Bessie back, and as I drove into my driveway after getting home from work one night, a neighbour stopped me as I got out of the car. she said, "Sam are you having any work done in the back?" "No" I said, "Why?" She then tells me that she saw a man come out of my front gate with a skill saw in one hand and a black box in the other. I don't think I even let her finish telling me before I said, "Oh no!" I just knew before I ran round the back, through the gate to the shed. The shed door which had been padlocked was really beaten up, lock gone, door bashed in and as I stood and stared, I then saw the cooler just inside the door with the lid up and half full of tools.

Looks as though the "low life" who was stealing here was interrupted. I am guessing the kid I had taking care of the pool probably showed up as this person was filling up the cooler, and he had to stop and leave in a hurry, but he still got away with some good stuff and it included a power screwdriver and a drill that I had gotten for George as a birthday gift a couple of years previously.

I cannot say how stressed I was. I went into the house, took care of my dog and called the police. I found a photo that I wanted my neighbour to look at, so I walked over there and asked her if this looked like the person she saw coming out of my yard. She said, "Yes, that was him." I knew it, slimeball again! The police showed up and went to look at the shed. I could not believe that they never took fingerprints, just looked around for a few minutes. I told them I had shown my neighbour a picture of a person I thought might have done it.

They informed me that I shouldn't have done that, as now I have put the idea in her head that it was the person in the photo. It should have been left to them. I lose again! So fix the shed girl and get on with life once more. Screwed without being kissed, and to think I could have put TWO slime balls in jail!

64   Funny Past Episodes

Now, I am going back to the episode I thought about that happened in the Bahamas, it seems very amusing now I think about it, but it could have turned out the opposite way. Jamie, my girlfriend, and I were in in the old pub as we called it, one night playing darts which I might add we were good at. We had played one, or two games of "301" when Dave came in with a couple of the dealers who were friends of ours. After an hour, or so Dave and company decide they want to challenge me and Jamie to a couple of games of "501", that's four players instead of two so we accept and we are all drinking and having fun. This goes on for five or six games and I think my partner and I kicked ass! Dave had had a few beers and as like most men, he does not take too kindly to be beaten by women. He becomes a little offish with me and in so many words, tells me to bleep off.

I decide I will, but I do not have a car tonight, I got a lift here with Jamie.

I leave the pub and walk past Dave's car in the parking lot. He had a Plymouth Barracuda. Most of the cars on the island came across from Florida, there were no auto dealers on the island if I remember correctly. The car that Dave had we thought was one of a kind on this island, WRONG! I started walking down the closest street from the pub, a long straight very dark road, rather creepy because there was hardly any lighting.

After I had been going for about ten minutes, a car pulled up on the other side of the road, a Plymouth fast-back Barracuda no less. I was so happy that David had come to pick me up, but I was not going to be nice to him after his tantrum in the pub.

I strolled across and opened the passenger door and the first thing I noticed was a small green plant in a pot on the floor. I had to step over it to sit in the seat which is what I did. David was not a plant guy! I folded my arms and just sat without looking to one side or speaking.

Suddenly, a voice said, "Excuse me. Where would you like to go?"

I was as close to pooping my pants as I had ever been, then and since. I looked across at the driver and realised I was in a total stranger's car. It happened that it was the same model as Dave's, that's why I got in without hesitation and it was very dark. I did wonder where the plant came from, should have known, Dave is still not a plant person.

The man whose car I was in sat and stared at me. He was slim with glasses, not very attractive, maybe in his late thirties, early forties. I told him, very nervously, "Please drop me off at the end of this road." I thank my lucky-stars that is what he did. It could have been a very different outcome and if it had been I would not have been writing this story.

Luckily, I got home before Dave came looking for me. When he did get home, he called me all the stupid blah, blah, blahs ever. He was right. I don't know what had possessed me, that word pride again I guess.

While I am reminiscing I thought of another episode that I went through on the island when my brain was not quite working even ninety per cent. I had worked in the casino one night until about one thirty a.m. I happened to be the closing girl, that was last cocktail waitress out after the last gambler left.

An oriental girl I worked with had asked me for a ride when I finished work so we walked out together. It was raining pretty hard and I had to go to the parking lot to get my car. It was an old Dodge Dart with the floor on the passenger side rusted and no light on the inside, but it got me to work and back for a long time. I had told Min to wait under the portico while I ran to get the car. I drove back to pick her up and after she got in the passenger side next to me, I was just about to drive off when the cashier from the small restaurant next door came screaming up the sidewalk. She was a large Bahamian lady and when she got to my car she opened the back door and jumped in, still screaming and pointing at a car about fifty feet in front of me outside the restaurant. I could just about see it through my windshield as the rain was really coming down. Tropical rain can be very heavy and hard to see through. As I stared at the car, I saw two people run from the building and jump into the car. It was very hard to see them, but I could see that they both had the type of hooded raincoats on that fishermen wear. They started to drive away and I finally understood what the Bahamian woman in the back of my car was trying to tell me. She had been held up with a gun and robbed. They took the days takings and the money from the register.

Well! Nancy Drew has nothing on me. I put my foot down and drove after them. My old Dodge kept up for about half an hour, more or less, and then I lost them. My next move was to go back to the hotel and call the police.

Poor Min and my Bahamian passenger, they must have been terrified and thought I was crazy, I on the other hand did not even stop and think of the consequences. I was definitely told in no uncertain terms by one of the policemen what an idiotic thing to do. He asked me, "If you had caught up with them what would you have done? They had guns, you could have all been killed."

Of course, he was right and I just told him it was an instant reaction when the cashier got into my car screaming and hysterical. The police sent us home. What a night! I never found out if the perpetrators were caught, but about a week later I was driving home from the pub (Where else?) and I noticed a car had pulled out after me from the parking lot and had followed me all the way to the apartment parking lot where Dave and I lived then pulled up next to my car.

I could not see who it was, or how many people were in the car as it was pretty dark. I sat in my car, locked all the doors and got very nervous. Could this be one of the guys from the robbery thinking I could recognise them, impossible? It was much too dark and raining too hard, so what was happening here?

Suddenly, there was a woman banging on my driver side window. I rolled my window down just a couple of inches. I had never set eyes on this woman. Who knows what her problem is? Suddenly, she is yelling and waving her arms in the air. "I know you've got my husband in there," she is shouting. I rolled the window down all the way and shouted back, "Excuse me. I don't know you and I have no idea what you are talking about." I decide to get out of the car and get eye level with this crazy woman.

I then, get out of the car and go round to the back and open the boot (Trunk to me now, boot to me then). I then open the back doors after she is satisfied that whoever she is tracking down (more like hunting down) is not in my car and maybe she has made a mistake following me. She takes off in a hurry, no apology nothing. In the meantime, he is making his getaway. WHAT A LUCKY GUY!

My apartment was very close by so I hurried and got home. Wow! What a week, and such a night "Nothing boring going on with me".

Where was I when I got rudely interrupted? I was going through the episode after George died when I was robbed and really taken advantage of. I remember one thing that will never ever exit from my brain. I was working one afternoon about two, or three months after George died and I started to cry. I could not control it. I guess I had to let things go. It was about two p.m. in the afternoon, one of my female customers told me to come to the ladies room with her. She was rather concerned about my frame of mind. I could not stop crying.

One of my managers showed up and told me to go home. Obviously, I could not work like that. I remember it was just after two p.m. A week later when I got my pay cheque, I was twelve dollars short That's is when we were paid six dollars an hour. I went into the office and asked the other manager who worked in the bar I worked in (The company owns more than one). "How come I am twelve dollars short on my pay cheque?" She reminded me that I was sent home early so I was written down for a six-hour shift instead of eight. Compassion would have been really nice!!

65   A New Home

I am now back to 2007 and getting ready to move into my new place. Hope I am not too confusing for everybody, jumping back and forth have to write it as I remember it. The huge yard sale helped me to get rid of plenty of stuff. I'm sure after I move I will gather more stuff. I think we all do it, get rid of it and buy more. The carpet in the home I am moving into is blue. I hate blue carpet so I am having it replaced before I move in. I have chosen a medium beige colour. It will go with anything.

Sue is going to take the dog to the new place while I deal with the moving company at the old house. The carpet should be in before the movers arrive with my stuff. The man laying it was there very early. Luckily, the distance between the new place and the old is only about a mile so I made a few trips to pick up odds and ends that did not need to be on a moving van.

I made arrangements to have my new furniture delivered the same day, it was, and the whole day worked out very well. All I have to do is unpack boxes and I am going to take my time with that.

How exciting to have new things! Fridge, microwave, a whole new living room and bedroom has lifted my spirits to no end. I know my dog is missing his pool and big garden. Sorry, George I had no option! The place is looking very nice now after a week of putting things away and arranging furniture, I have to start again I suppose.

I am back at work finally. Ugh! Not the place, I can deal with that, just the fact I have to work. Over four years I have worked here, time flies when you're having fun! I have a few female customers that at times cause me stress. Not sure what their problem is, but I guess I don't want to know. My graveyard bartender, the one on oxygen, has gone. He died a week after George and since then two or three more people, customers of mine have gone. I know at least one of them had a drug problem and another one was alcohol, there will be more. I have a large variety of customers going down that road.

Not anyone can do this job. It takes patience, compassion to a certain extent and in a local bar where one does not get a lunch break, or coffee break, not like union, enough energy to go eight hours without sitting. Although, I do know bartenders that sit every chance they get, it is a habit I have never gotten into.

I am now back in my routine. Glad to say all the sad parts seems to be over, hope it stays that way.

I am going to start saving now as I would like to spend my seventieth in England. I have taken a break since my last episode. As Christmas has suddenly arrived and I seem to be doing many more things than usual. Having a few friends round for an open house type thing for the holidays showing off my new place and furniture feels good! This is going to be two years since George died, it has flown by.

After New Year's Eve is over with I am going to concentrate on making a trip back home for my birthday, my seventieth!! I still have some money left after buying the mobile home and filling it with super brand new furniture. The round trip ticket to England costs over a thousand dollars and I need to save spending money. Luckily, I don't have to stay in hotels. If I had to do that I don't think I would be able to go back ever again.

Back to the grind and a couple of new faces in the bar. A couple of the bodies that go with the faces are definitely nuts. A couple of the girls, one in particular can be very normal, having a drink, putting a few dollars in a slot machine and suddenly all hell breaks loose, she explodes.

It becomes a calm bar, to a "One Flew Over the Cuckoo's Nest" scenario. . She was a roommate of one of my regular customers who left town. That is when all her problems started, well made them worse I should say. She did not work. Not sure how she was living day to day. I do know that a really nice guy, another one of my customers, helped her out, He was a handful at times too. If I served him shots of Jagermeister I had to make sure he did not have more than two or three in a short time. He was not a happy drunk. He always wanted to fight. Luckily, he was another one that lived in an apartment behind the bar so he could also stagger home. He passed away a couple of years down the road from now, 2010 I believe of a massive heart attack. Very sad. He was only in his late forties. I remember a saying that he said every time he came into the bar. It was, "Git-r-done Sam," miss him!

The woman he helped, wanted me to mention her name in this book but I decided against it, moods too many times, and if this becomes a hit, just a small one (not like a J.K. Rowlings) then she cannot suddenly dislike me and retaliate. I am so happy that my brain is still doing a good job, well now sensible wise.

If I write down everything I am remembering at this moment in time, this will be longer than "War and Peace"! I never did read that one, but I did get through "Hawaii." That took me a while, Michener, did draw things out a little.

I still have another few pages to go before I can finish this and whatever the outcome, published or not, I have really enjoyed sharing my life, or some of it with my closest friends. I am sure if they get to read this they may be surprised a little and hopefully forgive if I offended or upset anybody with my actions.

I have met the best people and made the best friends anyone could ever wish for.

Back to the bar for one or two more profiles of people that got my attention, sometimes in a bad way, but one has to deal with it as it's a part of the job. Alcohol can change a person's whole demeanour and sometimes not for the better.

I believe Matti was a working girl, a long time customer of mine. I think she may have had a hard life when she was young. She has never really discussed it with me. I just felt it.

We had our differences once, or twice, but solved them, life's too short. Now, her and I get along fine. She sent me hand made cards telling me she loved me, very nice!

There are far too many people to list, but those who made a difference and meaning to my life know who they are and thank you from the bottom of my heart.

Bud, thanks for helping me with this, it means a great deal to me, (Bud died before he could read the finished manuscript) also, (Jeep) who has read fifty pages at a time and suffered through my English spelling.

A workmate that helped me print, (my paper though) thank you too, before I change the subject and try to write another fifty pages.

A friend and bartender (Office), you are one of my favourite people and no, you cannot have the photo of me that is a little suggestive, when I am gone maybe! Also Jeremy, I could not have done this without you and Maggie, thanks for everything.

Back on track and getting ready to book a ticket to go back home for my seventieth. Wow! Am I really going to be seventy? It is about three months before I want to travel back to "Blighty" (England) and I am trying hard to buy my ticket.

I think Dave is arranging a party in the pub for me, his birthday too before mine so we get to celebrate together, can't wait!

About seventeen years of visiting this village, I have made some nice friends, lovely little place. One thing about living in Vegas, I can usually go back to England with a tan. Especially, if I go in September, makes me feel a little more attractive.

I'm sure I am speaking on behalf of lots of women when I say, "I hate my arms." I used to wear everything sleeveless. Now, I can't wait to cover them up. I have been very athletic in my life and I know for my age, I am in pretty good shape, but the arms, ugh! Then again, I think I have seen worse.

I am working hard in the bar at the moment and trying to save a little extra cash for spending money on my 'hols'!

A few new working girls try coming in lately, young, no form of ID. Cannot let them in I'm afraid, It's a sad world now, as far as I am concerned. Too easy to get drugs, food stamps, and disability at the age of forty something! Some of these customers I get do not want to work. The government is making it too easy for them.

Wish I could have had a little luck as far as money went, could have taken it a little easier in my old age. I am lucky that I have a sister who is always watching out for me, and I guess a job.

Occasionally, she will put money in my checking account. I wish I could return the favours tenfold! I try in other ways.

I do realise my big mistake was to buy the second mobile home, but my beautiful dog came first so I guess I did not have much choice.

If I could have got back what I paid for it things would have been much easier, but it did not happen. C'est la vie! I still have people I love and people who love me. What else does one need?

I finally buy my ticket to London, straight flight from Las Vegas to Gatwick. That is the smaller airport after Heathrow which is the largest one in the U.K. I am very excited about the thought of having my seventieth with my son and his new lady friend Mary and in the little pub on the beach next to the English Channel with a view of the White Cliffs of Dover. (phew! that was a long sentence) forgot the comma. Amazing when one is really wanting time to go fast, it doesn't happen, like the eight hours at work, slow, slow. Should not be wishing my life away, but need a break so bad!

66   70th In England

It's here, it's here. September that is and I am packing my bags. I bought a couple of nice new things to wear for a big bash, a long black woollen skirt and a top with sequin straps to match. It will hide a little weight that I have gained since quitting smoking. It has been a couple of years, but it is not easy to shed the pounds that seem to come on instantly. When one is young and tanned and slim, life seems a little easier, more than when you are going to be seventy and trying to pull everything in and buy wrinkle cream at twenty dollars a tube hoping it works in a few weeks, or less, but then after a little blush, a new haircut and a fake tan it's all good. Not half as bad as I thought it was.

I am on my way, sis and I have a quick lunch before she drops me off at the airport, have to be there at least two hours, or more before flight time. The 747 is a huge plane. Holds about 400 people I believe so I guess it takes a long time checking all those people in.

Although, I am very excited to be going, flying is not one of my favourite things anymore. I used to enjoy it years ago, now I definitely have white knuckle syndrome again on take-off and landing.

I think I calm down when I hear or see the liquor cart coming round!

Boarding begins. First Class (lucky buggers) then premium and finally peons. I have chosen an aisle seat way at the back, that way I can get up and down when I feel like it, ten or eleven hours is a pretty long haul. One thing good is a choice of movies (up-to-date), cocktails and dinner and breakfast. Wish I could take a kip (sleep) for an hour, or two, but I have never been able to do that. This big bird is up. Thank you Lord.

Twenty to thirty minutes in the air, vodka and tonic coming and pretty soon seat belt off. Settle down Sam you have a fabulous two weeks to look forward to.

I have been tipped off by a couple of friends in the village that a few of the men are going to dress up in suits and tuxedos and bow ties. Wow, how wonderful! Suddenly, time is forwarding fast, nearly in Gatwick on landing approach. That's about another half an hour. Time to go to the toilet and make myself look a little less red eyed. The landing was awesome, nothing to feel, smooth and easy Leslie is there behind the barrier waiting for me.

It takes a good thirty to forty minutes to get the luggage and go through customs and immigration. That's if there is not a problem with any of it.

Wonderful to see my son's beautiful face. Get the cases in the car and off we go. Les is driving me to Dave's about an hour and a half drive from the airport (the way Les drives) maybe it's over two not sure. It is a pretty easy drive on one of the motorways. We go to Dover and then go on the route to Kingsdown.

It's about twelve, noon. Les calls Dave who is in the pub and tells him we will be there about one p.m. I say, "Hi" to him on Les's cell and tell him how I will be very happy to see him. I can hear the background noise, sounds as though the pub is busy. It's Friday, best day for pubs.

Looking forward to seeing a lot of friends. Trouble is they seem to keep me up for hours after I get there and it usually finish's up that I am thirty hours without going to bed. It is mainly because of the time difference. England is eight hours ahead of Vegas so I lose the time when I arrive. Good job, I have the stamina to go with the flow and stay with the crowd, but great fun even at seventy.

The next day or two does catch up with me, but amazingly it is about the third day that the jet lag sets in and that is party night. It will not hinder me, or deter me. I am a descendant of a Viking (I think). Les and his new girlfriend Mary are going to stay in a little bed-and-breakfast near Dave's house and the pub, that way they won't have to drive if they party too much.

67 Dual Birthdays

Saturday is party night. David's birthday was Friday and mine will be next Tuesday so we decided Saturday would be good for everybody. When we arrive at the pub about eight pm I cannot believe how many people are there. This is wonderful. Seeing as I don't get to come here too often there are friends I have made from seventeen or so years ago, also our good friends Dave and I met in the Bahamas over forty years ago, wow! They make a point (The two couples) of making it to the pub to hook up with me every time I come over. I can honestly say that these four people are really good friends. Wish my girlfriend Rita could make it. Been friends for 60 years.

Her and I have known each other since we were teenagers, I think 15, or earlier. I wanted so much to have enough money to send her, to be able to stay with me in Vegas for a month.

It is just not happening. Not sure if it will before I check out. I have never understood how wealthy people get bored. (repeat) There is so much in life one can do and so many one could help, but I guess I will never know.

Back to the pub and the party. Dave had hired a one man band who is fabulous. Good music on the piano with the accompaniments. About an hour into this celebration I am dancing with my son. It's a lovely feeling. Nobody can know unless it has happened to them what it's like to lose custody of one's son when he is five years old and then struggle for years to keep in touch and try to see him.

Finally, I don't have that problem and have not had it since he was twenty-one. I made peace with his father when I went back to England for the first time after seventeen years. It took me a very long time to forgive him and lose my abhorrence toward him. I met with him because Les asked me to. I am sure his father heard I was coming back for a visit and wanted to make things right after all these years. Nearly thirty years, I believe. I gave him a hug and kissed him on the cheek after the three of us had gone to an old pub that his dad and I used to visit when we were young kids and dating. He could not impress upon me enough how happy he was that I had let bygones be bygones and had forgiven him for the ugly years he gave me. He passed away about eleven years ago, not quite sixty-one years of age. God rest his soul.

This is such a nice evening and the next thing blows my mind. Dave gave me an envelope with I assume a birthday card in it. When I opened the envelope and took out the card and after reading the funnies on the front page, I opened it up and saw all this money staring at me. I was flabbergasted and did not know what to say, or do.

After I read the card which was a comical one as usual (Dave never was romantic) I said to him, "I cannot accept all of this Dave". He replied, "It's a special birthday. I want to pay your fare." He never showed a lot of feelings. This was amazing and a really loving gesture. The man that he had hired to play music happened to be playing and old Tony Bennett song, "I wanna be around" so I started singing it softly to Les while we were still dancing. He suggested I should sing something with the piano player so after we finished our dance I asked him if he would mind if I sang a song.

He was all for it and showed me a book of songs he had, also music for certain ones that he played, but no words in his book. I found a song I love to sing and I know the words of it by heart. It was "Smile." It was quite amazing that we did not need to go over it at all and not worry about what key it was, it just happened and turned out beautifully. My girlfriends from Bahama days had never heard me sing, didn't know I did and were very impressed. Les and David the same thing, guess I did a good job!

Singing is something I love to do and I think I should have pursued it as a career when I was young, but let it get away, oh well! Another "C'est la vie."

The rest of our party turned into a super night for everyone, good food, good drinks and wonderful company. After this night is over, I have another couple of weeks in England before going back to Vegas and work, trying very hard not to think about it. I know somebody who will be very happy to see me when I get back, my beautiful pal George. He is camping with my vet while I am away.

I leave him there as he knows the best vet in the world, Dr. Mathews and the girls who work there. I think it keeps him about as happy as possible when I leave him.

Coming back from England is usually something that depresses me a little. I do get homesick and I miss my son and friends very much. Also, there are other things people in the United States may not understand, a roast pork with the crackling (skin) on top that snaps off when cooked, delicious. A pork sausage with hot mustard, no sausage in the U.S. tastes like one from a pub in England. Springtime, bluebells, daffodils and lambs everywhere in the countryside, I do miss that.

My girlfriend of 60 years Rita, my bridesmaid and I, usually try to get together for a day when I am there. We have lunch and reminisce about our young years. She was not a fan of my husband and always reminds me how bad he could treat me. There was an incident that she said I should write about, but I shrugged it off as I might come across as a suicidal idiot, but I have decided I will write it down. I guess to this day there are people who will never understand that I am a person who keeps stress inside and try not to show it, not good, but that's how I am made. I think Rita was one of those people that really could read me so I will try to explain this event that she really took control of.

279

68 Reminiscing Again

I was not having a good time with Jimmy, Les was about a year and a half old and we were all living with Jimmy's mother. I did get along with her most of the time, but she did things that got me so worked up like putting Les's woolen suits that my mother knitted him, in the copper in very hot water and they shrunk.

By the way, a copper was a large container about three feet tall, like a pot that heated water on legs., it was something we did washing in before washing machines.

She occasionally put coloured things in with whites which would make Jimmy's underwear coloured. He would yell at her and then I took the brunt of most of it especially, when she sometimes cooked a fresh chicken without taking the innards out first. I believe this period in time was when he started gambling. I was finding bills under the mattress for betting shops and bills that needed paying. I hope when my son reads this episode he will understand. I came to my wits end and I suppose I was not strong enough or old enough to deal with it.

One morning I was alone in the flat doing the ironing, Les was sleeping and it seemed that the more ironing I did the more depressed I got. I thought I would take a few aspirins and lay down more than I thought was the outcome.

Not sure how Rita was suddenly there, but the next thing I know is I am walking with Les in the pushchair, my hands tied to it, and she is next to me telling me keep moving and walking. How long and where we walked I will never remember, but she took care of me and delivered me back to the flat.

I do remember that Jimmy was there with his mother and a couple of relatives and I did act a little strange, I do remember that part. I was put to bed. To this day nobody knew about this event, only my best friend Rita. I love you babe.

It was after this that we moved back to Portsmouth. Rita and her hubby and baby, came to visit for Christmas. It really was not a great time. Rita hated the way Jim treated me and at one point smacked him across the face with a wet tea towel when he gave me a mouthful for no reason.

I have already written the outcome of this marriage, very sad really so now back to my seventies, amazing eh? Where does it all go? I am back in the Saloon and showing my customers the great pictures I have from my party in the pub in Kent. I am taking George to Lake Mead as often as I can so that the poor dog can get a swim, but I find that neither one of us can get into the water far enough where it is deep enough. The water has receded so much that the edge is very, very soft mud like quick sand.

I finally gave up on our usual beach and decided I would try the place where the marina used to be. The boats that were there have all had to be moved as the water became so shallow. I found a concrete ramp where George could just walk, or run mostly, into the water. He was in his glory!

I know how he feels. I really miss my pool too. Sharing a pool with other people doesn't do it for me, but beggars can't be choosers! If ever I become well off before I die I will buy a house with two bedrooms, a lovely garden with a pool and two golden lab retrievers. Nice to dream, of course if I am very rich, I will buy a house on the beach.

It has been a few weeks since I got back from London, seems an eternity. I have been living in this used mobile home I bought for a couple of years now. I sometimes wonder if I should have taken the apartment that I could have rented, where I could have taken my dog. I could have had money in the bank.

I know in a couple of years this place is probably going to need repairs, then the fun starts. I am seriously thinking about selling before that does happen.

I am also worried about George. He keeps choking and coughing especially at night. I get an appointment with Dr. Mathews and he tells me after an examination that George has a collapsing trachea, surgery is not an option and he gives me pills for him that may help a little. Luckily, I took insurance out from A.S.P.C.A. so it covered some of the cost. The pills were expensive.

Then he had a tumour under his tail which had to be removed that was about 400 dollars even with the insurance, poor thing! I hope he is not going to suffer. That will hurt me very much.

I do love the fact that I still have a garden, very small, but neat. A nice little square patch I have dug out and planted a few flowers, looks good, and I also have a small porch that I have put a two seater bamboo couch and two side chairs, a glass top table in the middle finishes it off. George is happy to have a nice cool lawn to lie on I'm sure, and there is a tree at one end that gives some shade. Need shade when our temperature gets into the nineties and the hundreds.

I only have twenty steps to my mailbox and the pool so I would say everything is very convenient. Let's just wait and see if I get lucky with all of it.

Thanksgiving nearly here again. Looking forward to Sue and kids coming and Jenny who works with Sue, lovely person. We don't do turkey very often. It's nice to do beef, or pork, or something different. We usually agree between us what it's going to be. I don't mind. I'll cook whatever everybody wants.

Wouldn't it be wonderful if my son could spend a holiday with me, a Christmas now and again, or even a Thanksgiving would be nice even though he does not celebrate this holiday in England, it would be nice if he joined us here, and Dave, what are the odds on him coming to stay with me? Nil, I guess.

I am now working on finishing this life story that I have been working on for over two years. My friend Bud will be relieved and will be giving a big sigh of relief. It is impossible for me to go on and on, there is still too much to write about. I am going to try and squeeze another five years into a hundred pages. There will be friends and family that might expect me to write much more about them, but I think I have expressed about as much as I can to paint a picture for people to understand and maybe enjoy some of my life's stories even the sad ones.

It is half way through 2010 and happy news. My niece, Melissa is getting engaged to her long-time boyfriend Bill. They have been with each other since high school about nine years.

Melissa has become a doctor of pharmacy and Bill has passed his bar so hopefully they will have a nice fruitful life. The wedding is in November. Something great to look forward to and even more exciting, Les is coming over to attend.

This is going to be a grand affair so I have to start looking for a nice ensemble to wear. Glad I have a few months to do this and hope I can find something that looks good that is not too expensive.

Melissa and Bill have a little celebration at Bill's parents house to celebrate their engagement and Bill passing his bar exam. Well done Bill! I'm sure it was not easy. The RING is absolutely gorgeous, a girl very much loved.

Sue is going to be busy helping Melissa with all the arrangements, a lot of work I know that. A wedding takes much organising. If it is going to be a large affair and have everything go smoothly. I believe they both have chosen one of our exclusive golf courses for the ceremony and then the reception inside one of the large rooms that are used for banquets. To actually be married on the golf course will be very different, looking forward to it.

Summer is nearly here and already it is a blasting heat. However, many years I have been living here, I still hate anything over 100 degrees. Don't give a monkey's if it is dry heat. Still too bloody hot. Cannot lay by the pool, cannot go for a nice long walk, only at six a.m. If one goes grocery shopping have to get back home in a hurry especially, if buying butter, ice cream, or meat. I keep a large cooler in the back of my car for the summer months. At least that lets me hang around a little longer after shopping.

On the other hand, it is usually only for about three months and we don't have snow and freezing weather very often. Great climate really.

This is what attracts people to move here. The population is growing rapidly since I moved here thirty-six years ago.

I liked it better then. Traffic was much easier and people seemed nicer. Maybe it's only how I feel, but if I was wealthy I would love to move back to England for six months a year and spend the winter months in Vegas, dreaming!!

I have kept my eyes open watching for sales in stores I like to buy clothes in. There is one particular place, Stein Mart, that sells just about anything to keep a woman's attention for an hour, or so. Shoes, jewellery, clothes and very nice goods for the home. Unique bowls and dishes, nice linens and I am giving them a good plug, eh?

I am in there one weekend about two months before the wedding and I saw a coat dress on a rack that really appealed to me. It was black and white with a zip up the front, a very large collar that could be lifted at the back and overall an attractive outfit. Now, I need to get a nice pair of high heel shoes and maybe a big floppy hat, look out here I come!

69   A Wedding Coming, My Four-Legged Friend Going

This wedding could not have come at a better time. It has been about a year and a half since I came back from England and the worst thing happened approximately a year, or so ago. My wonderful four legged friend started going downhill. The choking was getting worse and it was really bad at night. I had trouble sleeping and I know he did. Then he had trouble controlling his bowels so I was forced to shut him in the bathroom when I left for work. It was very hard on him, a large dog shut up for nine hours and it became very sad for me. I did not know if I could bear to take him to Dr. Mathews and put him down.

One morning I went to work and called my vet, fighting to hold back the tears. I told him what was happening with George and he told me to bring him in and he would take care of him for me.

My girlfriend of 36 years showed up for a coffee and she could tell I was upset about something. I said, "Rachel, I have to put my dog to sleep and I don't know how I am going to handle it!" Instantly, she said, "Sam, give me your house keys and I will go and get him and take care of it for you." She was not working at the time. Of course, I could not believe that she would do that for me, but she did and I will never be able to thank her for that stressful thing she did for me.

I think i cried nearly my whole shift. That was the dearest, gentlest creature anyone could wish for. I am going to miss him terribly. It must have been hard for Rachel to do that even though it was not her dog, she knew him and loved him. Thanks from my heart Rach.

The big affair is getting closer. I found a nice black large-brimmed hat, but I have to buy inserts to make it smaller. Found some in one of our larger stores, now fits perfect. I have not dressed up for a wedding since I don't remember when.

Pretty soon my invitation came in the mail. A very classy looking one, brown ribbon on cream coloured heavy parchment type paper, very attractive. My sister tells me that Dave will be sent an invitation. I told her not to expect him to come. He won't even come and visit me after all these years.

Not sure if it really is fear of flying for 11 hours, or meeting lots of people he doesn't know.

Either way, it won't happen, as much as I would love a visit from him. I guess in our later years it's very different from being in love with someone at twenty-six and I think I must have hurt him tremendously when I said no to his marriage proposal.

If only he would have never let me go and on the telegram he sent me five months after I left if he would have said, "Will you marry me? I love you, not, we are getting married immediately, ticket following. ." Guess I was being very feminist. I wanted "I love you," most women do.

I actually know that he does love me in his own funny way and I believe I am his soul mate. Not too many people have a soul mate so I am lucky.

On with the positive. My son is coming and spending a week with me. Can't wait to see him. It's been a couple of years. One of the reasons I would like to be well off is I could go to London much more and maybe even fly business or even first class. Am I dreaming again? Doesn't hurt, feels good.

Pretty soon we have to attend a rehearsal and dinner before the wedding. Les is now here and I think this is the first time he has seen this place I'm in now. He was here in 2006 after George died and I moved in here in 2007. I went home in September, 2008 and now it's 2010. It has been about three, or more years since he was in Vegas I'm sure.

He did his usual, renting a convertible mustang, guess mum is going to have to act like a "Cougar," or try.

Wish George was here to see Melissa married. He made her very nervous when she was a baby about two, or three years old, he had a loud voice, but when she got older she would sit on his lap.

He was wonderful with children and he was there to see her grow up into a beautiful woman. Peter, her brother, on the other hand, was very laid back and easy going. He also became a very nice handsome guy. My sister did a marvellous job with her children. Hope they know it.

Rehearsal coming up at the golf course. We can dress a little more casual than the wedding which is going to be very different from the run of the mill church do's. There is a special place that consists of a large hill and this is where Melissa will be coming from, very green and hidden from all the guests that are sitting at the bottom on the other side. Sue and Terry (her ex), have decided that they will both be walking her to the Rabbi which I think is super.

There will be five bridesmaids and male escorts to accompany them. I think about one hundred and fifty guests, give or take fifty or so, I did mention this is going to be a grand affair!

The rehearsal is over and we are on our way to a dinner with the selected guests who attended. Just a small gathering ahead of the big one to come.

I have just made up my mind that this life story is going to come to an end a little earlier than I was thinking. I am going to jump ahead after I have written about the wedding. There will only be a couple of events that became very important to me in the next three years so I have decided to put this love and tragic comedy to rest.

Wedding day is here. Les and I are both taking full advantage of having two bathrooms. I do miss that when I go to England, but then there are things that make up for that. To see my son in a nice suit is a sight for sore eyes. Wish I had another seventy years with him.

70 Leslie And I Looking Very Snazzy

I am finally dressed, hat and all and Les checks me out in the garden at my request. Everything is ship shape according to his viewing. We decided to have a quick cocktail in our bar, (the Office) where I know some of my friends will be and they can look us over before carrying on to the wedding.

It had been a long while since I wore high heel shoes, hope I can handle it for a few hours. Nothing more flattering to a woman's legs than high heels.

We had a big wow, when we walked in and funnily enough, somebody called me a cougar. That swelled my head a little. After one drink and lots of compliments we are on our way.

Wish Dave would have come. I could have had two men looking good in suits.

We arrive at the club house a little early. Good thing, we found a parking space in a hurry. Straight to the bar and already there are people I know in the lounge area. This place is pretty big. There are two or three large rooms that can be made into one and the bar area is a pretty good size. I suppose there are a lot of functions held here.

It is filling up fast and suddenly there are people yelling "Sam". It's amazing how many faces are appearing that I have not seen in years. Friends of Sue, friends of Terry and people who used to come into the bar when their kids were young, without the kids of coarse. It's going to be a memorable day.

After about an hour, we find out that there are golf carts taking everybody to the ceremony area. It is a lovely setting and views of the strip can be seen in the distance.

I think it's about five to a cart so Les and I are on our way to the canopy that is set up on this special green. We are seated in the very first row of chairs with friends of Sue's. A doctor and his wife, and Jenny, a lovely lady who works with Sue. There are a couple of ladies I have never met, next to the Chuppah, (A Jewish wedding canopy held by four poles and a cover on top), who are playing cellos, beautiful classical music.

Finally, the waited for moment, the groom and his henchmen are all in place, bridesmaids too and suddenly over the top of the hill coming into view is this gorgeous girl holding her mother on one side and dad on the other.

Not being prejudice because this is my niece, but this is one of the most beautiful brides I have ever seen. Not just the dress, the hair, the make-up which is not very much, but I think the whole picture. My nephew Peter is at the back of the Chuppah holding one of the four poles. I think this holding of the poles is some sort of tradition. I know the meaning of the Chuppah is supposedly when the wedding couple are starting their new home together.

The ceremony begins. One can hear a pin drop.

At last we are coming to the couple being wrapped in the Tallit, Jewish prayer shawl, and then the smashing of the glass. This lovely couple are now one, after all the years of courting, etc. Pictures, hugs, kisses and now golf carts coming to pick everybody up to take to the reception. Good job I'm thinking, as suddenly the weather has turned very chilly.

Around the room and the main table have beautiful tall flowers and on each guest table, very classy. I will be happy to sit, give my feet a break, and take my big floppy hat off. My son gets us a cocktail and we commence to relax and wait for dinner.

Nice menu, choice of three entrees. Les and I are having filet, can't wait I'm starving, but first there are toasts and speeches, actually pretty good ones. The best man's speech was awesome, very personable guy.

The food is here. Yippee! Very, very nice steak, great veggies and salad. A ton of fun and laughter at this do. Dinner is over and Melissa is being carried in on a chair above the groomsmen's heads, a little scary looking. Next is Bill's turn, guess it's some sort of tradition. Anyway, they are both danced around and finally let down.

The garter is the next on the agenda. This beautiful slim bride is sitting on a chair, alone in the middle of the dance floor in this great big room surrounded by about one hundred people. Bill makes his entrance and walks to her and kneels down. What we see next is unbelievable. Bill lifts Melissa's dress from the floor until it reaches her knee and then puts his head under it to look for her garter. It was hilarious, got the whole room's attention. Great move Bill!

71 Beautiful Wedding, Great Day

Soon, this day is over as far as weddings go. Les and I go for a drink in a local bar and then home. I have managed to get him a room in a casino close to my house so he can have two, or three days on his own to relax.

So Sunday night he takes off. I will see him for the next couple of days for a couple of hours here and there and I am back to work on Tuesday, he is leaving on Wednesday, boy a week goes so fast.

Leslie is gone. I will try to make Christmas in 2011 if I can manage to save the money, to England that is. It feels like it's going to be a long year, nothing exciting happening. I have enjoyed the last week immensely, now back to the grind.

I thought there was nothing to look forward to, but there really is, life, breathing, dinner and a glass of wine with my sister, drinks with best friends and now and again, karaoke.

Dave's seventieth this coming year, wish I could make it, know I can't, but I am trying hard for Christmas and New Year. That is a very happy time in England, very different to the U.S.A., or should I say Vegas which is a twenty-four hour town, not time for holidays and if one is in the "waiting on the public profession" then one day is the same as all the rest. Christmas, Thanksgiving, July the fourth, all the same if you are due to work on those days. Then that's what you do.

In 2011 Christmas and New Year's eve will be on a Saturday, Christmas day Sunday. In England when holidays fall on a weekend then an extra day off is added on so 2011 will be about four days as Boxing Day the 26th of December is also a holiday. A lot of people in the USA think that Boxing Day is something to do with boxing. It is actually a tradition started years ago when the rich people put their leftovers in small boxes and gave them to the poor and needy, guess that idea went down the drain. Now it's cardboard signs for money.

Suddenly, it's June and the temperature is increasing by leaps and bounds. Wish I had a cabin about five thousand feet up on Mt. Charleston. Should have bought one in 1976 when property was very affordable, too late now, (Good name for a song), in fact George and I were offered once acre on the far west side of town not far from the mountains for two-thousand dollars. We discussed it for quite a while and after lengthy conversations both wondered why we would want to buy an acre of desert miles away from the strip and absolutely desolate? Oh, how wrong could we have been? In the last thirty years it may be one of the most developed parts of Las Vegas. I don't really know, but I would think an acre in that area would cost a million, or more, that's if one could find it. Something else for me to dream about!

72   No, No, Not Moving Again, YES

I put the mobile home up for sale before the kids got married and sold it in February. Took a beating, but I am now in a senior living complex, closer to my sister and realising that I won't have to pay for repairs.

During the three months I have lived here I have made the apartment look very nice. I sold my large couch and very large chair and ottoman to the lady who bought my mobile home. It would not have fitted in the place I am in so I bought a small cream coloured sofa and a Queen Anne type chair in a coffee colour with a very small cream dot in the material.

I also had a very good friend put two ceiling fans in the bedrooms which did not have them. James is a very capable man. Seems to be able to put his hand to any job. He also painted one wall in the living room for me, a nice sage green. Just inside the front door was a small closet probably for vacuums and, or, ironing boards, or even coats.

James made it into a pantry for me. He put reinforced shelves in there so I have plenty of cans and jars stored and large appliances like mixers and heavy pans on the bottom. The rent is more than the space rent I had in the mobile park, but this is going to be easier. I am actually beginning to get used to living in an apartment. It is not as cramped as I thought it would be and I have a long-time friend living on the same floor a few doors away. She is the one who put me in touch with this place.

I met Claire when I worked in a hotel close to the strip. We both worked in public relations dealing with tourists coming in from California and states not too far away. The majority came in on buses and they were given slot play, comp food and we took care of their needs for a few hours while they were in the hotel for the day.

Boy, did we see some sights! Her husband, Henry and George hit it off when they first met and we would all get together in each other's homes. They had a nice room with a bar and a dartboard and at that time my dad was alive and he was a great dart player so him and mum and George and I spent lots of time playing darts with Henry and Claire and having great social times.

We shared Jewish holidays, weddings, Henry and Claire's son Lionel, soccer injuries (Adam, the eldest), and love break-ups with their daughter and her beau's. They also shared some of our really bad patches.

Henry died a year before George 2004, and times change, years go by, and Claire and I were not given a real easy way to go. We still see each other in the hallway and occasionally have a cocktail in my apartment. If I have friends round, mostly the girls for lunch, I always invite her to join us. We have a lot of years under our belts.

Summer and heat are nearly over. It is October 2011, and I have booked my ticket for London in December, as good as April in Paris, I would say. I am hoping if it is snowing even though it is beautiful at Christmas time, that it won't be as heavy as it was the last one I spent there in the snow.

The one drawback I have when I go for the holidays in the winter, is that I have to take winter clothes, which means that my luggage weighs heavy for only half of the clothes I could have for the summer, but then summer prices on the airlines are much more, no win situation!

Dave tells me we will be having Christmas dinner in the pub, joined by a few friends as in past years and it will be roast beef and

Yorkshire pudding, (Not a desert like popovers), veggies and roast potatoes, (my favourite), and Christmas pud.

He usually closes the pub about three p.m. then about ten of us celebrate. His chef and a couple of the cooks prepare our meal and wait on us and do a wonderful job before they leave for their Christmas celebration.

I have bought four beautifully decorated large battery operated candles to take with me. I thought it would be nice to put them on the table, make it a little more Christmas-like.

73   A Happy Christmas And New Year

I love this holiday, Dave does not. I thought when we lived in the Bahamas he enjoyed the holidays. I would not have known he didn't. Guess he put on a good front even when we had all of our friends for dinner before going to work. Most years the weather did not help to create a Christmas atmosphere, warm and sticky, but one year the temperature was only in the forties Fahrenheit, it was great!

The island we lived on had pine trees galore in certain areas so we were able to cut our own tree down. I think that was the year when a bunch of us finished work and went back to the house, lit a fire as it was cold enough and the best looking fireplace! Huge brick opening two sides that covered half a wall with one side just for logs. It's not often one lights a fire in the Bahamas and being Christmas made it even more special. We all got pretty loaded and played charades until the wee hours of the morning.

Al, a friend and a dealer from England, did one of the best I can remember. He stood in front of the fire and said, "Movie title, two words." He then held up one hand and bent his little finger. We all sat and thought and thought and drank some more to no avail. Okay, Al we give up. What is it? "Moby Dick," he said. I don't think I have ever laughed so hard since, but I guess I have.

New Year's Eve was not a night off for anybody even if it was your night off on the schedule. This was more so for the dealers than us cocktail waitresses. I remember one year I was off, but nobody else was, so nowhere to go with friends until about three a.m.

Now, I am on my way roughly forty-six years later to spend a New Year's Eve with people I love, friends and maybe my son. Not too many New Years have I been able to spend with him. Either he has a gig that I could not get to, or he is in London and I am in Kent. "One day maybe, Les, we have not had very many New Years and Christmases together over the years."

Sue and I and the kids have a holiday dinner at my place before I leave, and we exchange gifts. Who cares if it is a bit early? My friend Maggie and her boyfriend take me to the airport. Sis works on the day I take off and great to have friends that are always there for you. Les picks me up in London and takes me straight to Dave's It's a day, or so away from Christmas Eve which is on Saturday, have a feeling I am needing to put my drinking suit on.

My Son My Son

Les is coming back for Christmas dinner, not sure if Mary is coming with him. They have two dogs that need looking after and an independent cat. I always feel like I am home when I get to Dave's. Him and I have a great rapport and we both have the same sense of humour. The only time things get strained is when I start to tidy up in the house then he gets a little paranoid that I will move things to places where he won't find them.

There are very few women who could deal with his domestic environment and I know if I can get my writing made into a book, and he reads it, then he will agree with me.

The pub has been his life for the past thirty-four years and I guess the house was not a priority.

It's very sad really, if I was here I could make it lovely, but it's not my life, or concern. I just enjoy trying to make it nicer when I am there and I love the guy!

It is Friday night. I arrived this morning at ten a.m. England time, that is two a.m. Vegas time and it is now ten p.m. and I am about to go into the pub with Dave which means I have been up since Thursday morning at six a.m. in Vegas which means I am still hanging in after thirty-two hours, or so. How do I do this? Scary!

I'm guessing after seeing friends and having a few toddies, it will be quite a bit longer, and when I think my yesterdays are fading away, I am going to stay if it's all night. Dave is the one who decides what time it will be. He is the man in charge and when he says, "Last orders please," SOMETIMES HE REALLY MEANS IT.!!!

Reunion

When the place thins out, him and I often sit and have nice conversations about past years and I remember one time I was telling him about George, he said he would have loved to have met him. Obviously, that would never have happened, funny thing I think they would have really got along.

I tell Dave stories about when George and I had funny things that happened during our thirty years. One in particular that came to mind was when I was hosing down the cool decking one morning in January. I remember it was very cold and the water in the pool was about fifty nine degrees, outside temperature I think was around mid-forties.

It can get very cold in Las Vegas and we do have freezing occasionally. I had a pair of sweats, a tee-shirt, a thick hoodie and sneakers with socks on. My pal George, my Lab, was with me even he had not gone in the water this morning. I put a high powered nozzle on the end of the hose which washed the dust from the decking and would also wash the side walls in the pool when I put it in the water.

I started at the shallow end and worked my way up to the deeper end washing lounge chairs and cushions and got to the table and chairs and the umbrella in the table which we would leave in if it wasn't windy. There was a cement holder that it fitted in which kept it pretty safe.

I had gotten to the six foot end of the pool and as I finished the table, I backed up a bit too far and the next thing I remember was going under the water with the hose in my hand and coming back up to the dog looking at me as though I was crazy. My hood was full of water, and luckily I was close to the steps with a hand rail, so I grabbed the rail and climbed out.

It was not easy with my clothes and shoes full of water. I made my way across the lawn and turned off the hose. I then went to the bedroom window to knock on it and get hubby's attention, by this time I was freezing cold! I banged on the window hoping he would get up and come to the front door, (It was only about eight thirty and he did not get up that early). Anyway, no answer so I made my way to the front door. I did not want to go into the house dripping water everywhere so I started knocking on the door. I started taking all my clothes off and just as I had my hand on the door handle George opened it. He stood and looked at me with utter disbelief. I cannot imagine what he was thinking when he saw me, naked, hair dripping wet, my clothes and sneakers in a pile and the dog sitting there taking in the whole scene. George said, "What the blah blah blah are you doing?" I explained that I fell into the pool at the deep end while I was washing down the deck and the furniture. "George, hurry up and get me a towel and a robe, I'm really very cold." Then he realised what he was seeing. Glad we had a six foot wall in the garden, that would have made a great video for nosy neighbours.

This story gave Dave a laugh. I think we left the pub at around one thirty a.m. It will all start again tomorrow, but now David has become a dog owner and he has to make sure the Jack Russell, is not left in the house too long on his own. He is just a baby and needs to be taken out etc., wild little bugger!

Supposedly, Jack Russell's are a handful. I think he will give Dave a run for his money and plenty of exercise. The customers in the pub are really making a fuss of him when Dave brings him in.

One problem he has is jumping up at people. I suppose that's what puppies do. They have to be trained to control lots of bad habits, but he is beautiful, I miss mine.

Our dinner on the twenty-fifth is very nice. Dave even bought Christmas crackers for us to pull. A cracker is a tube shaped piece of cardboard, usually covered with very fancy paper and tied at each end with about three inches left for a person to be able to hold and pull. They have a little strip down the whole length inside which explodes very safely when pulled by a person holding each end of it. After it is pulled it splits in half and inside one finds a little novelty, or a paper hat which if getting one of those is worn during dinner, just fun! Some boxes of crackers are very fancy and very expensive.

I remember when David was leaving for the Bahamas in nineteen sixty-four. It was two weeks before Christmas and he drove me down to Hampshire from London to see my parents and say goodbye before he left. He bought them the most beautiful box of crackers I think they had ever had. Must have cost him a fortune. Hard to believe that was forty-seven years ago and Les was five years old when I met Dave. I wish he had been given the opportunity from his father to spend more time with me.

The court had said reasonable visitation, but that did not happen and when I think of all the summers he could have spent his school holidays in the Bahamas with Dave and I, it breaks my heart.

I think Les thought I was dating David while I was still with his father and that was not so. Dave and I worked together and when I lost custody, he was there to console me. It was not until a few months later that we went out for a drink together.

Les was nearly six when I left England. Hard decision for me, but I had someone I cared a lot for and I know who cared for me and not being allowed to see my boy when I wanted, I think I made the right choice even though it hurt very much to leave my son and not know when I would see him.

I am so glad I kept up with birthdays and Christmas and letters now and then, this kept us close and now he is fifty-two and I am seventy-three. It's as though we were never apart.

New Years' eve is our next party night, pretty sure Les and Mary will not be coming. I'm sure they have parties and arrangements made. Dave and I have a nice relaxing week having fun with (Jack the Ripper), that's what I am calling the dog. His nails are very sharp and when he jumps on me my skin tears. It's getting very thin now, too much sun bathing, smoking whatever, it stinks!

A few days go by and Dave tells me that he isn't feeling right. He thinks he has a cold coming. Well, he was right! It has made a little hole in our New Year's celebration, but I will go on my own and share a couple of hours with friends. I think he would rather be left alone anyway, not a good night to feel rough and stay home, but nothing worse than aching, coughing, sweating, etc., not even booze helps.

I dressed up and spent a nice visit with people I met years earlier. I could not seem to really enjoy it without Dave so I only stayed an hour after midnight then went home. He was already in bed and I crept around not wanting to disturb him, but he was awake and asked me if I enjoyed my night.

About two days later I started coughing and felt like crap, guess I have it coming, thanks Dave. I am down, what a shame! We were invited to a lovely home cooked Sunday roast at friends of his. He had had to call them and tell them we are both sick and can't make it.

I felt very bad about that one! I wanted a great roast beef and Yorkshire pudding, and our friend who cooked this would only have three people for lunch instead of five, or six. Sorry hon would have loved it.

Nearly time for me to leave this beautiful little place in Kent and go back to London to spend time with Les and Mary before going back to the U.S.A. Little did I know, that this would be the last Christmas dinner and New Year's Eve party I would be spending with Dave in the pub.

74 Another Event Coming

When I got back to Vegas, I was told wonderful news. Melissa is having a baby sometime in July. I think she is a little worried right now thinking something might go wrong. That is because her mum and I both had stillborn babies. We have talked to her and reassured her that it is not hereditary. Unfortunately, it is something that just happens. I can really understand how scared she must feel. It is the most devastating thing that can happen to a woman.

When Melissa gets to her third, or fourth month our family and Bill's parents are going to share her ultra sound experience with her and we will all find out the sex of the baby, can't wait.

I am back in the Saloon working my butt off, but guess I am lucky to have a job that hires me for two days a week, pays the bills. I am grateful for that.

One thing I know, we are all worth more than minimum wage, seven twenty-five an hour is what the state rate is. This is a very hard stressful place to work a lot of the time.

I am very lucky that I have friends that come to see me pretty regularly especially, working Tuesdays and Wednesdays, I gave one of my shifts away, hope I can get by with two. Not the best days for bartenders who rely on tips and especially working eight a.m. until four p.m. shift.

Pushing on, it's now early February and I am with my sister and nephew at Melissa's ultra sound exam along with Bill's mother and father. This modern technology is amazing. It is so mind boggling to sit and see a picture of a baby moving inside of a woman's belly.

Finally, the doctor doing this procedure asks us if we are ready to know the sex of the baby. It's a boy, wonderful, due in July!

Another happy event to look forward to and Melissa tells me it could be a July fourth baby. That will really be a celebration.

When George was alive we always had and Independence day party, with a wonderful back yard like we had why not?. We took advantage of it at every opportunity and if it was very hot, as July is, we had a misting system along the top inside edge of the patio.

I used PVC pipe and glued it all together and had holes drilled into it for the little misters, hooked it up with a piece of pipe to the hose and faucet on the ground at the end of the cover. We turned it on and it reduced the heat under the patio by about ten, or more degrees, felt awesome, I did a great job there.

The pool water was always very warm, as it was a dark surface and the black lava rock around the back held the heat. This was all was a few years ago.

Do not really celebrate the fourth much anymore, watch the shows and fireworks on TV but if the baby comes on that holiday, I will definitely be doing it.

It is our spring now, great weather at this time of year and also September through November is usually super. I won't be going to England for Christmas. My shift falls on the holiday, but if I can save enough I would love to go for New Year's Eve. Usually, takes me a year to save the money for my fare and a little to spend.

Funny really, I always dreamt and wished someday I would be able to fly first class, guess not! I have a nasty feeling that I am going to be working until I am eighty years old. I suppose if I am capable it will be okay if I can look half way decent and still walk up and down for over eight hours. Maybe by then I could get a nice raise!!!

It's now the end of June and we are all waiting anxiously for baby Adrian to arrive, Adrian is the name chosen for him

July the fourth nearly at an end and no baby, but wait! Melissa has gone into labour. Hope she does not have to go through that too long. At least nowadays hospitals have plenty of drugs on hand. I'm sure that makes it much easier. Not quite like a little gas and air fifty-two years ago.

Sue is going to call me when the baby is born and then we can visit when Melissa has had time to relax. He arrives on July the fifth. I think it is Bill's father's birthday, not hundred percent sure that it is. What a nice present for him, a grandson. He is a beautiful baby.

Sue is now a grandmother and me a great aunt, did not make grandmother, no problem, dealt with it. I am so sure my son would have loved to have had kids, but it just did not happen for him. This new baby is going to be very well cared for. Melissa's baby shower was unbelievable. I have never seen so many gifts at a baby shower ever! Her and Bill worked hard to become the professionals they are so they deserve to have a good life.

I am not happy that I cannot be in England for Christmas, mainly the reason being that I have to work on those days, but I am going to try hard for New Year's Eve. I need tips, lots of tips. I think most people would be very surprised about the amount of customers who do not tip the bartender and there are those that will actually steal your tips if you are not watching. I never learnt to pick up my tips straight away even when I worked in the casino. I would not stand too long waiting for a gambler to tip me. I used to think it was a little embarrassing. The girls were always telling me, "Sam, wait for a tip."

The place I work in now is two hundred times different from an exclusive casino in the Bahamas. I could wait in front of some of these people all day and still get stiffed. One cannot make a person tip. They do, or they don't. It is just a little bit upsetting when you wait on a person for two, or three hours and they cash out a good jackpot and don't leave you anything. Have to take the good with the bad, but I know one thing, I am worth more than minimum wage! I know I am good at my job, I have been told by a few customers over the years.

September is here, specifically the sixteenth, my birthday and Mexican Independence Day. A little ironic when I think I was married to a man of Mexican heritage. This is my seventy fourth and I am remembering so many things from years ago which I have to write about before I go any further with this year.

Girls I worked in the casino with, who I am still in touch with, in fact a few of the dealers too who are on the internet. Amazing how we all still relate to the island. We have a get together on line it's great.!

Now a few funny things my sister did when she was living on the island between England and France.

I remember one time she was going to visit mum and dad on the mainland, and the plane landed, small plane, small airport, grass runway.

Anyway, Sue gets off of the plane and walks to the small arrival area. She has one of her knees wrapped in a large bandage and is walking with her legs apart, pretty ugly looking gait, (Not as good as a horse).

Mum says, "What on earth have you done to your leg?" Sue takes her out of earshot from dad and tells her that there is nothing wrong with her leg. She has a large lump like a boil in between the cheeks of her bottom so to disguise the walking funny part she wrapped up her knee, hilarious!

Her and I used to get into these laughing bouts that went on for a long time and most of them were about stupid things, but the lump turned out to be a pilonidal cyst. It is usually the result of an ingrown hair and moisture that gets infected. I believe if I remember correctly, that Sue went through two or three procedures in Jersey that did not take care of the problem. I think the final surgery that took care of her back was in Las Vegas many years later.

This problem came and went for a few years and if I think back in time, the last surgeon managed to fix it and it never came back. She had a hard time, for a long time, with that problem.

I am looking forward to the Ryder Cup which is being played this year. I have not played golf for years, but I still love to watch it. Even though I became an American citizen, I am still English and when Europe and England are playing against America I have to support the country I was born in. This particular tournament is only played every two years with the best players teamed up, playing for the U.S. and the U.K. and Europe. It seems I will be working on Sunday the last day of competition, hope I get to see some of it. I believe Europe is holding the cup at the moment which means that the states have to win to get the Ryder Cup back.

I am at the bar working the eight until four shift, last day of golf. Yesterday, things were not going so well for the team across the pond, but today looks totally different. Our team is playing fantastic golf and suddenly things are going our way.

I have a busy shift going on and four young guys come in. One of them I have served before a while ago. Anyway, they got drinks, all gambled on one machine that they could stand around and were enjoying watching the golf when a nightmare walked in! A homeless female who was on medication, possibly a schizophrenic who was not allowed in the bar, but would show up now and then and walk in and cause a scene.

Most of the time I could handle her and sometimes it was an impossible task, this day was that. I ran around and mentioned to most of the customers to please ignore her and she will go away, but there are people who just have to aggravate a situation. She picked on my four guys playing slots and watching golf and then it was my turn. I will not put on paper the names she called me. I am sure most of you can figure it out.

We have polite ways of using these words in England, but how would this poor soul ever know that? I tried to help her and calm her down for a few years now, but today I have to call for help.

I dialled 311 which is not an emergency number and low and

behold, I had two nice policemen show up! I explained that I needed her out of the bar and was there any way they could help her, take her to the hospital, or somewhere that would do something for her?

Their hands are tied, I found out. If they called an ambulance and she refuses to go there is nothing they can do. If she does go they cannot keep her in the hospital. Do we think money has something to do with this picture? If I won the lottery, (Not in Vegas, we don't have one) I would be able to help lots of these people that I deal with every week and me too!!! Finally, a little peace on my afternoon, needless to say my four nice guys left. Who can deal with this crap? I guess the bartender can.

When I have a day like this sometimes I wish there would be a TV channel, or news reporter that could sit here for a few hours and see what we deal with.

75   I Love Remembering

I am now going back in time again to when my son was small maybe three years old. It's amazing to me that I remember all this stuff and also wonderful that I can. I would love people to share this with me. What a great seventy years!

Les awoke me one morning with one of my paint brushes (That I had left in a jar of paint thinner to clean, in the loo behind the toilet) in his hand. I had started painting our flat with a light grey paint, just the wooden door frames and the base board then I had some maroon wallpaper just for the long hallway. Well, lovely little Leslie had found the brushes that I had left in soak behind the toilet and pulled one out and proceeded to help me paint the place while I was sleeping. When I opened my eyes and finally was able to focus, (It was very early in the morning). I thought, oh no! Then I got out of bed and I guess the look on my face really scared him. He started crying and shaking.

I walked out of the bedroom and the first thing that hit me was the grey paint in plenty of places that I didn't want it. Then I noticed his pyjamas which were yellow with little animals on them, were now mostly grey in lots of places and animals disappeared!

How could I get mad and shout at him? He was a little boy who was curious and adventurous. I had to get the paint remover and start getting his artistic work off of the floor and other places. Luckily, I had not papered yet. I think the jamas have had it. About two hours of scrubbing, I finally cleaned all the paint off of the floor and walls and doors, he had been very busy! Now, it's time for a nice breakfast scrubbing can make one hungry. I had given Les a couple of cookies and milk to keep him going while I got rid of his dirty deed. Two eggs, bacon with fried bread are in order. Lovely memories.

How lucky was I and am I? Working with great people most of my years, still do. really nice kids, and Joe who manages the cleaning of the place and covers our back if we have a problem with a rowdy customer, or someone out of hand.

Thank-you all for being nice workmates and often helping me get things done when my old bones are hurting. You might have to do it for a few more years if I can handle working that long.

I have just received an email from Dave. He has decided to retire in December. The second will be his last day from what he tells me, so this really is the last Christmas I would have in the pub were I there.

He is going to have a great party I'm sure, for his thirty-five years. Wish I could be there and then he is taking two weeks off for himself and going to the mediteranean for a nice break.

The new landlords in the pub are going to take care of Jack, Dave's dog, which is really super for him. He can relax for two weeks, (Dave too)!

September, October and November are nearly over with. The thirtieth is my sister's birthday. I find it hard to believe she is going to be sixty-four. That means I will be seventy-five next year. How bloody awful!

We celebrate the Thanksgiving holiday, Sue and the kids and this year a new family member, Adrian, nearly five months old, cute and good looking. I think we have a family trait going on here, (Okay, I guess I am a bit vain, but why not)?

Christmas Eve is over and Christmas day I am working. I make sure that I take food for Christmas day, just ham rolls and pickles and chips. I figure any sort of food is welcomed as some of the people I have coming in Christmas day do not have a meal at all.

The next day is Boxing Day, the 26th of December, and I explain to some of my customers what Boxing Day means. They think it is actually something to do with boxing. I tell them it came from a custom, years ago in England when the wealthy would box up their leftovers at Christmas and give to the not so fortunate. I suppose it is carried on here to this day. The homeless and down and out are able to get a meal from shelters and many organisations that take care of the not so lucky people. Not all cardboard signs.

There are people who come in the bar on my shift that I am sure do not want to help themselves. I think they take drugs every chance they get, they panhandle and live under trees on empty lots and cover themselves with anything that they can find, old tarps, paper and who knows what else. I do try to help the ones that I believe are genuine and I am always being told by people in the bar to stop taking money from my tips to buy a drink for someone or lend another one a couple of dollars. Guess you can't teach an old dog new tricks.

76   David Retired, Not A Happy Visit

Thursday, the twenty-seventh, I am leaving for my home land at four thirty p.m. on one of those big scary 747s, but can't wait. Dave is getting back from his holiday and staying the night at the airport hotel before I land in Gatwick at ten thirty a.m. on the twenty-eighth.

This is a first, him picking me up at the airport. My son usually does it. What a nice surprise.

Unfortunately, things did not go as smooth as I hoped. After I landed, it took at least an hour and a half to clear customs and immigration. I have two citizenships, therefore two passports. I stood in the line for the U.S. as it was the shortest, but there was a hitch of some kind with a previous passenger so it held all of us up. The line for the U.K. and Europe which was three times longer than the one I went to has totally gone.

When I finally picked up my cases and made it to the gate where Dave was waiting, I could see he was a little stressed after waiting a lot longer than he expected and I think he thought he had missed me.

We found his car after first going to the wrong floor in the parking garage then a couple more bloopers and we are on the rainy road to Dover. After about half an hour of driving, I think things are much calmer. This trip takes about an two hours if the traffic is easy and it seems to be. I am glad about that as Dave does not have too much patience. I on the other hand am very happy and excited to be here. I love coming home whenever possible. It's still home to me.

It seems very strange arriving at Dave's and not going into the pub. It will be closed for a while for the renovations to be completed according to what he tells me. From what I gather, a brewery who is selling their beer in the pub, leases the place to the new people who are working for them and the brewery is the one remodelling the place. I will miss my New Year's Eve in there, but Dave tells me that we are going to a French restaurant with friends. Sounds wonderful and very much different to the usual celebration. It was a lovely New Year's dinner and spending time with people you like makes it even better, great company.

A week has passed and I am noticing that Dave is not his usual self. He seems to be picky and his sense of humour is not as good as it always has been. In fact, I don't feel as easy and relaxed as I have in past years.

An incident occurred that upset me quite a bit. Les had asked the guys in the band if they would do a gig at a local pub in the village near where Dave lives. I had never seen them play before on any of my trips and this would be a treat for me. Les tells me he will play for nothing and the rest of them will do a cheap night. I made a mistake and told Dave this. He got very upset with the fact that when they played in his pub he paid them a lot more. I tried to explain to him that Les had asked them for a favour as I was visiting and they all agreed.

David does not have a son that he only sees once a year and I don't think he realised that this was a very nice gesture on the bands part. He had been drinking when I told him so I excused most of it, but it did make me cry. I am an emotional person and it did hurt. I think the first month of being retired has not sunk in with him and maybe he feels lost. He is certainly not his old self.

I feel a little like an intruder. I have never felt this way in fifty years! We had one or two more get-togethers with friends even going to one of those was a bit tense. The car window was open on my side when we arrived at their house so I pressed the button to close it. When Dave went to get out of the car the door would not open. He tried the door lock and then started yelling at me to not touch anything as though it was my fault.

Finally, he got out of the car. I was not going to let this make me cry. I have done that already since getting here. The door lock on the driver's side kept playing up for days before I left. I was actually happy when I found out I had not caused this problem. He had to get it fixed after I left.

The last event that really, really upset me was when Dave took me to the train station for my journey back to London where Les would pick me up.

I got my ticket and he carried my two cases on to the platform. I had my purse and a small carry on type hold all. The train was due in about four, or five minutes. He put the cases in front of me, kissed me goodbye and said, "I have to get to the bank. Have a good time." Then he took off. I did not expect this, he just left me there

He always helped me on the train with my cases. They are pretty weighty and I know I am capable even though I am seventy-four. It was just a surprise to me that he did this. The train pulled in and I started to drag the cases one at a time to get them on. There was a couple on the platform with a young boy and the man came over and helped me get the cases into the carriage.

What a relief that was. I thought I would not manage before the train pulled out. Silly thing to think. I'm sure the conductor was watching me from the end of the train. The gentleman who helped me showed me a special place where one puts suitcases and he did it for me.

After I sat down and got myself a little more relaxed for the two hour train journey, I noticed the little boy had a problem. A rash of some kind that covered his face and more. The couple told me that they were taking him to Great Ormond which is a hospital for kids.

The beverage cart came around with tea, drinks and sandwiches. The couple ordered tea and snacks for their son so I made a gesture to the man in charge of the cart that I would take care of whatever they ordered. They were reluctant to accept, but I insisted. The man has already offered to help me off with the cases when we get to Waterloo where Les will be waiting for me, I hope.

When the train gets there this kind couple go out of their way to see that I am safely on the platform before the train leaves. I wish them all the best for their son and thank them very much for helping me.

Les is here and he is a little upset because the train was late and he did not know if I would be on it. He had called Dave to see if I was on this one and Dave tells him he is not sure as he left me on the platform. He never actually knew for sure if I caught that train. That did not sit well with my son. I told him to forget it. Dave was not himself at all. I am very hurt and did not feel that he was just a little happy to see me.

I did not even call when I left England. I sent him an email when I got home and let him know how I felt, we sorted it out and we are back to where it should have been and how it used to be. I am very happy about that. Not sure why he was like that, but I have excused it. There had to be a reason. Retired and alone, instead of company in the pub every day, that could have been one reason.

Not a very happy two weeks for me and won't be going next Christmas, have to work. My girlfriends have nagged me for years, why doesn't he want you? Why this, why that? I think I know him very well. He has been alone too long and I would be in the way (Whitney Houston, I will always love you) That's the best way I can describe it, but he does love me, I know that. Guess that is about the most I am going to get. If he ever does get close and loving it's usually when he is drunk. That's how he is made. Nobody knows him like I do! A shame really. I think we could have had a good partnership together.

I got lucky when I met George and had nearly thirty nice

years with him. Two thousand thirteen is flying by nothing much changing. Veteran's day is coming up and I decide I will go to the Vet's cemetery and visit George's grave site. When I have in the past I have put a can of Lite beer in his vase. He loved his beer. This time I am taking a nice green plant.

I make a point of going very early in the morning. It is much less crowded. When I get there I see the hundreds of flags that are put at the graves. Small U.S. flags cover the whole place. It took me a while to find George's stone number.

Then I realised there were many more rows since I was here last. I finally found him and put the plant in the holder and then cried and got very upset and had to leave. I think he would understand I really hate going there, too emotional, miss you George.

On a lighter note, I have been told by my good friend Maggie that I am having a birthday party for my seventy-fifth. Put on by her at her house along with her significant other Jeremy. What a nice thing for them to do, a lot of work. I know I have held parties for years, but love to do it and I know my good friend Maggie does to.

Adrian is one year old in July and Melissa and Bill gave him a party at a place that caters to children of all ages. A very fun place for kids. All the slides and things they play with are surrounded by protective foam and rubber so that they do not get hurt. I don't really agree with a party for a one year old.

I don't think they have a clue to what's going on, but I suppose parents are different nowadays and a big party for a baby is the thing to do living in Vegas. I am glad that my birthday is in September which means it could be cooler and more comfortable for an outside do. Maggie has a nice patio and a pool. Perfect for outdoor parties.

I am really looking forward to this seventy-five years of my life shindig. Hard to believe I got here. Don't feel old, don't act old and I don't think I look old how great is this? Now, I have to go through the closet for a week and find something that will go along with my frame of mind. It definitely has to be something that covers the top of my arms, (hate them) and black is always flattering so hunt for stretchy, long, maybe legs. Found it! Jumpsuit way in the back of the closet has not seen daylight in about five years. I tried it on and it fits fine still. All I need to do find a fancy belt. I have a ton of those too, so I'm set.

What an absolutely fantastic party. Tables with pictures of me during different stages of my life. How did these get here? Must have shown them to friends at some time and a sneaky person took them and made copies. The food was awesome, in fact, my ex brother-in-law brought me sushi. What a nice thought. He knew I loved sushi.

Maggie has done a lot of cooking and people have brought a variety of dishes. This is a banquet! If I remember rightly, this party went on for a few hours and I had friends that came up with very unique things. One was my picture on the front of a small booklet that are found in taxi cabs, advertising hotels and restaurants etc., in Vegas.

Another friend Bud, put my picture on Caesar's marquee on Facebook, very clever fake.

I had a bowl given to me with money in it that everybody had collected.

Diane, a girlfriend of twenty years, gave me the most beautiful card and put seventy-five dollars in it. (she is also gone now), I was touched and taken aback with this as her and I had a few differences over the years. Not any more, too old for any crap! The money my friends put in the bowl was very generous.

I have awesome friends and I know there are at least thirty people who want to buy this book if I can get it published. I was really working on closing this out at six hundred and fifty hand written pages, but I still have one, or two more things to talk about so it may be six hundred and fifty-two.

I started writing this in March of 2012. It has been two and a half years. Incredible how time slips away. I will be seventy-six in two days. I hope this will be finished on the sixteenth of September, Mexican Independence Day.

77 A Nice Ending For A Seventy Year Journey

Post party and creeping towards December and I have to work Christmas again, but I suddenly thought how nice it would be to go to England at Easter. I mentioned it to my girlfriends in England and Beryl told me she could possibly get me a friend ticket with British Airways which is the airline she has just retired from.

I always fly on Virgin Atlantic every time I go, but Beryl could save me about three hundred dollars. That would be wonderful.

It takes me a lot of saving to take that trip. We talk after Christmas and I tell her I can pay for my ticket when I get my refund from the IRS which will be some time in February I hope. I have some saved for spending money. I do like to share when I go out with friends to eat and drink, etc. And I like to buy groceries when I stay with Les and Mary. Then I go to Dave's and do the same thing. Everyone is very good to me and I guess they know deep down that it is not an easy road for me.

I do love to go home. After fifty years, I still get homesick and I think if I had money I would love to live in England six months of the year. I have done my duty for gifts to the family and friends at Christmas. I am now concentrating on my trip home in April.

A hot cross bun at Easter is one of my favourite things, I really am looking forward to it. To me one of these warm buns with real butter on it is as good as a gourmet dinner.

Les is picking me up on April 10th which is a Thursday. Mary is in Bali taking a course on vegan food preparation along with the use of spices which is something she wishes to pursue. I hope she really does well with her venture.

Les and I go out and eat and needless to say drink a few cocktails. We need to after not seeing each other for a year and a half. Mary arrives home the next day and we socialise, the three of us.

Saturday, Les is taking me to Dave's and a friend in the village who has lost his wife unexpectedly has hired the band for a charity evening, it must be devastating for him.

She died after only a few weeks illness. The band Les plays with was a favourite of hers so her hubby arranged a tribute to her in one of the local pubs and hired the band to play. It would be a couple of hours after Les dropped me at Dave's.

When we arrived at the house Dave forgot that I had asked him to shut Jack up until I had a chance to get in and get prepared for him. When Dave came out to the car to greet me, Jack was with him. Excited is not the word, I cannot believe after not seeing me for a year and a half, that he got so worked up, jumping up like mad, he took the skin from the back of my left hand. I was not a happy camper with that, but I got lucky as far as the legs were concerned!

I have just arrived and already I am bleeding and needing band-aids on my hand. My skin is so thin and it tears so very easily especially on my legs. I'm not sure if Dave sees the importance of the situation. I really don't think he realises what damage the dog's nails can do to me. How can I bitch and be mean? I have just arrived and will deal with it for now anyway.

Les Dave and I go into the pub next door for a drink before Les has to go to the pub up in the village to get ready for the gig, pubs everywhere! Dave and I are going to stay and have a couple more cocktails and talk for a while.

This turns into more than a couple of drinks, and two hours later we decide it's time to walk up to the pub where the band is. It is about two hundred yards give or take including a pretty good uphill climb half way. I think this good stroll helped us to start the party again when we got there.

It was a very successful night and everybody donated to a charity for brain diseases of every kind. Met lots of friends including our friends from the islands who I always see when I go to Dave's.

We see them again a couple of weeks later when the six of us go to dinner in Dover at my favourite restaurant. It is a little cozy Italian place. Dave has been taking me there for over twenty years since I first went back to England to see him.

The day before I leave to go back to London, Dave is playing in a golf tournament in France so I am staying with Jack all day. I was NOT going to do any cleaning whatsoever, but I weakened and did a lot of jobs to make the kitchen look nicer. It's so rewarding when it was a mess and now it looks great.

Another really good friend from Bahama days, who now lives about forty minutes away, comes down to the pub next door at lunch time and my friend Nancy, who lives in the village, joins us both for lunch. Great lunch on a beautiful sunny day on the beach. Who could ask for more?

I say goodbye to the girls and tell them, "See you in a year hopefully," and go back into the house which is about a two minute walk behind the pub down the alley, Jack is so happy I'm back. Now, I am going to do more jobs and cook the chicken that Dave feeds him every day. Boiled chicken at night and dog food for breakfast. He is very spoiled and why not?

I finally finish working and the dog and I go for a walk on the beach. I wish I had enough money to come home and rent a flat here, it's a lovely little place. Going to settle down and watch a movie that Dave left me after I feed the dog and make a cuppa. It is about nine p.m. and I have viewed the movie. It was very good.

I decide the dog and I will go out for another walk. I have not walked him on the beach in the dark so a flashlight is in order. He has gotten very used to me in the past two weeks, so I do not need a lead. I did put a collar on him just in case I have to grab him in a hurry.

Dave calls me about ten p.m. from the docks in Dover. They have just gotten off of the ferry from France and he wants to meet me in the Pub next door. I get a little blush and mascara on, change clothes and walk to the pub with the flashlight in hand. The back alley is very dark at night. I am glad it is only about thirty steps. There are two, or three people I know inside which makes it nice. The new publican's wife is working behind the bar. She is very congenial person. I feel at home again. Her hubby is on my side drinking! He, too, is very friendly.

Pretty soon his highness arrives. He says he has had a very nice day and a wonderful meal in a little place in Calais. Then he proceeds to get all worked up. He had been into the house and left his wallet there. He does not have any money on him. Wow! It is the end of the world, "Dumb Shit." I say, "After fifty years, I don't think I'm too worried. I have enough with me."

We go back to the house after a couple of hours and after calming the "Ripper" down, Dave hands me a bag. "For you," he says. Inside was a bottle of Christian Dior's, "Miss Dior", a fragrance I have been wearing for over forty years. It is a beautiful soft scent. I do not buy it very often because it is too expensive for me. Dave must of written down the name before he went across to France and purchased it in the duty free shop on board of the ferry. I was very taken back. He is not a very outgoing person with feelings. This took a lot of thought. Now, I feel very special.

Friday lunchtime and it's time to catch the train back to London. It's different this time. Dave waits with me until the train arrives and puts my cases on, kisses me goodbye and I am gone, hate it!

Les is at the other end. He always is. I love him so. I spend the next three days relaxing and spending a day with my great pal Rita. We walk the embankment next to the River Thames taking pictures of the Tower of London and the Tower Bridge. We had a nice lunch. Real fish and chips and then she helped me pick out a couple of souvenirs to take back to Vegas. Her and I have been friends since we were very young. A great feeling to have such a close friend.

Time to fly out. I always tell Les when we say goodbye that I am not going to cry and I always do. The flight back was full and bumpy. Not like the one coming over that was empty and bumpy. I take one day off before going back to work. I think I would probably enjoy it more if I knew I didn't have to work a couple of days, I'm sure it would be very different if that were the case and I was doing it to keep busy.

Already, I miss my son. I miss Dave and I miss the beach. I am so thankful I have a family and friends on this end.

Melissa is having another baby. Super! Her and Bill are having a 'Is it a boy, or a girl party' after her ultrasound. Bill has the envelope with the result in it and Melissa is having a cake made with blue or pink inside. She will not know until Bill opens the envelope what the result is. She gave the bakers the sealed envelope and they made the cake the appropriate color unbeknownst to her. A very original way of doing things.

We all gather at the house, have a wine, or a cocktail as I did, and wait for Bill to open the envelope and Melissa to cut the cake. It's blue inside of the cake, another boy. I think I see a little disappointment on Melissa's face. She was hoping for a little girl.

Sue and I both tell her how wonderful two boys will be. The new baby boy is due at the end of September. The month of September is going to be very special for my good friend Maggie as well, she is going to be eighty. Another big do for me to get ready for.

It is now only a week away from Maggie's birthday and friends are getting a party together in the office bar, (my bar).

This is definitely going to be the end of my story on my seventy-five years of my life and this book. I hope if I do get lucky and can share this, that everybody will enjoy it and not judge me for anything I did to hurt anyone and for my silly mistakes.

I have love for my family and friends and I have enjoyed all the places I have been and things I have seen and done.

I lived in England and swam in the English Channel. I have lived and worked in the Bahamas and had a "Good evening, how are you?" from Cary Grant in the casino one night while I was working, could not even answer I was so gobsmacked (so shaken up or amazed). Sunbathed on a white beach and swam in the turquoise waters of the Atlantic and the Gulf of Mexico. I have visited Canada, France, Scotland and Wales. I have lived in Jersey, a part of the Channel Islands, in between England and France along with spending a few hours in Bermuda. I have had the spray from Niagara Falls on my face and have had my feet in a freezing mountain stream in Vermont. I also went to what felt like the top of the world in New York's Empire State building, and have flown in a single engine plane through a very nasty storm in the Gulf Stream. I played the piano at the Royal London College of Music and was awarded an honours certificate at age ten for playing Beethoven's Fur Elise. I have also had a little tinkle on a piano in Las Vegas once owned by Liberace.

Working as a bartender at seventy-six years of age makes me proud even though it is very tough to do sometimes, and finally I sang with the "London Strums", the band that my son plays with.

This has been an enjoyable journey, happy, sad and sometimes very hard, but after two years of writing I think I have accomplished what I set out do, and that was to write about my wonderful life.

(good name for a movie).

"Sometimes the past cannot be ignored
Or forgotten. I have done neither."